A teacher's guide to classroom research

Fourth edition

David Hopkins

with the assistance of Elpida Ahtaridou

Open University Press

Open University Press
McGraw-Hill Education
McGraw-Hill House
Shoppenhangers Road
Maidenhead
Berkshire
England
SL6 2QL

email: enquiries@openup.co.uk
world wide web: www.openup.co.uk

and Two Penn Plaza, New York, NY 10121-2289, USA

First published 2008

A catalogue record of this book is available from the British Library

ISBN-13 978 0335 22174 5 (pb)   978 0335 22175 2 (hb)
ISBN-10 0335 22174 2 (pb)   0335 22175 0 (hb)

Library of Congress Cataloging-in-Publication Data
CIP data applied for

Typeset by RefineCatch Limited, Bungay, Suffolk
Printed in the UK by Bell and Bain Ltd, Glasgow

The *McGraw·Hill* Companies

For Jeroen, Jessica and Dylan with love

In short the outstanding characteristic of the extended professional (teacher) is a capacity for autonomous professional self-development through systematic self-study, through the study of the work of other teachers and through the testing of ideas by classroom research procedures.

Lawrence Stenhouse
An Introduction to Curriculum Research and Development

Learning experiences are composed of content, process and social climate. As teachers we create for and with our children opportunities to explore and build important areas of knowledge, develop powerful tools for learning, and live in humanising social conditions.

Bruce Joyce, Emily Calhoun and David Hopkins
Models of Learning – Tools for Teaching

Appreciating a phenomenon is a fateful decision, for it eventually entails a commitment – to the phenomenon and to those exemplifying it – to render it with fidelity and without violating its integrity. Entering the world of the phenomenon is a radical and drastic method of appreciation.

David Matza
Becoming Deviant

And what is good, Phaedrus,
And what is not good –
Need we ask anyone to tell us these things?
Robert Pirsig
Zen and the Art of Motorcycle Maintenance

Contents

Preface to the fourth edition

It is now well over twenty years since this book was originally published and the educational landscape in Britain and most other Western countries has changed dramatically since 1985. One of the most dominant changes observed since then is the increase in centralized policy-making, however, far from undermining the role of 'teacher-researcher', it has in my opinion made such a professional ethic all the more necessary. Educational research and educational literature increasingly suggest that 'top-down' change does not necessarily 'mandate what matters', and that it is the work of teachers, that is most influential in determining the achievements of students. If we are serious about enhancing the quality of education in our schools, teachers need to be more, not less, involved in curriculum development, school improvement and pedagogy.

It seems to me that the major difference between now and the mid-1980s is that teacher researchers have to increasingly take a whole school and at times systemic perspective. They now have to interpret and adapt policy to their own teaching situation, to link their classroom research work to that of other colleagues and whole school priorities, as well as to the process of teaching and learning.

It is a great privilege to have the opportunity to update a book at regular intervals, for it allows one to keep pace with what has proven to be a rapidly changing educational scene. In successive editions of *A Teacher's Guide to Classroom Research*, I have tried to take new perspectives into account while retaining the structure and simplicity of the original book. In the second edition I placed more emphasis on the importance of viewing teacher research within a whole school context. In particular, I emphasized the crucial role of classroom observation in supporting teacher and school development and added a new chapter on linking classroom research to other whole school initiatives. In the third edition I argued that not only should teacher research be a whole school activity, but that it should also focus unrelentingly on the teaching and learning process. It has become increasingly apparent to me that if teaching and learning are not the centre-point of our classroom research efforts then the achievement of the young people in our schools will continue to lag behind the aspirations we have for them. And more importantly we will have failed them during the most crucial learning opportunity of their lives. As we pursue an increasingly ambitious educational reform agenda it is vital that we take the opportunity to create a discourse around teaching and learning in our schools and communities. In this fourth edition, I extend this perspective to embrace and emphasize the importance of moral purpose, the personalization of learning and the importance of locating teacher research within a systemic context. This reflects my recent experiences as a national policy-maker and international consultant.

In preparing this fourth edition, I have revised and updated the text. I have also added a number of additional examples and cameos that reflect the increased focus on teaching and learning. In a few places I have rearranged certain sections in order to accommodate other necessary revisions. In addition I have rewritten the last four chapters. The first significant change was to expand the original Chapter 9 into two separate chapters to accommodate new experience and knowledge about analysing and then reporting classroom research. The second was to take the opportunity to re-write the chapter on teaching and learning to expand the discussion on learning *per se* and to accommodate the current emphasis on personalized learning. Third, I combined the discussion in Chapters 11 and 12. This was partially to drop some material that was arguably tangential to the more conventional role of the teacher-researcher, but mainly to make a further argument about the role of teacher research in systemic reform. In so doing I have emphasized their importance in the creation of increasingly powerful learning communities in our schools, in enhancing the professional judgments of teachers, in networking, and the contribution classroom research can make to whole school development.

In the preface for the second edition, I mentioned that since the initial publication of the book I had become the proud father of Jeroen, Jessica and Dylan. Their mother tells me that my writing and practice has become much more learning and classroom focused since they have become part of my life. Whatever the truth in that, it is certainly the case that as they have developed their own individual learning histories they have consistently challenged my own ideas on education and forced me to rethink and rewrite. As I have written elsewhere, I am continually trying to adjust my educational thinking to keep pace with their development. As I was preparing this fourth edition I learned of how well our three children had fared in a variety of national examinations and tests (Jeroen – A levels, Jessica – GCSE and Dylan – KS3 SATS). I am pleased to report that by and large they did fulfil their potential and are now securely embarked on the next stage of their educational journeys.

Despite their relative success, what I still wish for Jeroen, Jessica and Dylan, is that they not only meet and if possible surpass existing educational standards, but that they also find learning exciting, compelling and intrinsically worthwhile. I wish them to become competent and develop sound, secure and healthy self-concepts to help them face the challenges that await them. It is here where the personal and the professional converge. What I want for my children is, I believe, the same as what most teachers wish for their students. There is a striking quality about fine teachers – they care deeply about the young people in their school. Most teachers came into teaching because they wanted to make a difference. Classroom research by teachers is one way of focusing educational efforts to ensure that this difference is being made.

The book continues to have a modest aim: it is to provide teachers and students with a practical guide to doing research in their own classrooms and to link these research efforts to the extension of their teaching and learning repertoires and to whole school developments. Despite the proliferation of texts on action research in recent years, I believe that there is still a place for a practical and straightforward introduction to teacher-based classroom research; particularly one that is committed to teacher and school development. In this way, the book complements the existing literature rather than competes with it.

In rereading the book again I was struck once more by how far the original text was influenced by the work of Lawrence Stenhouse and how relevant his ideas still are for us today. Given the great educational challenges that we continue to face, more people of his stature are needed who have a vision of education and can translate it into a coherent philosophy and a pragmatic course of action. On my office wall there is still the quotation from Stenhouse that is on his memorial plaque in the grounds of the University of East Anglia:

> It is teachers who, in the end, will change the world of the school by understanding it.

I hope that in some small way this book continues to contribute to that aspiration.

David Hopkins
Argentiere Mont-Blanc
1st September 2007

Acknowledgements

I am grateful to the late Mike Bruce, Don Cochrane, Peter Norman, the late Jean Rudduck and especially Ann Kilcher for the care with which they reviewed the original manuscript; and for conversations that clarified my thinking on this and other matters. Their friendship and professional collaboration has meant a great deal to me. Suzzane de Castell, Gill Harper-Jones, Pat Holborn, my now deceased sister Mary Schofield, Louise Pelletier and David Pritchard also provided material and intellectual support at critical and opportune times: my thanks to them too. A number of colleagues and students graciously allowed me to use some of their material as illustrations and examples in the first edition. In this regard, I remain indebted to Stan Auerbach, Judy Byer, Heather Lockhard, Sandra Meister, Marianne Schmidt, Ann Waldo and Harvey Walker. The three anonymous reviewers of the original book proposal made comments that encouraged me to revise and improve that manuscript. I anticipate that at least two of them were satisfied with the outcome.

The original argument of the book was developed from ideas first published in the *CARN Bulletin*, the DES booklet *Planning for School Development*, the *Empowered School*, *Managing Schools Today*, *Phi Delta Kappan*, *School Organization* and *The Times Educational Supplement*. Finally, I must also acknowledge the Deakin University Press, the Ford Teaching Project and Universitetsforlaget AS for allowing me to reproduce copyright material.

In preparing the second edition of this book, my colleagues at Cambridge were characteristically generous in taking time to review and help me with the manuscript. I am particularly grateful to Mel Ainscow for his thoughtful and creative comments, and more generally for exploring with me the boundaries of professional partnership. Colin Conner, Dave Ebbutt and Julie Howard also reviewed parts of the manuscript and made helpful comments. I am grateful to the Bedfordshire LEA/University of Cambridge Institute of Education 'Developing Successful Learning Project', Howard Bradley and Rob Bollington, Jere Brophy and Tom Good, Walter Doyle, Rex Gibson, David Hargreaves, Pamela Hughes, David Jeffries, Denis Lawton, James McKernan and The Sanders Draper School for letting me use some of their material in that edition. John Skelton, my publisher at Open University Press, was most supportive throughout.

The task of preparing the third edition was greatly eased by the assistance of Julie Temperley and John Beresford. They both made numerous and helpful suggestions for updating the text and through our discussions shared with me their own experience of facilitating teacher research. Once again my colleagues were more than generous in allowing me to include work that we had published elsewhere. In this respect I am grateful to Mel Ainscow, John Beresford, David Fulton Publishers, David H. Hargreaves, Alma Harris, David Jackson, Barbara MacGilchrist, Collette Singleton and Ruth Watts. Thanks also to Shona Mullen of the Open University Press who is one of the best, and most supportively critical editors with whom I have had the pleasure to work.

In the interval between the second and third editions I had the privilege of working with networks of schools in Nottinghamshire, Derbyshire, Bedfordshire, South Wales, Leicester and Walsall on our 'Improving the Quality of Education For All' (IQEA) school improvement project. This work has focused more than ever before on strategies for teaching and learning and the facilitation of action enquiry and classroom-based research. As always, I have learned a great deal from the commitment, enthusiasm and sheer professionalism of colleagues involved in those networks. It is here that the energy for the transformation of our school system lies. My thanks and admiration to them.

In preparing this fourth edition I have had the inestimable support of Elpida Ahtaridou whose enthusiasm for the project, commitment to the concept of classroom research and assistance in preparing Chapter 10 and editing the text generally has greatly enhanced what follows. I am most grateful to her. I spent most of the period between the publication of the third and fourth editions working in Government. Apart from being a remarkably formative period for me personally it also convinced me of the importance of the teacher research role in the realization of broader system goals – hence some of the new emphases in this edition. It gave me the valuable experience of working alongside great national institutions such as DEMOS, the National Strategies, the National College for School Leadership, the Innovation Unit and the Specialist Schools and Academies Trust. I am also profoundly grateful to those headteachers who I met during this period who so openly shared their enthusiasms and frailties, successes and failures with me and from whom I have learned so much. I also need to acknowledge the outstanding teachers such as Rebecca Jones and Christine Artington and those whose names I have been unable to locate, and who have allowed me to showcase their work in this new edition.

Last but not least, I would like to thank Jane Reed and Kathryn Riley who with such willingness and collegial spirit have provided me with resources which undoubtedly have enhanced the quality of this edition.

1 A teacher's guide to classroom research

This is a practical guide for teachers who wish to undertake research in their classrooms and schools for the purpose of improving practice. Classroom research, in the sense that I refer to it here, is an act undertaken by teachers, to enhance their own or a colleague's teaching, to test the assumptions of educational theory in practice, or as a means of evaluating and implementing whole school priorities. So, when I write of classroom research or of the teacher as researcher, I am not envisioning scores of teachers carrying out technical research projects to the exclusion of their teaching. My vision is more of teachers who have extended their role to include systematic reflection upon their craft with the aim of improving it.

Although lip service is often paid to this idea, we live in an educational system that tends to limit individual initiative by encouraging conformity and control. Teachers and pupils (and society too) deserve better than that. Undertaking research in their own and colleagues' classrooms is one way in which teachers can take increased responsibility for their actions and create a more energetic and dynamic environment in which teaching and learning can occur.

The origins of teacher research as a movement can be traced back to the Schools Council's Humanities Curriculum Project (HCP) (1967–72) with its emphasis on an experimental curriculum and the reconceptualization of curriculum development as curriculum research. The HCP, in its attempt to encourage a non-partisan and critically reflective attitude to teaching on the part of teachers, had a radical and controversial influence on teaching in British schools during the 1970s.

Following HCP, the concept of teacher research was nurtured by John Elliott and Clem Adelman in the Ford Teaching Project (1972–75). The project involved 40 primary and secondary school teachers in examining their classroom practice through action research. These teachers developed hypotheses about their teaching which could be shared with other teachers and used to enhance their own teaching.

At about the same time, Lawrence Stenhouse, who directed the Humanities Curriculum Project, further popularized the concept of 'the teacher as researcher' by utilizing it as the major theme in his influential book, *An Introduction to Curriculum Research and Development* (Stenhouse 1975). Encouraged by the considerable impact that Stenhouse had on the theory and practice of curriculum and teaching, and the popularity and publicity enjoyed by the Ford Teaching Project, the teacher research movement mushroomed. As well as burgeoning teacher research groups in the UK,

Australia, the USA and Canada, there are pockets of teacher-researchers in Scandinavia, France, Chile and many other countries. Although teacher research was not an entirely new concept in the late 1960s, it is from this period that it became an identifiable movement.

Much, however, has changed in the context of education in most Western countries since the concept of the teacher as researcher became popular. The main difference between the 1970s and the first decade of the 21st century is that classroom research has to be seen within a whole school and increasingly system context. It is no longer sufficient for teachers to do research in their own classrooms, without relating their enquiries to the work of their colleagues and the aims and direction of the school and the system as a whole. We need to strive consciously for a synthesis between teacher research, school development and system reform. That is why this book is not just a primer on classroom research techniques, it also attempts to relate teacher research to whole school development and the wider context of education.

All books emerge out of a specific set of individual circumstances that have influenced the author, and this book is no exception. The journey that preceded this book is still continuing, and so the story remains unfinished. But two influences in particular have been crucial in developing the ideas presented here and provide a context in which to consider the book. The first is the work of Lawrence Stenhouse whose intellectual and personal example still challenges me. In the HCP and his other work, Stenhouse was primarily concerned with the concept of emancipation. He wrote (1983: 163):

> My theme is an old-fashioned one – emancipation . . . The essence of emancipation as I conceive it is the intellectual, moral and spiritual autonomy which we recognise when we eschew paternalism and the role of authority and hold ourselves obliged to appeal to judgement.

There are three levels at which this concept of emancipation can operate – at the level of the student, the teacher and the school.

At the level of the student, emancipation refers to the ability to stand outside the teacher's authority on forms of knowledge, and to discover and own it for oneself. It was in the HCP that Stenhouse most notoriously signalled his commitment to this theme. In that project he was principally concerned with the emancipation of pupils through a particular teaching strategy. There were three elements to this aspect of the project: the use of discussion, the use of documents as evidence to inform discussion, and the assumption by the teacher of the role of neutral chairperson. By adopting this approach, Stenhouse was moving away from a teacher-dominated classroom to a setting where pupils, unconstrained by the authority of the teacher, could create meaning for themselves on the basis of evidence and discussion.

If HCP was in part a curriculum designed to emancipate pupils, the phrase 'teacher as researcher' was intended to do the same for teachers. Teachers are too often the servants of heads, advisers, researchers, textbooks, curriculum developers, examination boards or the 'Department of Education', among others. By adopting a research stance, teachers are liberating themselves from the control and command situation they often find themselves in. Stenhouse encouraged teachers to follow the specification of a curriculum or teaching strategy, but at the same time to assess it critically. Such curriculum proposals and teaching specifications are probably intelligent but are not necessarily correct. Their effectiveness should therefore be monitored by teachers in the classroom. By adopting this critical approach, by taking a research stance, the teacher is engaged not only in a meaningful professional development activity, but is also engaged in a process of refining and becoming more autonomous in professional judgement. This applies as much to the National Curriculum and 'personalized learning' as it did to the HCP.

The third level at which emancipation can operate is that of the school. Here it is a question of the school liberating itself from a bureaucratic educational system. The image of the 'ideal' type of emancipated school is represented by the words 'autonomous', 'creative', 'moving' or 'problem-solving'. These successful schools take the opportunity of the recent changes and use them to support developments already underway or planned for in the school. They adapt external change for internal purposes. In the most successful or emancipated schools, there is also a realization that successful change involves learning on the part of teachers. This implies that successful change strategies involve a seamless web of activities that focus on, are integrated with and enhance the daily work of teachers. This can result in quite profound alterations to the culture of the school and the ways in which teachers, heads and governors work together towards the goal of student achievement. More recently we have seen the emergence of the system leader, who is driven by a commitment to the improvement and sustaining of other schools as well as their own. It is here that the genesis of system transformation lies.

The second influence on this book is much more personal. During the 1970s I trained as a teacher and taught, worked as an Outward Bound instructor and mountain guide and read for postgraduate degrees in education. Although somewhat different activities, they were all characterized by a desire, often hesitant and naive: to create ways in which people could take more control of their own lives. Irrespective of the context – practice teaching, an 'O' level history class, counselling a 'delinquent' pupil, assisting in a youth club, on the rock face, out in the wilderness, or discussing ideas in a seminar – there were similarities in overall aim and pedagogic structure.

Later, as a teacher in a Canadian university, I taught courses in curriculum development, analysis of teaching and classroom research, and found in Stenhouse's work a theoretical framework within which I could put my ideas into action. The book emerged from that experience, more specifically from a course I taught in classroom research and some papers I wrote on the topic (Hopkins 1982, 1984a, b). Thus, the book is based on a set of ideas that have the enhancement of teacher judgement and autonomy as a specific goal, and is grounded within the practical realities of teachers and students.

My interest in classroom-based work, although always in my mind linked to school improvement, assumed a broader perspective while teaching at Cambridge and Nottingham Universities between 1985 and 1996, and 1996 and 2001 respectively. Much of my work then was concerned with assisting teachers, schools and local authorities (LAs) to handle and reflect on the change process. I learned an enormous amount from them, as I did from my involvement in the evaluation of the Technical Vocational

Education Initiate, the then Department for Education and Science[1] projects on Teacher Appraisal and School Development Plans, and in particular our school improvement project IQEA. I have also been fortunate to have worked over a slightly longer period with the OECD's Centre for Educational Research and Innovation (CERI) on a number of school improvement-related projects. This work has helped me to see the teacher's role in the wider context of the school as an organization and workplace. In particular, it has impressed on me the crucial importance of the culture of the school in sustaining teacher development.

I am by background and temperament a school improvement activist. Over the past thirty years or so I have self consciously located myself at the intersection of practice, research and policy. It is here that I felt I could best contribute to the process of educational reform. Reflecting back over this time, one of the initiatives of which I am most proud, as is seen later, is the work I did with the IQEA school improvement project where we collaborated with hundreds of schools in England and elsewhere in developing a model of school improvement and a programme of support. More recently however I have found myself as a national policy-maker concerned not just with regional networks of schools but with a part responsibility for transforming a whole system. Having served a parliamentary term as the Chief Adviser to three Secretaries of State – Estelle Morris, Charles Clarke and Ruth Kelly – I have now returned to an international role in educational leadership, where hopefully I can use this relatively unique experience to inform practice, policy and research in education. These experiences have convinced me that not only should every school be a great school, but that this is now a reasonable, realizable and socially just goal for any mature educational system. Inevitably this fourth edition emphasizes some of the issues I wrestled with in government – the importance of moral purpose in system reform, the primacy of personalized learning and the absolute necessity of getting all parts of the system moving in the same direction.

It is this commitment to a practical philosophy of emancipation and empowerment as well as a particular set of individual circumstances that underpin the argument in this book. After this introduction, a few case studies of teacher-based research are given to provide a context for what follows. In Chapter 3, two arguments are considered for teacher-based research – the need for professionalism in teaching, and the inadequacy of the traditional research approach in helping teachers improve their classroom practice. In Chapter 4, action research, which has become the main vehicle for teacher research, is discussed and critiqued; from that discussion, six criteria for teacher-based research are suggested. Chapter 5 discusses the ways in which teacher research problems are formulated and initiated. Chapters 6 and 7 describe the principles and practice of classroom observation, and in Chapter 8 various other ways of gathering data are described. Chapter 9 outlines a method for analysing these data and Chapter 10 discusses how to report and disseminate them. These six chapters constitute the heart of the teacher research process. There is in Chapter 11 an explicit focus on teaching and particularly learning as well as an emphasis on the importance of personalized learning. In arguing that pedagogy should become the heartland of classroom

---

[1] The government department responsible for Education in England is now called Department for Children Schools and Families (DCSF).

research, I review the research on effective teaching and models of teaching and provide practical examples of three common models of learning and teaching. The discussion in Chapter 12 locates the role of the teacher-researcher in the broader systems context. It first explains the nature of system reform and then identifies the four drivers for system reform that teacher-researchers can play a central role. In doing this I connect the discussion in previous chapters to the themes of teacher and school development, in particular the creation of a culture that promotes networks and professional learning communities within and outside the school.

A continuing emphasis throughout the book is the importance of establishing a professional ethic for teaching. Implicit in this idea is the concept of teacher as researcher. The teacher-researcher image is a powerful one. It embodies a number of characteristics that reflect on the individual teacher's capacity to be, in Stenhouse's phrase, 'autonomous in professional judgement'. A major factor in this is the teacher's ability to think systematically and critically about what they are doing and to collaborate with other teachers. Central to this activity is the systematic reflection on one's classroom experience, to understand it and to create meaning out of it. By becoming self-conscious, collaborative and critical about their teaching, teachers develop more power over their professional lives, extend their teaching repertoires, and are better able to create classrooms and schools that are responsive to the vision they and we have for our children's future.

Further reading

The key source for any teacher-researcher is still the work of Lawrence Stenhouse and in particular his *An Introduction to Curriculum Research and Development* (1975). Although he died before making his own comprehensive statement on classroom research by teachers, Jean Rudduck and I (Rudduck and Hopkins 1985) edited his published and unpublished writing to make such an argument in *Research as a Basis for Teaching*. Until the mid-1980s most of the work on teacher research was either philosophical discussion (Kemmis 1983, 1988), reports by researchers (Elliot and Adelman 1976) or teachers' own accounts of their research (Nixon 1981). Since that time however, there has been a dramatic growth in the number of books on the topic. Pride of place must go to John Elliott's (1991) *Action Research for Educational Change*, which traces the development of the teacher research movement, describes its methodology and explores how it can be 'a form of creative resistance' to centralized policy-making. Other books that attempt in different ways to link teacher research to school development and educational change are Helen Simons' (1987) *Getting to Know Schools in Democracy*, Rob Halsall's (1998) collections on *Teacher Research and School Improvement*, our own *The Empowered School* (Hargreaves and Hopkins 1991) and *The New Structure of School Improvement* (Joyce *et al.* 1999). However, more recently there is an increasing number of books that more directly link teacher research with school improvement as the *Improving Schools through Collaborative Enquiry* (Street and Temperley 2005), *Guiding School Improvement with Action Research* (Sagor 2000) and *Teacher-led School Improvement* (Frost *et al.* 2000). Much else of relevance to the theme of 'classroom research by teachers' has been published recently, and I have referred to them in the Further Reading section at the end of the most appropriate chapter.

2   Classroom research in action

Often the phrase classroom research brings to mind images of white-coated (or grey-suited!) educational researchers undertaking research in a sample of schools or classrooms and using as subjects the teachers and students who live out their educational lives within them. Often this image is correct. This book, however, is about another kind of research in which teachers look critically at their own classrooms and use research primarily for the purpose of improving their teaching and the quality of education in their schools. But even the phrase 'classroom research by teachers' can sound a little daunting. It might be useful therefore to begin with some examples of teachers who have engaged in systematic enquiry with the purpose of understanding and improving their practice.

The first three case studies were written by teachers. The first report begins as an exploratory case study that through the reading of literature on learning becomes a focused systematic inquiry. The second is an interesting example of how the process of research can reveal surprising insights that necessitate the re-think of the research focus. The third example is the most systematic one and illustrates the use of quantitative data in some detail.

The next five examples reflect the focus in this fourth edition of the book on teaching and learning and school improvement. The first pair demonstrates how learning can be shared between departments in a school. The sixth example is written by John Beresford, the research officer on the IQEA project, describing how he collaborates with schools in providing data on teaching and learning styles to assist in defining the focus of their improvement strategies. The seventh is by David Jackson who, at the time of writing the cameo, was Head of a longstanding IQEA School, Sharnbrook Upper School and Community College in Bedfordshire. (David was until recently Head of Research at the National College for School Leadership.) This vignette describes how the school improvement focus on teaching and learning is organized at Sharnbrook, and how students are involved in the process.

The final example is different from the others in a number of ways; as it illustrates in a more sophisticated manner the use of 'quantitative' methods than the third case study and it was also written by Lawrence Stenhouse.

In each of these cases, the teachers are engaging in classroom research for the express purpose of improving the quality of educational life in their classroom. This is no deficit model of improvement. However, the teachers involved are genuinely interested in understanding the dynamics of their own teaching style. They believe that 'you do not have to be ill to get better'. The motivation for doing so may be varied – a research degree, natural curiosity, a stimulating article or talk – but the process and its implications are essentially the same. Taken together, these cases illustrate the range and benefits of doing research in your own classroom and provide examples of the reflective professional in practice.

CASE STUDY

The first example is a case study by Rebecca Jones, a school teacher at Llanrhidian Primary School. Her research was initiated because of the school's involvement with The International Network for School Improvement project set up by Swansea LA.[1]

School context

The school serves a large area of North West Gower, comprising the communities of Llanrhidian, Llangennith, Llanmadoc and several small hamlets. The school accommodates children between the ages of 1 and 11 who are taught in split age group classes.

Selecting the focus for the project

As a group of colleagues we began by making a list of what we believed to be the characteristics of a good learner. We then went away to consider these characteristics in relation to our own class and to draw out any of our own conclusions about what makes an effective learner.

In the weeks that followed the meeting, I observed my Y1/Y2 class with these factors in mind. My primary area of interest was the children's communication skills since it was clearly the 'better learners' in the class who were more articulate and better able to express themselves. It was these children who were much more likely to approach me to discuss the aspects of their work they were finding difficult or were enjoying and to question me about it. Many children in the class however seemed to expect me to second guess the difficulties they were having instead of attempting to formulate an appropriate question.

Reading about children's learning I became increasingly interested in children's questioning and a lot of what I read strikes a chord with my own personal experiences. For example the fact that very young children are enthusiastic communicators and seem to have an innate ability to ask questions.

We have all been driven to distraction by the young child who asks question after question in their insatiable quest for knowledge about the world around them. So I had to

---

[1] The then International School Effectiveness Centre and now The International Network for School Improvement and part of the London Centre for Leadership in Learning (in 2005) was invited by Swansea LA to work with a group of schools to study the effectiveness of the learning and curriculum in their schools through classroom enquiry. This example was one of the case studies teachers produced during the project. It has been edited and published with the permission of Rebecca Jones and of Jane Reed, Head of the International Network for School Improvement.

ask myself why it was that in my infant class of 5–7-year-olds this instinctive ability to ask questions was not apparent.

The audit process

We began with the question: 'How can we get children to ask the types of questions that will further their learning?' This was then broken down into 5 focused questions, which could form the basis of our research project. I used the Y1s as my target group from my mixed Y1/ Y2 class:

1   What are children's current attitudes towards question-asking?
2   Which children in the class ask the most/least questions?
3   What types of question are currently being asked by the children?
4   Does curriculum area affect the frequency and type of question being asked?
5   Does current planning facilitate the asking of questions across the curriculum?

Question 1

I began by conducting a class discussion to find out what were the children's current attitudes towards question-asking. I prepared a set of questions to form the basis of the discussion. I divided the children into two groups to interview separately, to allow the less confident children to be interviewed together thus preventing the more forthcoming children from dominating the discussion. I taped the discussions so that I could analyse the data later.

The children participated enthusiastically in the discussions and I was amazed that they held such well-developed views on the subject.

Although both groups were adamant that they were not frightened to ask me a question several children expressed a concern that their questions might be regarded as 'silly' or 'not good'. Some children felt concerned that their questions may be deemed irrelevant.

My second main finding was even more disconcerting. The children were not at all sure about when it would be an appropriate time to ask me a question. In general, they seemed to believe that it was OK to ask me a question if it's *not* in lesson time. Dinner-time, play-times and the end of the day were all suggested as good times.

It seems that the children strongly believe that their questions are not of importance and that maybe only teacher questions have a place in the classroom. The children seem to view their questions as interruptions.

Question 2

I carried out a survey over the course of one normal school day to record the frequency of each child's questions. I planned a typical days' lessons and deliberately did not open the class up for questions at any point to see how many spontaneous questions were asked.

The results highlighted the fact that on the whole the children asked very few questions. Only 8 questions were asked in total and most arose from the children requesting help with their work.

The second part of the survey gave the children more scope for asking questions since I carried out two focused lessons, one in history and one in science, that were conducive to children's questioning. I planned appropriate breaks in the lessons to invite the children's questions.

To answer my question about who was asking the most questions it was one of the students who asked 5 in history and 8 in science. Another student asked 5 questions in science but only 1 in history. Three children asked no questions at all.

Questions 3 and 4

Classroom observations lead me to the conclusion that the types of questions asked by the children tend to be functional. Such as 'should I underline the heading?' or they relate to lack of understanding of tasks – 'what am I supposed to do on question 5?' Such questions are unlikely to lead them to significant further learning and rarely arise from a real curiosity in a subject. However, when I made room for children's questions by planning opportunities into the lesson, the children asked questions which demonstrated that they were able to reflect on what had been learnt and were genuinely curious to find out more. In such lessons I found that listening to the children's questions enabled me to assess how much of the lesson had been understood and to plan subsequent steps.

To assess the impact of the curriculum area on children's questioning I carried out a survey over one normal school day but this time recorded the children's questions according to subject. The results highlighted again that the children are asking very few questions regardless of curriculum area. No questions were asked in the maths lesson and the most asked was 3 in a drama session – most questions related to the children's need for further explanation of tasks.

I wanted to analyse the frequency and type of questions asked by the children given the optimum conditions, i.e. lessons with planned opportunity for question asking – so I used the tape recording of the history and science lesson described earlier to analyse the questions asked.

The science lesson produced the most questions from the children. Twenty-six were asked in total whereas the history lesson of the same length produced only 14.

I then categorized the questions according to 5 groups. Nine of the science questions were found to be unanswerable. It seemed that some children had difficulty formulating a good question and also maybe that some children were asking any old question for the sake of it. In history, 14 out of 14 questions were researchable.

My conclusions from this piece of research are that in science the children need to ask more observable questions and perhaps more testable questions that would lead to investigation. In history there is a need for more subjective questions that focus on the thoughts and feelings of people from the past.

Questions 5

I scrutinized my Y1/Y2 planning across the whole 2 year cycle and noted down where activities had been planned which would promote the asking of questions. I found planned opportunities in language, science, history, Welsh, geography and R.E. but less specific questioning activities in maths, IT, art, music and technology. This has obvious implications for my future planning.

Summary of main findings

The main findings from the audit phase could be grouped into four main areas.

- *Attitudes*: Children often see their questions as irrelevant. Some children equate question-asking with interrupting.
- *Time for questions*: Children didn't know when question-asking was allowed. Lesson-time was clearly identified as being an inappropriate time for children's questions.
- *Question type*: In a normal day, questions tend to be functional but when lessons were planned appropriately, good quality questions were raised.
  Most questions asked in science were researchable or unanswerable and in history all were researchable only.
- *Who asks the questions?*: Some children are naturally better at asking questions than others. Some children have difficulty formulating an appropriate question.

Targets and success criteria

In the light of these findings we formulated a success criteria list outlining what we hoped to achieve by the end of the project:

1 *Children's attitudes*

- Improved attitudes to the asking of questions
- Children to recognize the value of their questions as well as teacher questions in the classroom.
- Children to gain an understanding into why question-asking is desirable.

2 *Question type*

- Children to ask 'good' questions at appropriate times, which clarify or further their learning (Learning skill).
- The children need to ask more testable questions in science, which might lead to investigation (Attainment/Achievement skill).
- There is a need for more subjective questions in history (Attainment/Achievement skill).

3 *Time for questions*

- More planned opportunities for children to ask questions during lesson time and across the school day (Teaching skill).

4 *More children asking questions*

- Some lessons need to be planned deliberately to improve children's questioning techniques (Teaching skill).

Implementation and strategies

A second class interview was held which focused on two main points: first why children should ask questions in class, and secondly when would be an appropriate time to ask questions. The children obviously couldn't be given a free reign to bombard the teacher with questions at any time, certain boundaries needed to be set. The discussion highlighted a problem, that there may be times when a child has a burning question, which cannot be asked due to inappropriate timing. To overcome this problem Y1/Y2 children are now encouraged to jot such questions down on a sticky note. If related to the current lesson the question can then be asked at a more suitable point, i.e. when the teacher has finished speaking.

To encourage the children to ask their questions which deal with issues not being covered in current classwork they are now asked to stick their question post-it to the whiteboard. Time is set aside each week to discuss selected questions from the board. After such sessions the children are often motivated into researching themselves their questions, and interestingly a more constructive use of the school library has been noted. Sometimes research is continued at home and it is now a common occurrence for children to come to school armed with encyclopaedias with pages earmarked for my attention.

To encourage more testable questions in science a question board has been added to the class interactive science display on which children are invited to attach their topic related questions. The electricity topic evoked a wealth of questions. Some of the questions needed to be answered through research but many naturally led the children into scientific investigation. Examples include 'Will two bulbs light in a circuit?' and 'How do you make a buzzer buzz?' With the equipment at hand the children were able to answer their own questions through immediate experimentation.

The last two terms have begun by introducing the new topic to the children and inviting them to pose any questions they would like to see answered through their class activities. The ensuing 'brainstorm' then provides a framework for some of the term's work. This approach has given the children a greater deal of motivation towards their classwork by offering them an ownership of their learning. The brainstorm is referred to weekly to see whose question is being answered.

The children also use questions now to help each other edit their creative writing. The children take turns to sit on the 'author's chair' to read their compositions aloud. The audience is allowed to ask any helpful questions that may enhance the author's work e.g. 'what was the setting?' 'Why did the main character leave home at the beginning?' Questions such as these often highlight parts of the story where important details have been omitted and any ambiguities in the story line.

Evaluating and monitoring the strategies

During the winter term 2001 while continuing with the development work I also began to turn my attention to monitoring and evaluating the success of the project. First I carried out a final questionnaire with the target group of children who had just moved into Y3 and so were no longer in my class. I asked their opinion of the strategies that had been in place during their time with me. The children's comments showed a surprising awareness of the benefits of the activities to their learning. Here is a selection of some of the most revealing comments;

- *Sticky note boards*: 'If children asked a question it meant they didn't know it and so they could learn more things'; 'If the teacher is busy you can stick it on the board instead'
- *Topic planning charts*: 'We get to know things we want to learn about'; 'Other children might need to know the same sort of things as we do so it helps them learn too'
- *Children should ask questions because . . .*: 'The teacher will know what we need to learn'; 'It's easier for the teacher to know what we don't know'

I also carried out a selection of focused lesson observations while the children were engaged in some of the activities described above. On the advice of Jane Reed, the Head of the School Effectiveness and Improvement Centre I devised a recording sheet that allowed commentary of the lesson on three different levels. The first section of the sheet required a description of the activity taking place. Secondly I would make a reflective/analytical statement about the significance of the activity in terms of the project's aims and objectives. The third section allowed a speculative comment about the activity, i.e. what were the implications of the activity for future project work. Lastly I would note any unintended benefits or impacts.

Findings

Through the wide range of activities carried out during the last few terms the children have demonstrated that they certainly are eager to ask questions and when given appropriate opportunities they do ask them. Children need to be given time to articulate their questions and this must be planned into lessons and not left to chance.

I found some curriculum areas easier to plan with a questioning approach than others so decided to concentrate on improving the children's questioning skills in English, science and history.

I found that getting children to raise questions about texts gave them a much more sophisticated understanding of plots and characters. During 'hot-seating' activities the children seemed naturally to ask the character about their motives and relationships with others. The child on the hot-seat had to reply in character and refer back to events in the story to substantiate their answers. In this way the children were able to move beyond a literal understanding of text as they began to make inferences and deductions.

Encouraging children to ask the kinds of question that will lead to investigation is at the very heart of successful primary science. The term's science topic always produced more children's questions than any other curriculum area. I found that the questions dealt with more complex aspects of the topic as the term progressed and the children's understanding and knowledge developed. During the topic on electricity Jennifer (age 6) asked, 'How do we light the bulb?' and a few weeks later asked 'Do two bulbs light in a circuit?'

Her second question shows that she now has the answer to the first question and is ready to move to a further level of understanding. Also the second question demonstrates that she can use subject specific terminology (i.e. circuit).

History also seemed to naturally lend itself to a question-asking approach. The children asked the most pertinent questions and those they genuinely wanted answers to when they had an identified audience. The children prepared questions for our class trip to Cefn Coed

Colliery Museum to ask the guide. Having done a good deal of work already on the topic of mining the children had plenty of questions already in their minds which they were now able to ask our expert. The questions revealed a strong interest in the lives of the children and horses who worked in the mines which we were able to follow up back in class. Of course in light of the trip there were more questions which arose back in class, the answers to some began to take us beyond the realms of the children's understanding. In this way question-asking, like the learning process, is never complete. Questions generate more questions and the teacher needs to be aware of the appropriate point to stop the questions and to consolidate existing knowledge and understanding.

From interviewing the children at the end of the project it is evident that the children gained great enjoyment and satisfaction in investigating and researching questions raised by themselves. They demonstrated greater motivation towards class activities knowing that they had had an input in the planning stage.

Outcomes from the project

Children are more likely to ask good quality questions when the learning activities are well structured with a tight focus.

It was observed that children asked better quality questions when they had prior knowledge of the study area and had already participated in classroom activities relating to it. When children were invited to ask questions about a brand new topic there was evidence of children offering questions because they felt they had to. In these cases there were more instances of unanswerable questions. This was particularly the case when the new topic had a very broad focus e.g. 'Houses and Homes'. Topics such as 'Mould' and 'Electricity' produced the best quality questions.

Evidence gathered from talking to the pupils demonstrates they understand question-asking as a tool to their learning.

During the final interviews with the target group I asked the children to complete the sentence 'Children should ask questions because . . .'. Eight out of 11 children made a direct reference to the benefit of question-asking to their learning.

Evidence from lesson observations shows that children ask good quality questions when they are given first hand experiences.

When the children were engaged in practical tasks such as observing mouldy food, making electrical circuits or seeing which materials are attracted to a magnet, their questions arose spontaneously and from genuine perplexity or interest.

Good quality questions are raised when the children have opportunities to talk to each other.

An unintended outcome from the project has been the improved group work among the children. Many of the activities introduced in the development phase required the children to work as a pair or a group. As a result the children have much better skills of co-operation and collaboration and have become quite mature in their ability to turn-take and delegate responsibility. The talk observed within the groups was often purposeful and sustained. Children were observed discussing their questions and refining them when necessary. One question from one child would often trigger another child's question.

CASE STUDY

This second report was produced by an infant school teacher concerned with the behaviour of black boys in her school. It shows how she quickly discovered that the introduction of anti-racist teaching was a bigger priority.[2]

Anti-racist teaching in a multicultural school

Background

The research was triggered by an assumption: that an increase in extreme behaviour in the school could be linked to an increase in the number of children from ethnic minority groups, especially boys with a Black African background. The original aim was to investigate ways to support this group of children to prevent them becoming disaffected at such a young age. What the research actually uncovered was something shocking: that I was racist.

I discovered that I was clearly influenced by the stereotypes of certain groups of people, and because of this made assumptions about their behaviour and the reasons for it. The fact is that those demonstrating 'out of control' behaviour were not part of any one ethnic group. The focus of the research therefore moved on to look at developing anti-racist practices within the school.

The school setting

This research took place in a larger than average infant school serving a community in the thirty-sixth most deprived local authority in England. The educational background of parents is generally very low. Attainment on entry is well below average, particularly in terms of children's development in communication, language and literacy. The school population is predominantly white, but with a growing number of families from a range of ethnic minority groups.

Research method

The research used an ethnographic approach, which consisted of finding out people's opinions and experiences including my own. I shared my concerns and aims with the participants, regularly discussing my findings with them. The purpose of the exercise was

---

[2] This report is published by the General Teaching Council for England (GTCE) (http://www.gtce.org.uk/networks/achieve/learn/antiracist_teaching).

to deepen our understanding of how we were responding to the changing ethnic profile in the school.

I kept a journal of events as they happened and documented questions I couldn't answer that arose from them. I would then re-visit these events over time and evaluate them in light of my reading and discussions with participants. This proved to be a powerful tool to use in honestly examining my own thinking and practice.

I interviewed a range of parents and teachers to find out what they thought about their own education, their own ethnicity, and their experiences of racism. I asked what they thought about existing provision in the school to promote anti-racism and any suggestions they had for improvements.

Findings

Teachers on the whole felt that not enough was being done to promote anti-racism. They were concerned that, although the multicultural approach of learning about other faiths, food and traditions was valuable, it was not enough to ensure equality of provision. However, they were unsure what else they could do. They felt that often they did not deal with issues through fear of saying the wrong thing.

Parents were largely pleased that their children learned about other cultures. Those from minority ethnic groups felt that racism was something they had to put up with, as it was never going to go away. They advised their children to grow a thick skin and ignore racist remarks. Many felt their job opportunities were fewer because of the colour of their skin, and they all felt they had to work harder than white people to gain recognition for the things they did. One parent felt it was good that protective legislation was available, but pointed out that though this did offer some protection it did not change attitudes and had the effect of silencing racist views and sending them 'underground'.

Pupils were initially surprised as teachers became more confident about initiating discussion related to ethnicity. However, they very quickly began to join in and initiate discussions themselves.

The impact of the research

The major impact of this research is a change in the attitudes of teachers, pupils and parents alike.

Teachers are now more confident in being proactive in teaching in an anti-racist manner, both through the curriculum and by recognizing and dealing with racist incidents. Opportunities to highlight and discuss differences are actively sought within the curriculum.

Pupils are comfortable to bring up issues of 'race' and ethnicity, allowing dialogue that promotes equal opportunities and enables misconceptions to be dealt with. Teachers and pupils are more confident to discuss issues of ethnicity as part of class groups. PHSE has become a major vehicle in promoting these discussions, although history, art, religious education and dance are other areas that are developing an anti-racist approach.

Parents who were involved with the research have said they feel listened to and valued, and there has been a marked improvement in relationships. Work with parents is in its infancy, though, and still needs development.

CASE STUDY

This third example was written by Christine Arthington, a design and technology team leader from High Tunstall School and was commissioned by the National Teacher Research Panel for the Teacher Research Conference 2004.[3]

Using data to ensure gifted and talented students achieve their full potential in design and technology

Aims of project

The research set out to look into the provision for Gifted and Talented (GAT) pupils within design and technology at Key Stage 3 in a Hartlepool school, which was currently using a standardized ability test known as Middle Years Information System (MidYIS). Two questions were considered:

- Are test results from MidYIS a reliable indicator for technology GAT pupils?
- Does a more creative delivery encourage GAT pupils to produce higher-level ideas and to be more satisfied with their projects?

Context

The project looked at the effectiveness of identification data across one year group of 230 students in an 11–16 comprehensive school. The study then continued through action research involving two groups of approximately 22 mixed ability students, one acting as a control group and one as the test group.

Summary of main findings

Identifying gifted and talented pupils in design and technology (D&T). Evidence indicated that:

- the MidYIS testing was a useful general tool for initial identification of GAT pupils;
- individual components of the overall grade needed to be considered – particularly non-verbal, maths and skills – for identification within D&T;
- analysis of the MidYIS data was very useful when considering underachievement;
- clear guidelines were essential to help identify GAT subject specific talents; and
- reference to professional judgements helped to ensure that special talents were not missed in the identification process.

---

[3] This research report was commissioned by the National Teacher Research Panel for the Teacher Research Conference 2004, and is published by the DCSF, (http://www.standards.dfes.gov.uk/ntrp/lib/pdf/Arthington.pdf).

Implications for delivery of the curriculum were that:

- an emphasis on creativity and individual choice could help to stimulate the interest and motivation of GAT pupils;
- strategies to teach and develop creativity were of benefit to GAT pupils;
- ability grouping appeared to help in creating a climate conducive to stimulating the imagination as part of the design process; and
- pupils needed a 'safe' environment in which they can be encouraged to demonstrate innovative ideas in D&T without fear of ridicule and failure.

Background

High Tunstall School is an 11–16 comprehensive with 1150 students on roll. It is part of Hartlepool Excellence in Cities action zone but does not have a high proportion of disadvantaged families. Prior to the research, identification of GAT pupils in school was carried out by teacher nomination. Within the D&T department, staff used professional judgement, based on pupils' class work, when identifying individuals as GAT, with little reference to performance data. This led to a large number of pupils being nominated with little coherence of standards across the department.

To address such discrepancies the school introduced the Middle Years Information System (MidYIS) – a standardized ability test carried out within four areas: vocabulary, maths, non-verbal and skills – for the 2001 Year 7 cohort. Through analysis of these results, pupils could be sorted by rank order and a quantitative measure applied to identify the relevant GAT pupils. The author was keen to discover whether these general tests accurately reflected D&T ability and talent.

In addition, OFSTED has long reported that 'making is better than designing' in D&T, with pupils being taught practical techniques rather than being encouraged to have innovative ideas. One common factor, firmly established in the many checklists for GAT (George 2001: 42), is an ability to demonstrate creativity. Hence the author also decided to investigate the effects of a more creative delivery method.

Teaching processes and strategies

The author made a simple modification to the delivery of the next textile project by introducing a group design exercise in the first session, prior to any specific material knowledge being taught. She was keen to explore whether this produced more creative designs than the previous technique of designing at a later stage. This exercise was intended to create a non-threatening environment in which pupils felt comfortable to take risks and not to be too concerned with the practicalities of construction. The opinions of the test group were then compared with a control group who had had a 'teacher led' delivery (traditional emphasis on making) to examine if the more creative delivery (stressing experimentation and discovery) encouraged GAT pupils to produce higher-level ideas and to be more satisfied with their projects.

Findings

Results of identification by current staff nomination system

Different teachers have identified almost half the cohort as GAT over the course of the year (see Table 2.1); clearly there was a problem with the current system. The author reflects that this could be due to:

- the lack of agreed detailed criteria or baseline assessments;
- pupil's individual preferences for different themes;
- staff personality differences; or
- undue influence of attractive presentation, which may also have influenced nominations, as it does not necessarily reflect ability.

Other factors could be pressure of work on staff leading to lack of quality time for assessment of potential, lack of differentiation or challenge in the curriculum, emphasis on 'making' rather than creativity and national assessment criteria not being sufficiently rigorously applied.

Identification according to MidYIS test results

If the GAT were identified as the top 20% of pupils ranked by overall MidYIS score, then 44 pupils become the cohort. However, if the GAT were identified using only one individual category such as non-verbal score, a different cohort would be the top 20% as can be seen by the figures in Table 2.2.

Table 2.1 Staff nominations of GAT pupils after each project

	Autumn	*Spring*	*Summer*	*Consistent nominations in same category*	*Total of different pupils nominated*
Top 5%	16 total 12 girls 4 boys	17 total 13 girls 4 boys	13 total 9 girls 4 boys	5	
Top 10%	22 total 20 girls 2 boys	24 total 23 girls 1 boy	19 total 9 girls 10 boys	1	
Top 20%	16 total 14 girls 2 boys	20 total 13 girls 7 boys	34 total 23 girls 11 boys	2	
Total (Cohort 219 pupils)	54(23.4%) 46 girls 8 boys	61(26.5%) 49 girls 12 boys	66(28.6%) 41 girls 25 boys	8	107(48.8%) 70 girls 37 boys

Table 2.2 Summary of ranked MidYIS test results

	Total size	20%	Top 50 pupils ranked by MidYIS overall score	Number of pupils not in overall top 50 MidYIS group but in top 50 of individual test areas			
				Vocabulary	Maths	Non-verbal	Skills
Year 7	219 total	44 total	50 total	15(30%)	10 (20%)	15(30%)	19 (38%)
2001	105 girls	21 girls	25 girls	4 girls	6 girls	8 girls	11 girls
cohort	114 boys	23 boys	25 boys	11 boys	4 boys	7 boys	8 boys

Table 2.3 Staff nomination of pupils compared to MidYIS testing

Top 50 pupils in each area	MidYIS	Vocabulary	Maths	Non-verbal	Skills
Number of pupils missed by staff nominations	22 total	24 total	20 total	20 total	22 total
	4 girls	6 girls	2 girls	5 girls	5 girls
	18 boys	18 boys	18 boys	15 boys	17 boys

Comparison of staff nomination and MidYIS testing

Despite 107 pupils of the cohort being nominated as GAT under the current system, 22 of the most able, according to MidYIS, were never mentioned. Many factors may have contributed to this including underachievement, attendance, behaviour problems and gender differences. The quiet pupil who does not demand attention (Wallace 2000: 31) and the 'academically able' pupil who may not necessarily be talented in D&T could also have affected nominations. Some pupils may have under/over performed in the Table 2.2 tests and some may argue that 'pencil and paper' tests do not accurately reflect D&T ability. Nevertheless, on consideration of these various factors, it was decided to identify GAT pupils within the sample groups as those with an overall MidYIS A grade.

Outcomes following a change of curriculum placing more emphasis on creativity

Textiles is a totally new experience for the Year 7 D&T groups. The original, teacher-led, control group were provided with experience of materials and equipment prior to producing ideas for a storage hanging (traditional emphasis on making). With the test group, an ability based group design exercise employing a strong emphasis on 'safe risk taking' was used. Pupils were encouraged throughout the project to investigate and try out the skills necessary to implement their original ideas and discover for themselves which restrictions had to be placed on the construction phase.

The results show the range of ideas produced (see Figures 2.1 and 2.2) and, when asked, all pupils agreed or strongly agreed that the exercise had been useful. Group 1 (most able) made use of a good range of different ideas and utilized annotation effectively to produce designs that were creative and functional. Group 6 (least able) demonstrated the

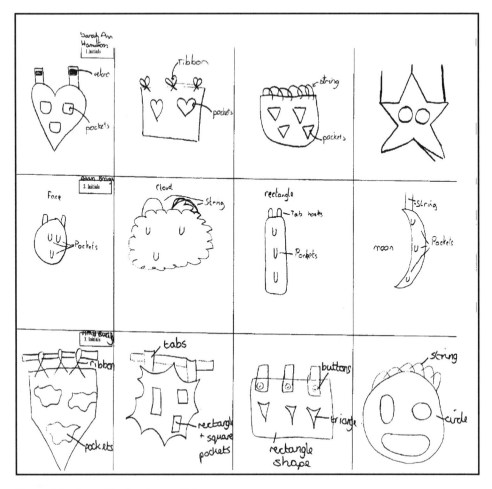

Figure 2.1   Group 1's ideas (most able).

'developmental' rather than 'new' aspect of designing. No annotation is present and many of the ideas are reworked versions of another. This group found the exercise particularly difficult, as they had to think quickly, one minute per idea.

Questionnaire results
A questionnaire, developed from an Australian study by Anne Fritz (1998), was administered to both groups under exam conditions. It was emphasized that there were no 'wrong' answers and pupils were encouraged to be as truthful as possible. Fritz identified three factors that significantly defined the D&T learning experience (satisfaction, ease and independence) and the results were considered in relation to these.

When looking at satisfaction in Figures 2.3 and 2.4, the GAT pupils in the test group were more positive than those in the control group indicating a better learning experience for these pupils. However, the non-GAT pupils in the test group were less satisfied than those

Figure 2.2 Group 6's ideas (least able).

in the control – perhaps because they were required to do more 'thinking' and make more individual decisions.

With regards to 'ease' in Figures 2.5 and 2.6, the majority of normal pupils in the control group felt that they had finished the project easily and none were disappointed. However, in the test group, 50% experienced difficulty in completing the work and 10% were disappointed. The author concluded that this was due to the more demanding approach delivered to this group producing a better-differentiated experience for the pupils.

Pupils in the test group felt more independence than pupils in the control group according to Figure 2.7. This demonstrates the individuality of the more creative approach and allows pupils to take more ownership of their work.

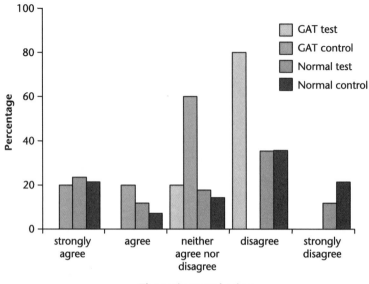

The project was boring

Figure 2.3 Disagreement on 'The project was boring'.

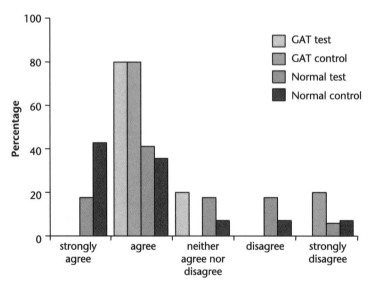

It was worth all the work

Figure 2.4 Agreement on 'It was worth all the work'.

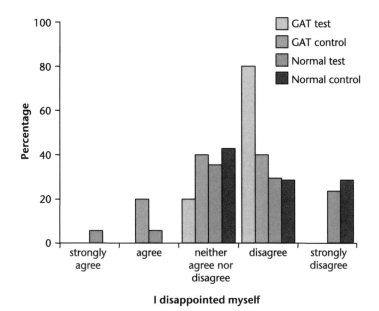

Figure 2.5   Ease: disagreement with 'I disappointed myself'.

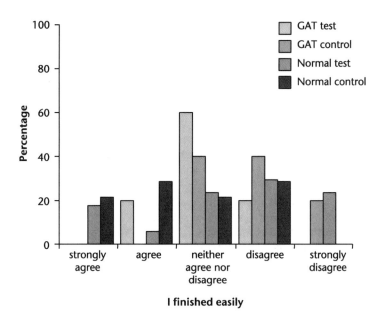

Figure 2.6   Ease: agreement with 'I finished easily'.

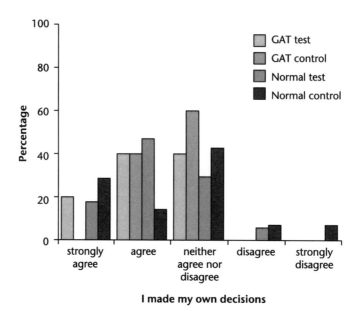

Figure 2.7 Independence: agreement with 'I made by own decisions'.

Final outcomes

The final wall hangings that were produced demonstrated the better creativity of the test group. For example, the shape of the backgrounds and number/type of suspension methods was more varied than that of the control group. On comparing the overall outcomes of both groups it is clear that the test group demonstrated more creativity than the control group but that the standard of construction was similar.

These results lead to the conclusion that, by arranging pupils within groups by ability and introducing a simple creative design exercise at the start of the project, GAT pupils were more satisfied with their work and produced higher-level initial ideas.

Research methods

Students take the MidYIS test on entry to the school and data from these results were analysed to identify prospective GAT individuals. Design and technology staff were also asked to identify GAT students in their teaching groups, under the current system of using professional judgements, at the end of each project session resulting in three sets of identification data for examination. These two sets of identification data were then compared in terms of which students made up the top 20% of the year group, and hence were classed as GAT, to explore if the same students were identified by each method. A questionnaire was then designed, incorporating some features of a study by Anne Fritz (1998) in Australia, that compared the views of winners of D&T awards with 'ordinary' pupils. The objective of the questionnaire was to explore the affective responses of students to the different delivery styles used in the test projects.

Conclusion

Identification

This small-scale research project provides evidence to demonstrate inconsistencies resulting from systems of teacher identification of GAT where there are no clear guidelines to work from.

When considering alternative methods of identification of GAT pupils, colleagues may wish to reflect on whether generic tests such as the in-school MidYIS provide an accurate diagnosis of ability in the D&T processes. Nevertheless, it is clear that in this study MidYIS testing did give an independent assessment of general ability against which D&T talents could be assessed and underachievement considered. Through the limited examination of the different test area scores done here, I feel that non-verbal, maths and skills scores of pupils should be taken into account when producing initial ability lists for consideration. I would suggest that the overall top 50 plus 'extras' from these areas form an initial short list from which the top 20% can be selected by specialist D&T staff. This is in line with the DfES (2002) recommendation for use of both quantitative and qualitative methods for identification.

Focus on creativity

The results demonstrated that pupils found the emphasis on creativity to be more challenging and motivating than the traditional style of delivery. The GAT pupils in the test group were more satisfied with their projects than the GAT in the control group. The variety of ideas produced initially by the group exercise showed a good range of imagination, although many of these were later simplified to accommodate production issues. Overall this proved to be a good method of enriching the curriculum for all and in particular for the GAT pupils. With further improvement and development of strategies/resources to extend this focus, the level of differentiation within the group could be additionally enhanced.

However, for this approach to be most successful, it seems to be important that pupils of similar ability work together at the designing stage in order to stimulate more creative ideas. Once the focus of the project has been established, pupils can work effectively in friendship groups with GAT pupils offering support to the less able during construction. This, in turn, helps them to consolidate their own skills.

CASE STUDY

The fourth and fifth examples should be treated as a pair. These have both been conducted as part of the NCSL-CfBT Research Lesson Study project supported by the Teaching and Learning Research Programme and the Economic and Social Research Council in England. The project aimed to provide network and school leaders with the appropriate tools to conduct research.[4]

Fourth example

> KS3 subjects: science, modern foreign language (MFL), English as an additional language (EAL)
> Pedagogy: literature across the curriculum
> Research lesson question: How can we use MFL techniques to boost pupil achievement in science?

Four research lessons studies, three research partner teachers

An analysis of pupil data revealed a group of Year 9 pupils who were predicted to achieve Level 4 in science in Key Stage 3 tests. Their class teacher felt they knew the science and were held back in test scores by their early developmental stage in English, which was causing them to fail to articulate the science he felt they knew.

He worked with colleagues from the MFL department. They used a research lesson to establish the degree to which his hypothesis may be correct – using non-verbal assessment methods to ascertain the pupils' levels of scientific understanding. They then brainstormed approaches using language learning techniques which may help develop the pupils' abilities to structure, sequence and express their scientific understanding in written answers to questions. The science lessons began to incorporate activities such as cut up instructions to sequence, structured cloze test and DARTs activities which pupils did in pairs and groups. The research lessons were used to establish ways of making these more effective by close observation of focus pupils.

Findings and outcomes

Pupil attainment expressing science orally and in writing soared. All but one of the pupils predicted to attain Level 4 in fact attained Level 5.

Fifth example

> KS3 subjects: science, music, EAL.
> Pedagogy: peer tutoring

---

[4] Examples four and five were published by Networked Learning Communities/CfBT (2005) *Network leadership in action: Networked Research Lesson Study in practice. Booklet 2*, Nottingham: NCSL, p. 6.

Research lesson question: How does peer tutoring in music work – and how can the science department learn from the technique in order to improve science teaching and learning?

Three research lessons studies, four research partner teachers plus seven ITT students

An advanced skills teacher in science wanted to find out how a successful science department, in a multilingual school, could learn from an exceptionally successful music department. What techniques could be replicated or adapted? Research lessons were used to identify how peer tutoring was used and how pupils utilized and benefited from the techniques. Only this level of study would enable understanding of the process in sufficient depth to begin to design similar approaches in science.

A sequence of lessons was observed and captured on video. The research partners made more and more targeted use of the video to enable subsequent studies of the developments and behaviours of the focus pupils.

Findings and outcomes

The study enabled the research team to be very explicit about the component parts of the peer tutoring which was in use so successfully and to analyse how these worked. They produced artefacts to illustrate these (please see www.nlcexchange.org.uk for details). They also produced evidence of the enhancement of pupil learning of music, English acquisition, self-esteem and confidence to learn. The next quest is to use research lesson study to implement what was learned in science.

Analysis

These two examples both show careful studies, which have enabled learning to travel between departments in the same school. The research teachers took care not to make assumptions about what 'peer music tutoring' or 'writing about science' might involve.

They used the research lessons to ensure that the understandings were deep and shared across the subject boundaries, before attempting to solve the issues. But both also show how the learning about how to teach, which the teachers gained, impacted upon pupil learning and achievement – in the first of the two cases, dramatically improving upon predicted Key Stage 3 and GCSE grades (their validation test). All these colleagues had taught together for some years, but it has been research lessons study which has opened the doors, or glass walls, between departments and subject areas.

CASE STUDY

In this vignette, the sixth example, John Beresford, the research officer on the IQEA project, describes how he collaborates with schools in providing data on styles teaching and learning to assist in defining the focus of their improvement strategies.

There is already an extensive literature on the component parts of effective teaching (see, for example, Chapter 10) but less on the process of matching teaching strategies to students' learning styles. Much of the matching of teaching and learning styles has been extremely speculative, based upon the premise that if a sufficient variety of strategies are employed, then a catch-all effect will apply.

The need for some form of dialogue between teachers and students about teaching and learning methods in the classroom has increasingly been recognized by a number of the schools in the IQEA project. These schools have shown themselves willing to discuss with students their views about what constitutes effective teaching. It is also clear that they regard some acknowledgement of student learning preferences, in the teaching which takes place within their classrooms, as an element of effective teaching in its own right. They have also called for an easy-to-administer research instrument that can both help them match what goes on in classrooms more closely to the preferences of their students and provide clues about where to develop the teaching repertoire of their teachers and the learning repertoire of their students.

In order to undertake an audit of the teaching strategies used in its classrooms, and a survey of students' views on those strategies, we developed instruments based on the work of David Kolb. Kolb's (1984) seminal work, *Experiential Learning*, effectively reconceptualizes Piaget's work on developmental learning into four distinct and authentic learning styles, with no implicit hierarchical structure. These four learning styles can be represented as quadrants in a grid where the two dimensions of perceiving and processing information have been juxtaposed, and Kolb also gives useful descriptors of each learning style.

Our colleagues have further identified a range of classroom activities and strategies associated with each of the four learning styles (see Fielding 1994) and from this have produced an observation schedule which can be used to record the incidence of these various activities in a lesson (Beresford 1998). Each activity is coded according to the learning style for which it caters. As each activity occurs in the lesson, its incidence is noted. No assessment is attempted regarding the effectiveness of the various strategies within the context of the lesson. At the end of the period of observation the different number of strategies and learning activities employed by the teacher is totted up and recorded, in the boxes provided, against the appropriate learning style. Hence the lesson can be said to have a particular profile corresponding to the combination of numbers in the boxes. These can be converted into percentages of the total number of strategies and activities used.

In order to assess students' preferences for these characteristics teaching activities, we drew up a similar schedule on which students were asked to indicate which of the activities they preferred. The schedule consists of a list of classroom activities directly related to the teaching strategies listed in the observation schedule. By scoring 'Don't Like' responses as 0, 'Don't Mind' as 1 and 'Like' as 2 and adding the total for each of the learning style categories, a profile similar to that derived from lesson observations can be derived for each student. By adding the totals of all students in a particular group, a group profile can be obtained. These profiles indicate individual and group learning style preferences (see Beresford 1998, 1999).

The schedule is versatile inasmuch as it can be used to gauge individual's learning preferences as well as group ones. Students' preferences in individual subjects can be assessed as well as their general learning preferences. Some schools have used the schedules to find out which strategies the students feel are most effective in the teaching of an individual subject, but most have felt that their students lack the necessary analytical skills to arrive at such a judgement. The schedule can also be used to assess any gender differences or differences between year groups.

CASE STUDY

In the seventh example, David Jackson who, at the time of writing the cameo, was Head of Sharnbrook Upper School and Community College in Bedfordshire, describes how the school improvement focus on teaching and learning is organized at Sharnbrook, and how students are involved in the process.

Sharnbrook Upper School and Community College was established as a 13–19 upper school in 1975 to provide comprehensive education for 32 villages situated in rural mid-England. Sharnbrook's school improvement model is now a continuous, whole-school initiative deeply embedded into our work. At its heart is a fluid group (cadre) of staff committed to working in partnerships and together around areas of mutually agreed enquiry. During the eight years of involvement with IQEA we have had almost as many different modes of operation for the school improvement group, but certain characteristics remain consistent. Some of these are that:

- The school improvement group is led by two staff operating in a co-leadership model.
- The school improvement group breaks down into trios of staff, each engaged in a separate enquiry designed to generate knowledge and understanding about the school's work and to indicate directions for improvement.
- Each of these partnerships undertakes a sustained process of enquiry within the school, drawing also from the knowledge-base within the field and from good practice elsewhere, and, as an outcome of this data-gathering, suggests improvement to the school's practice, supports the implementation of improvements and then enquires further into their effect upon student learning or the wider school community.
- Each partnership tries to ensure that all those who contribute towards their research are involved, too, in the process of making meaning from the data and, where feasible, in the implementation of outcomes.
- Each partnership also commits to connect with the wider constituency of staff,

students, parents and governors in order that all who need to do so can share the emergent journey.

- The school facilitates opportunities for each partnership to lock into consultation and decision-making structures, as appropriate, so that findings from the enquiry will be implemented.
- The entire school improvement group commits to monitoring the value of their own work and to critique each other's practice.

It goes without saying that staff at all levels of the school are involved, including newly qualified teachers, support staff and, more recently, students. Each partnership is entirely free of status positions within the more formal organizational structure of the school and offers leadership opportunities to a variety of staff. Some partnerships might be involved with significant whole-school issues (for example, assessment strategies to improve student achievement) while others may be engaged in focused classroom research activity (questioning technique, or cooperative groupwork). The scale of the intended impact is less significant than the quality of the knowledge deriving from the enquiry. A piece of classroom research, for example, can have equally powerful whole-school impact if the knowledge (about seating arrangements, starts and finishes of lessons – or whatever) is sufficiently significant and widely owned.

By 1997 we had incorporated into the model a group of students who were empowered to operate their own 'school improvement group', complementing and mirroring the style of the wider group. As the student voice dimension of our work evolved, we wanted more authentic and active involvement than 'passive voice'. Between a third and half the staff were, at this stage, involved any one year, focusing exclusively on enquiry and improvement issues.

The 1999/2000 model retains the concept of trios, but reverts to a focus specifically upon teaching and learning. Following a workshop with the whole staff, six areas of classroom practice were identified, and each of the trios has adopted one of these areas mandated by the whole staff. The first 'enquiry' task for each of the partnerships is to develop a powerful theoretical understanding of their particular teaching and learning focus – by researching the knowledge-base, observing classrooms, visiting other schools, or whatever. The trio will then practise and develop their skills in the classroom, providing in-house coaching for one another. The next phase will be to engage in action research with students to seek to validate the impact of this approach upon learning. Throughout this process the remainder of the staff (all staff not involved in one of the partnerships) will choose one of the areas, creating associate groups of about 15 staff for each partnership, who will follow the course of events, engage in workshops and generally become immersed and prepared. When (or if) the action research process validates the impact of the model, the associate staff will be asked to adopt the approach in their own classrooms and to be coached by the trio engaged in the original work.

This is a huge over-simplification of the model, but even described at this level it gives indications of the infrastructural and cultural changes that have evolved through the work of the various models. These would include:

- the opening up of classrooms and classroom practice and the legitimization of in-class coaching;

- the creation of a language to talk about teaching and school improvement;
- the integration of enquiry and professional development approaches;
- the value and authenticity of the student voice and the significance given to their perceptions as learners;
- the willingness of all staff to embrace the value of the development work emanating from the school improvement group;
- the ownership by the whole staff of the school improvement approach;
- the power of a sustained school improvement journey to win over those initially sceptical or even cynical;
- the expansion of leadership capacity.

CASE STUDY

The final example is taken from a paper by Lawrence Stenhouse (1979: 71–7; reprinted by permission of Universitetsforlaget AS). He describes, in the first person singular, the fictionalized predicament of a teacher who turns to the research literature for advice on which teaching strategy to use.

I teach social studies in the form of a human issues programme covering such topics as the family, poverty, people and work, law and order, war and society, relations between the sexes. I wonder whether I should include race relations. A complicating factor is my style of teaching controversial issues to adolescent students. I set up discussions and use evidence such as newspapers, stories, pamphlets, photographs and films. I act as neutral chairman in those discussions, in order to encourage critical attitudes without taking sides. In short, I have been influenced by and am in the tradition of the English Humanities Curriculum Project (Stenhouse 1970).

I am very concerned that my teaching should contribute positively to race relations in my multiracial society, if that is possible. I wonder whether I should teach about race relations at all. If so, I wonder whether it is appropriate in this case to take the role of neutral chairman, even though this is a teaching convention and not a position professing personal neutrality. So I turn to a research report on 'Problems and Effects of Teaching about Race Relations' for enlightenment (Stenhouse *et al.* 1982, cited in Rudduck and Hopkins 1985).

Here I find that the project has monitored on a pre-test, post-test basis two different strategies of teaching about race relations, one in which the teacher is neutral (called strategy A), the other in which the teacher feels free to express, whenever he feels it appropriate, his committed stance against racism (called strategy B). Strategy A was conducted in 14 schools and strategy B in 16 schools. The samples are not true random samples because of problems of accessibility of schools and students, but I know something about this from my study of education at college (Campbell and Stanley 1963). Control groups have been gathered in the same schools as the experimental groups whenever this was possible, though this was not possible in all cases. I came across this table (see Table 2.4) of results on a scale purporting to measure general racism.

Table 2.4 Scores on the General Racism Scale of the Bagley-Verma Test[a]

	Experimental sample			Control sample			
Teaching style	Pre-test mean (S.D.)	Post-test mean (S.D.)	Direction of shift and t-value difference of means	Pre-test mean (S.D.)	Post-test mean (S.D.)	Direction of shift and t-value difference of means	t-value for difference between the experi-mental and control groups
Strategy A							
Experimental (n = 258)	17.24	16.51	1.71	16.06	17.61	2.11*	2.83**
Control (n = 124)	(10.05)	(10.25)		(9.66)	(10.49)		
Strategy B							
Experimental (n = 359)	17.25	16.17	2.27	17.42	17.87	0.72	1.91
Control (n = 180)	(9.61)	(9.78)		(9.93)	(10.58)		

[a] A decrease in score represents a decrease in racism.
* P < 0.05; ** P < 0.01.

This seems to help me a good deal at first sight. My neutral strategy is strategy A. Attitudes in the strategy A group seem to improve and, though the improvement does not quite reach even the 0.05 level of significance, the control groups, left to general influences, deteriorate in attitude significantly and the comparison of experimental and control shows at least by one criterion a 0.01 level discrimination in favour of teaching about race relations by strategy A. Strategy B does not look markedly superior to strategy A, so I don't seem to need to change my teaching style. So it seems that research has helped me by enabling me to decide the right style in which to teach about race relations.

But, oh dear, here's a problem. On a later page the same data are presented in a different form to show the situation in individual schools and this seems to complicate the issue as shown in Table 2.5. Now, looking at this table, I personally feel that, given comment codes A, B or C, I certainly ought to proceed, given comment codes D and possibly E, I should proceed with great care, and given codes F and G, I might be better to give a lot more thought to the matter. In seven out of 12 schools, the result seems encouraging, in four schools results seem doubtful and in one of the 12 rather alarming. How do I know what category my school will fall into? This is really rather disturbing for my decision. Perhaps I should shift to strategy B. Let's look at the strategy B table (see Table 2.6).

Oh dear! This is no better. Here eight out of 15 schools are reassuring, three are doubtful and three are alarming. Strategy B seems no refuge.

Can it be that statistically significant discriminations between two treatments when presented through means and standard deviations can mask such a range of within-sample

Table 2.5 Differences between pre- and post-test school means for the experimental and control groups on the General Racism (GR), Anti-Asian (AA) and Anti-Black (AB) Scales of the Bagley-Verma Test: Strategy A

1	2	3	4	5	6	7	8
School code	Experi-mental GR	Experi-mental AA	Experi-mental AB	Control GR	Control AA	Control AB	Comment code
03	−1.83	−0.35	−1.22	–	–	–	C
07**	1.58	0.54	0.31	−0.86	0.21	−0.71	G
09	−0.22	0.55	−0.90	2.11	1.45	1.09	A
10*	−0.63	−0.18	−1.54	–	–	–	C
13	−0.85	0.37	−1.29	−0.89	−0.56	−0.67	D
17	−2.50	−1.17	−1.78	–	–	–	C
18	1.70	2.40	0.90	6.63	4.38	3.75	B
19	0.37	−0.04	0.62	–	–	−D	
29	−3.42	−1.75	−1.67	2.0	0.87	−0.25	A
31**	−0.12	0.77	0.65	0.34	0.50	−1.16	D
32**	−1.61	−0.70	−0.83	−0.07	−0.77	−0.38	A
39*	1.20	−0.50	1.05	–	–	–	D
Mean of strategy A controls (individuals)				(1.30)	(0.83)	(0.49)	

* 5–25% non-white; ** over 25% non-white.

Table 2.6 Differences between pre- and post-test school means for the experimental and control groups on the General Racism (GR), Anti-Asian (AA) and Anti-Black (AB) Scales of the Bagley-Verma Test: Strategy B

1	2	3	4	5	6	7	8
School code	Experi-mental GR	Experi-mental AA	Experi-mental AB	Control GR	Control AA	Control AB	Comment code
01	−3.51	−1.60	−2.57	−1.75	1.43	−1.34	A
02	0.00	−0.67	−0.10	2.43	1.22	1.43	A
04*	1.04	0.10	0.24	–	–	–	E
05	−2.27	−0.34	−0.97	–	–	–	C
06*	−2.00	1.29	−1.30	0.55	0.34	−0.52	D
08	1.09	0.30	0.07	−5.40	−1.20	−2.33	G
09	−2.89	−0.22	−1.97	2.11	1.45	1.09	A
11	−1.58	−0.48	−0.53	–	–	–	C
14**	−0.33	0.39	0.91	–	–	–	D
15	−2.25	0.17	−1.42	–	–	–	C
20	−0.39	0.05	−0.22	−1.15	0.86	−1.43	F
21		−1.77	−1.32	−1.19	1.59	1.04	0.59
24*	0.19	0.37	0.60	4.93	1.07	1.65	B
30*	3.79	1.27	2.16	–	–	–	E
33	1.00	0.43	0.38	−0.83	0.83	−0.08	G
Mean of strategy B controls (individuals)				0.90	0.71	0.30	

* 5–25% non-white; ** over 25% non-white.

variance as this? It can indeed. In the psycho-statistical research paradigm, the effects are not 'other things being equal'; they are 'by and large' or 'for the most part'. So doing one thing is only sometimes better than doing the other! This, apparently, depends on your school context or school environment or perhaps yourself or your pupils.

What I have to find out now is whether teaching about race relations by strategy A is good for my pupils in my school. However, that reminds me that I haven't looked at pupils as individuals, only as means and standard deviations. Suppose I took these data and looked at them in a way that depicted the fate of individuals. How about a histogram of change scores. There are, of course, problems with such scores but, bearing them in mind, I'll give it a go (see Figures 2.8 and 2.9).

My goodness, it looks as if the same teaching style and the same subject matter make some people worse as they make other people better. One man's meat is another man's poison. If I teach about race relations, some people get worse. But if I refuse to teach about race relations, even more people get worse. I suppose I should have thought of that anyway. I know that when I teach literature some people come not to like it, but I believe that even fewer would enjoy literature if I didn't introduce them to it all.

I need to steady myself. After all, engineers don't always build exactly the same bridge. Nor do chess players always play the same game. There must be ways of fitting action to situation and perhaps even to individuals in that situation.

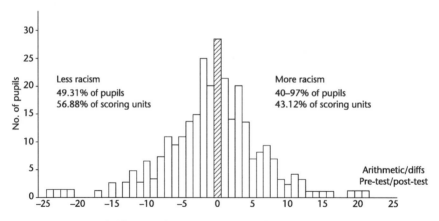

Figure 2.8 Histogram of differences between the pre- and post-test scores on the General Racism Scale of the Bagley-Verma Test: Strategy A experimental (n = 288).

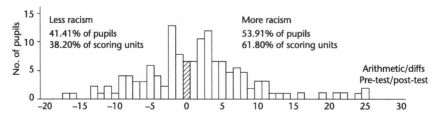

Figure 2.9 Histogram of differences between the pre- and post-test scores on the General Racism Scale of the Bagley-Verma Test: Strategy A control (n = 128).

I've clearly got to think things out for myself. Does this mean that research cannot help me? What was that piece in the paper by Cronbach they gave us in Ed. Psych? Here are my notes. And here it is:

> When we give proper weight to local conditions, any generalization is a working hypothesis, not a conclusion.
>
> (Cronbach 1975: 125)

That seems to mean that the results of research need testing in local conditions. What research gives me is most often not findings about all teaching but hypotheses about my teaching.

This is a bit of a shock, but it makes reasonable enough sense. And the hypotheses I've got are already of some use. I must test whether strategy A works well for me in my class-room, whether I can sustain its logic in practice and whether it is giving good results in attitudes. At the same time, I know that even in a good result some individuals may be deteriorating in attitude.

What I am going to do is this. I'm getting a student to come in and pre- and post-test my pupils and a control group in my school. But I'm also going to tape our sessions on race relations on a portable cassette-recorder. To do this, I have to tape other lessons too, so that I don't seem to be concentrating on race. I've started this. I'm explaining to the students that I'm doing a study of my own teaching and that this should help me to teach better. And I'm beginning to get them talking about how well my teaching and their learning goes.

Of course, there's a problem about how to handle the tapes. I played some at home and tried a Flanders Interaction Analysis (Flanders 1970) on them. It did tell me that I talked too much, but not a lot more. Then I tried the Humanities Curriculum Project analysis, which worked quite well because I was involved in discussion teaching. But I want to look at pupil behaviour as well as teacher behaviour. I'm beginning to ask myself whether I can develop a theory of individuals who cause me concern in class. I don't even need paper to do that. I can play cassettes in my car as I drive to and from work.

The more I come to study my own classroom, and my own school as well, the more I come to understand why the research provides case studies of classrooms. Comparing other people's experiences with my own throws up all sorts of illuminating possibilities – hypotheses, I mean.

At the end of this session, I'm going to try to set up a club in the district for teacher-researchers. They have clubs for people who tinker with motorcycles to get more per-formance from them, so why not the same for teachers who are tinkering with their teaching?

I'd like to set about testing Piaget. Most of his experiments are a kind of teaching. And I have a feeling that if I work with a small sample, like he did, I'll find out quite a lot for myself. I've got a better laboratory than he had: it's a real classroom!

I'm not sure if I'm doing research. I am testing hypothesis by experiment as systematic-ally as a busy job allows.

The Shorter Oxford English Dictionary says that research is: 'Investigation, inquiry into things. Also, habitude of carrying out such investigation.' Well, it is beginning to become a habit.

Further reading

There are a number of sources for further examples of classroom research by teachers. In *A Teacher's Guide to Action Research*, Jon Nixon (1981) presents a series of descriptive accounts by teachers of a variety of classroom research projects. Extended illustrations of teacher research are given by Michael Armstrong (1980) in *Closely Observed Children*. Classic examples of classroom research in this tradition, although involving the participation of an external researcher, are found in Smith and Geoffrey's (1968) *The Complexities of an Urban Classroom* and Stephen Rowland's (1984) *The Enquiring Classroom*. Jean Rudduck and her colleagues (Hull *et al.* 1985; May and Rudduck 1983; Rudduck 1981) have produced collections of teacher research accounts as a result of their funded research projects. During the 1980s, the Classroom Action Research Network (CARN), the Ford Teaching Project, and the Teacher–Pupil Interaction and the Quality of Learning (TIQL) project (Ebbutt and Elliott 1985; Elliott and Ebbutt 1985a, b) all published accounts of their classroom research activities that were available from the Centre for Applied Research in Education, University of East Anglia. More recent collections of teacher research case studies are found in *Action Research in Classrooms and Schools* (Hustler *et al.* 1986), which mainly focuses on secondary schools, and Rosemary Webb's (1990) *Practitioner Research in the Primary School*. Four other books that contain detailed examples of classroom research as well as descriptions of method and philosophical discussions are *Collaborative Action Research* (Oja and Smulyan 1989), Richard Winter's (1989) *Learning from Experience*, Atweh *et al.* (1998) *Action Research in Practice: Partnership for Social Justice in Education*, and Burnaford, Fischer and Hobson (2001) *Teachers Doing Research: The Power of Action Through Inquiry*.

Governmental interest in the 'teacher as researcher' concept has recently contributed considerable legitimacy to the movement. As a consequence, the research papers published by the DCSF (www.standards.dfes.gov.uk/ntrp) the National College for School Leadership (NCSL) (www.nscl.org.uk), the Teacher Training Agency (TTA) (www.tda.gov.uk) and the GTCE (www.gtce.org.uk) provide a rich and important source of classroom research case studies, as do the articles in *TOPIC* (published by the National Foundation for Educational Research) and *Improving Schools* (published by the Institute of Education, London). Homerton College publishes teachers' research accounts under the aegis of the Homerton – Schools' Research Circle.

3 Why classroom research by teachers?

In asking the question 'Why classroom research by teachers?', one is raising a whole series of issues around the topics of professionalism, classroom practice, the social control of teachers and the usefulness of educational research. Each of these issues provides a rationale for teacher research. For example, classroom research by teachers can be justified by references to professionalism because systematic self-study is a hallmark of those occupations that enjoy the label 'professional'. Unfortunately, the teacher's claim to professionalism sometimes falters at this definition. In this chapter, however, I will focus on three other themes that justify and, indeed, make imperative a concept of classroom research by teachers. The first is the link between classroom research by teachers and the establishing and refining of professional judgement. The second is making the focus of classroom research the curriculum and teaching learning. The third is the inappropriateness of the traditional research paradigm for helping teachers improve their teaching. I conclude the chapter with a reflection on the nature of classroom research itself.

'Autonomous in professional judgement'

Lawrence Stenhouse (1984: 69) described the ideal role of the teacher like this:

> Good teachers are necessarily autonomous in professional judgement. They do not need to be told what to do. They are not professionally the dependants of researchers or superintendents, of innovators or supervisors. This does not mean that they do not welcome access to ideas created by other people at other places or in other times. Nor do they reject advice, consultancy or support. But they do know that ideas and people are not of much real use until they are digested to the point where they are subject to the teacher's own judgement in short, it is the task of all educationalists outside the classroom to serve the teachers; for only teachers are in the position to create good teaching.

This is a very different image from the contemporary approach to schooling that is based on the assumption that instructions issued from the top – from the minister, the director of education or headteacher – are put into practice at the appropriate level lower down the organization. This approach to education tends to equate schools to factories which operate on a rational input–output basis, with pupils as raw material, teachers as mechanics, the curriculum as the productive process and the school leaders as factory managers.

This image of schooling stands in direct contrast to the aspirations of the teacher research movement. John Elliott (in Nixon 1981: 1) has observed that 'the teacher as researcher movement emanated from the work and ideas of Lawrence Stenhouse'. Crucial to an understanding of Stenhouse's intellectual position is, as we saw in Chapter 1, the notion of emancipation (see Stenhouse 1983). In this context, emancipation refers to the process involved in liberating teachers from a system of education that denies individual dignity by returning to them some degree of self-worth through the exercise of professional judgement.

In terms of curriculum and teaching, the path to emancipation involves reconceptualizing curriculum development as curriculum research, and the linking of research to the art of teaching (Rudduck and Hopkins 1985). When viewed through this particular lens, centrally imposed curricula are in danger of becoming prescriptive blueprints that tend to inhibit autonomy in teaching and learning. On the other hand, the process model of curriculum, as described by Stenhouse (1975), is liberating or emancipatory because it encourages independence of thought and argument on the part of the pupil, and experimentation and the use of judgement on the part of the teacher. When teachers adopt this experimental approach to their teaching, they are taking on an educational idea, cast in the form of a curriculum proposal, and testing it out within their classrooms. As Stenhouse (1975: 142) said:

> The crucial point is that the proposal is not to be regarded as an unqualified recommendation but rather as a provisional specification claiming no more than to be worth putting to the test of practice. Such proposals claim to be intelligent rather than correct.

The major consequence of doing this is that teachers take more control of their professional lives. Curriculum content does not prescribe what one has to do, or makes teachers feel uncertain with what they are doing. Teachers who engage in their own research are developing their professional judgement and are moving towards emancipation and autonomy. This idea is so central to the concept of the teacher as researcher, that I describe in Chapter 11 a series of practical ways in which teachers can refine their professional judgements. It is important to note that although this approach encourages new teaching strategies and implies a different way of viewing knowledge, it is not inimical to the idea of a National Curriculum or other curriculum guidelines, such as National Literacy or Numeracy strategies.

Curriculum and teaching as the focus of classroom research

Successful implementation of any centralized innovation requires adaptation by teachers at the school level. It is not an either/or situation or a straight choice between 'top-down' or 'bottom-up' – it is a combination of both. As Denis Lawton (1989: 85) argues in his book *Education, Culture and the National Curriculum*:

> [we need] more curriculum development which is at least partly school-based. This is not to suggest that the centre–periphery or 'top-down' models of curriculum development are completely outmoded: it is a question of balance. It would be unreasonable to expect every school to develop its own curriculum from first principles, but it would be equally foolish to attempt to impose a detailed, uniform curriculum on every school, leaving no room for school-based development geared to specific local needs.

This balance is maintained through the professionalism of teachers. As Lawton (1989: 89) further comments:

> The increasing desire of teachers to be treated as professionals rather than as state functionaries, has encouraged a tendency to look for ways in which teachers could solve their own professional problems at a local level rather than react to more remote initiatives. Hence the emphasis on the school as the obvious location for curriculum renewal, the in service education of teachers, the evaluation of teaching and learning, and even educational research.

The crucial point that Lawton is making is that the claim of teaching to be a profession lies in the ability and opportunity for teachers to exercise their judgement over the critical tasks involved in their role, namely curriculum and teaching. Most centralized school systems prescribe what is to be taught to pupils, but require the teacher to put the curriculum into practice. At a very basic level, this involves the teacher in some form of 'translation' of the curriculum policy into schemes of work or lesson plans. More emphasis on research-based teaching would, I believe, result in better 'translations' of centralized curriculum into practice and in teachers who are more confident, flexible and autonomous.

Over a quarter of a century ago, Stenhouse made essentially the same point by suggesting that classroom research be used as a means of testing curriculum ideas. The context of that proposal is worth reproducing in full (Stenhouse 1975: 142–3):

> I have argued that educational ideas expressed in books are not easily taken into possession by teachers, whereas the expression of ideas as curricular specifications exposes them to testing by teachers and hence establishes an equality of discourse between the proposer and those who assess the proposal. There is, of course, no implication as to the origins of the proposal or hypotheses being tested. The originator may be a classroom teacher, a policy-maker or an educational research worker. The crucial point is that the proposal is not to be regarded as an unqualified recommendation but rather as a provisional specification claiming no more than to be worth putting to the test of practice. Such proposals claim to be intelligent rather than correct.
>
> I have identified a curriculum as a particular form of specification about the practice of teaching and not as a package of materials of a syllabus of

ground to be covered. It is a way of translating any educational idea into a hypothesis testable in practice. It invites critical testing rather than acceptance.

I have reached towards a research design based upon these ideas, implying that a curriculum is a means of studying the problems and effects of implementing any defined line of teaching.

The uniqueness of each classroom setting implies that any proposal – even at school level – needs to be tested and verified and adapted by each teacher in his own classroom. The ideal is that the curricular specification should feed a teacher's personal research and development programme through which he is progressively increasing his understanding of his own work and hence bettering his teaching.

To summarise the implications of this position, all well-founded curriculum research and development, whether the work of an individual teacher, of a school, or of a group working in a teachers' centre or of a group working within the co-ordinating framework of a national project, is based on the study of classrooms. It thus rests on the work of teachers.

Here Stenhouse is linking classroom research by teachers firmly to the curriculum and teaching. This is an important point that may have been lost in all the talk about the gathering and analysis of data. Teacher research is not an end in itself, but is inextricably linked to curriculum change and the adoption of new teaching strategies. It is also at this point that teaching becomes a profession.

Problems in traditional approaches

Perhaps the most unfortunate aspect of traditional educational research is that it is extremely difficult to apply its findings to classroom practice. The final case study in Chapter 2 is a good illustration of this. In a quandary about which teaching strategy to use, the fictionalized teacher went to the research literature for guidance. His subsequent experience was as frustrating as it was predictable, because the literature contains few unequivocal signposts for action. This dilemma is widespread: teachers quite rightly (in most cases) regard educational research as something irrelevant to their lives and see little interaction between the world of the educational researcher and the world of the teacher.

Arthur Bolster (1983: 295) asked the question, 'Why has research on teaching had so little influence on practice?', and his response to the question is worth quoting:

The major reason, in my opinion, is that most such research, especially that emanating from top-ranked schools of education, construes teaching from a theoretical perspective that is incompatible with the perspective teachers must employ in thinking about their work. In other words, researchers and school teachers adopt radically different sets of assumptions about how to conceptualize the teaching process. As a result, the conclusions of much formal research on teaching appear irrelevant to classroom teachers – not necessarily wrong, just not very sensible or useful. If researchers are to generate knowledge that is likely to affect classroom practice, they must construe their inquiries in ways that are much more compatible with teachers' perspectives.

Most researchers, when they enter classrooms, bring with them perspectives derived from academic disciplines. Their view of how knowledge evolves and how it is determined are firmly established by their formal training. The world view that guides researchers' actions is consequently at odds with that of teachers. The teacher derives their knowledge of teaching from continual participation in situational decision making and the classroom culture in which they and their pupils live out their daily lives. So one reason why traditional educational research is of little use to teachers is because of the differing conceptions of teaching held by teachers and researchers. But there are other problems.

Research in education is usually carried out within the psycho-statistical research paradigm. This implies tightly controlled experimentation and the testing of hypotheses by assessing the effectiveness of a treatment across randomly selected groups through the use of statistical analysis. This approach is based on the agricultural research designs of R.A. Fisher (1966) in the 1930s. At that time, educationalists, desiring to link research to action, began to utilize the very successful 'agricultural–botany' designs of Fisher in educational settings. This has continued (and increased) down to the present day as can be seen by the myriad of postgraduate theses that use this research design. The basic idea underlying Fisher's designs is that experiments are conducted on samples, usually divided into a control and an experimental group, with the results generalized to the target population. The point is that samples are randomly drawn and are consequently representative of that target population.

Stenhouse (1979) describes Fisher's approach like this:

> The strength of Fisher's paradigm is the recognition of random sampling, in which a sample is drawn such that each member of the target population has an equal chance of being included in the sample because it is a device of chance . . .
>
> In Fisher's agricultural setting, the hypotheses were not derived from scientific theory . . . They were hypotheses regarding the relative effectiveness of alternative procedures, and the criteria of effectiveness was gross crop yield.
>
> The result of an experiment of this kind is an estimate of the probability that – other things being equal – a particular seed strain or fertilizer or amount of watering will result in a higher gross yield than an alternative against which it has been tested . . . It is in applying experimental methods to teaching and curriculum evaluation in the schools that researchers have used the Fisherian model. The assumption is that one teaching procedure or curriculum can be tested against alternatives as a seed strain or fertilizer can in agriculture, i.e. procedures can be tested against yield without a real theoretical framework.

This approach to educational research is problematic, particularly if its results are to be applied to classrooms. First, it is extraordinarily difficult to draw random samples in educational settings (e.g. a random sample of schools, pupils and teachers would have to be drawn separately). Second, there are a myriad of contextual variables operating on schools and classrooms (e.g. community culture, teacher personality, school ethos, socio-economic background, etc.) that would affect the results. Third, it is difficult to establish criteria for effective classroom or school performance. Even if one could resolve these difficulties, there are, as Stenhouse (1979) points out, two deeper problems that relate to the nature of educational activity.

First, the 'agricultural–botany' paradigm is based on measures of gross yield (i.e. how much produce can be gathered in total from a section of land). That is an inappropriate measure for education. As teachers, we are concerned with the individual progress of students rather than with aggregated scores from the class or the school. Our emphasis is on varying teaching methods to suit individual pupils in order to help them achieve to the limit of their potential. Stenhouse (1979: 79) puts the paradox like this:

> The teacher is like a gardener who treats different plants differently, and not like a large scale farmer who administers standardised treatments to as near as possible standardised plants.

The second deeper problem relates to meaningful action. The teacher–pupil or pupil–pupil interactions that result in effective learning are not so much the consequence of a standardized teaching method but the result of both teachers and pupils engaging in meaningful action. And meaningful action cannot be standardized by control or sample. This is a similar argument to the one commonly used against those who overrate the utility of behavioural objectives. Behavioural objectives provide an excellent means for the teaching of skills or evaluating rote learning, but they tend to be counter-productive with more complex and sophisticated content areas. In the instance of rote learning, one can accept the parallel with standardized treatments, but not so easily with poetry appreciation. Here pupil response is the result of individual negotiation with the subject, mediated through and by the teacher – namely, a form of meaningful action. In this case, education as induction into knowledge is, as Stenhouse (1975: 82) memorably points out, 'successful to the extent that it makes the behavioural outcomes of pupils unpredictable' and, therefore, not generalizable. The implications of this line of thinking for teacher-researchers is to encourage them to look outside the psycho-statistical paradigm for their research procedures.

To summarize, I have made two points in arguing that the traditional approach to educational research is not of much use to teachers. The first point is that teachers and researchers do not conceptualize teaching in the same way. They live in different intellectual worlds and so their meanings rarely connect. Second, the usual form of educational research, the psycho-statistical or agricultural–botany paradigm, has severe limitations as a method of construing and making sense of classroom reality. For these two reasons, teachers and those concerned with understanding classroom life have increasingly adopted different approaches to classroom research.

The nature of classroom research

So far in this chapter I have been arguing for classroom research by teachers on three grounds: the first being its role in refining professional judgement; the second being its focus on the key professional activities of teachers; and third, the inadequacy of existing research paradigms for teacher researchers. There is, however, a further issue on which to reflect when discussing the importance of classroom research: the nature of the research activity itself. This is an issue that has vexed teacher-researchers and those that comment on it for some time.

As a precursor to the discussion, let me quote from Ebbutt (1985: 157):

> If action research is to be considered legitimately as research, the participants in it must, it seems to me, be prepared to produce written reports of their activities.
>
> Moreover these reports ought to be available to some form of public critique. I would go as far as to say that if this condition is not satisfied by participants then no matter how personally and professionally valuable the exercise is in which they are engaged, it is not action research.

While I would agree with Ebbutt's call for written reports and critique, particularly by other teacher-researchers, I disagree with the implication that unless the research is published it is not research. It seems to me that many current commentators on classroom research have a misplaced conception of what research actually is. Michael Armstrong (1982) exemplified this position well:

> I have grown impatient with the concept of 'research'. In the context of a study of education it has acquired too narrow a connotation especially in regard to criteria for rigour, evidence and validity. I prefer the word 'enquiry' . . . The form of enquiry which I have in mind is grounded in the experience of teaching and in particular in that practice of sustained observation which is inseparable from good teaching . . .

Armstrong seems to be saying, 'Let's call it enquiry and let's keep it in the classroom and then we won't need to tangle with such questions as what counts as research.' Hull *et al.* (1985) complicate this position even further. They appear to say, 'Let's call what Armstrong does self-monitoring "an investigation of one's own practice in private" but let's recognize that there is also teacher research.' They argue that teacher research (Hull *et al.* 1985):

> . . . must feed a tradition – from which individual researchers can derive support. In this way it is quite different from the activity which has been called 'self-monitoring' where a teacher uses some of the data-gathering techniques developed by researchers to record instances of their own practice as a basis for reflection. The self-monitoring teacher makes no claims to be methodologically reflexive. He or she does not undertake responsibility either to introduce

'system' into the investigations or make accounts of the studies available to other teachers. Self-monitoring is essentially a privatised encounter between a practitioner and practice. As such it has immense value. We conceive teacher research however, as potentially the root of a tradition of enquiry into educational processes which might stand alongside the academic tradition as an alternative body of knowledge rooted firmly in practice.

These claims are to me both confused and pedantic. The dichotomy that Armstrong and Hull and their co-workers point to is just not there. Armstrong's *Closely Observed Children* (1980) is one of the best teacher research studies. It is sensitive, insightful and profound; it is research at a high level of sophistication, imagination and rigour. Armstrong is doing teacher research in general, and himself in particular, a grave disservice to claim otherwise. One can readily appreciate Armstrong's 'impatience with the concept of research' but to call it something else is not to change anything. What he is impatient of is narrowly defined psycho-statistical research that has little to say to teachers, not research *per se*.

Research, enquiry and self-monitoring are all aspects of a similar activity because they all require systematic, self-conscious and rigorous reflection to be of any value. The problem is that psychological research, with its emphasis on statistical manipulation, has captured the educational imagination to such an extent that most people cannot think of research in any other terms. But criteria, such as validity or internal consistency, are necessary if teacher researchers are to escape the sentimental anecdote that often replaces statistical research designs in education, and gives teacher research such a bad name. Enquiry, self-monitoring and teacher research need to establish standards and criteria that are applicable to their area of activity, rather than assume (and then reject) criteria designed for different procedures.

Teacher research, like enquiry and self-monitoring, is a form of research. These forms may be presented to different audiences and formulated in different ways, but all are attempts to create meaning out of complex situations. And the meaning is only valid when it is subject to certain methodological standards. It is naive to argue that just because we call what we do enquiry or self-monitoring instead of research we can escape the demand for valid judgement. That is throwing the baby out with the bath water. It is equally incorrect to assume that just because we engage in research, we have to follow the criteria of the psycho-statistical research paradigm. If these criteria are inappropriate then other more suitable methods, like the ones discussed in subsequent chapters, have to be sought.

There are two important points to be drawn from this discussion. The first is that classroom research by teachers is a valid form of research because it results in hypotheses generated through a rigorous process of enquiry and grounded in the data to which they apply. This meets contemporary criteria for research. In the article to which I have already referred, Ebbutt (1985: 157) cites:

> Shulman's conception of what counts as research, that it is 'a family of methods which share the characteristics of disciplined inquiry' . . .

1   arguments and evidence can be examined

2   not dependent solely on eloquence or surface plausibility
3   avoids sources of error when possible and discusses margin for possible errors in conclusion
4   can be speculative, free wheeling and inventive.

This, it seems to me, is an accurate description of classroom research as it is being described in this book.

The second point is that it is important for teacher-researchers to open up their work to critique and, if possible, to publish it. It is pleasing in this respect to see the publication of teacher research reports in England by the Training and Development Agency (TDA), the General Teaching Council for England (GTCE), the Department for Children, Schools and Families (DCSF) and the National College for School Leadership (NCSL). The importance of public critique in classroom research is that it encourages a discourse among teachers, that is research-oriented and committed to action and the improvement of practice. It is the sharing of our experiences and the social and intellectual benefits that emanate from it, not the meeting of some abstract academic criteria, that provide the logic for publication and critique in classroom research. But the important point is that the mere fact of publication cannot be a judgement on the nature of the process that led (or did not lead) to publication.

In this section, I have argued strenuously against those who claim that teacher research is not really research. Their position is untenable because: (1) it is a capitulation in the face of the norms of traditional research; (2) it devalues the quality of teacher-research efforts; and (3) it avoids the necessity of establishing a rigorous methodology for classroom research. For these reasons I am calling the form of research in which teachers do research in their own classrooms for the purpose of improving practice, teacher research. The phrase, teacher research, has the advantage of being simple and identifies the major actor and the process involved. It is in this sense and with this aspiration that the terms 'classroom research by teachers', 'teacher-based research' and the 'teacher-researcher' are used in this book. It is the description of such an approach to classroom research that provides the substance of the following chapter.

Further reading

The notion of professionalism used in this chapter comprises a major theme in two of Lawrence Stenhouse's books: *An Introduction to Curriculum Research and Development* (1975) and *Authority, Education and Emancipation* (1983). An important discussion of the historical background to the nature of teacher professionalism is included in Dan Lortie's (1975) *School Teacher*. An excellent wide-ranging discussion of the practical implications of professionalism is found in Donald Schön's (1991) *The Reflective Practitioner* and (1996) *Educating the reflective practitioner: Toward a new design for teaching and learning in the professions* . . A more contemporary discussion of reflective professionalism in teaching is found in the contributions to *Quality in Teaching*, edited by Wilf Carr (1989). Zeichner and Noffke's (2001) discussion on classroom research and its direct link to the teacher profession and Sachs's (2003) *The Activist Teaching Profession* (part of the *Professional Learning* series) plea for teachers to participate and contribute to a more democratic society are also of interest. For a more detailed exposition of Stenhouse's critique of the traditional approach to educational research, see *Research as a Basis for Teaching* (Rudduck and Hopkins 1985). An entertaining and comprehensive review of the arguments against traditional educational research as well as an alternative approach is found in *Beyond the Numbers Game* (Hamilton *et al.* 1977). These arguments are also well rehearsed in Winter's (1989) *Learning from Experience*, Carr and Kemmis's (1986) *Becoming Critical*, Elliott's (1991) *Action Research for Educational Chang* and Carr (1995) *For Education*. A broader perspective on this 'alternative approach' to educational research is found in texts such as Lincoln and Guba's (1985) *Naturalistic Inquiry* and in their chapter in Denzin and Lincoln's (2005) third edition of the *Sage Handbook of Qualitative Studies* entitled 'Paradigmatic controversies, contradictions and emerging confluences', Sara Delamont's (1992) witty and perceptive *Fieldwork in Educational Settings* and Colin Robson's (2002) comprehensive and wise *Real World Research*.

4 Action research and classroom research by teachers

In the previous chapter, I outlined a series of problems associated with the traditional approach to educational research that limits its usefulness for teachers who wish to improve their practice. There are, however, at least two other research traditions to which teachers can turn. One tradition is associated with the work of sociologists and anthropologists. Social anthropological, ethnographic, phenomenological, naturalistic and illuminative research are examples of these research approaches. These are long words that describe essentially the same approach – one that attempts to understand a social situation and to derive hypotheses from that effort of appreciation. The procedures that such social scientists have developed for analysing fieldwork data are used in this book as a guide for making sense of classroom data. They are described in some detail in Chapter 9.

The other research tradition that stands in contrast to the psycho-statistical paradigm and has a strong link with contemporary social science research is the method known as action research. In recent years, teacher-researchers have adopted the label 'action research' to describe their particular approach to classroom research. In this chapter, I describe and critique this application of action research, and from the discussion propose six criteria for classroom research by teachers.

Action research

Action research combines a substantive act with a research procedure; it is action disciplined by enquiry, a personal attempt at understanding while engaged in a process of improvement and reform.

Here are four definitions of action research. The first is by Robert Rapoport (1970), who says that action research:

> aims to contribute both to the practical concerns of people in an immediate problematic situation and to the goals of social science by joint collaboration within a mutually acceptable ethical framework.

The second is by Stephen Kemmis (1983), who writes:

> Action research is a form of self-reflective enquiry undertaken by participants in social (including educational) situations in order to improve the rationality and justice of (a) their own social or educational practices, (b) their understanding of these practices, and (c) the situations in which the practices are carried out. It is most rationally empowering when undertaken by participants collaboratively, though it is often undertaken by individuals, and sometimes in cooperation with 'outsiders'. In education, action research has been employed in school-based curriculum development, professional development, school improvement programs, and systems planning and policy development.

The third is taken from a paper by Dave Ebbutt (1985), who not only gives a definition of his own, but also quotes from Kemmis. He writes that action research:

> is about the systematic study of attempts to improve educational practice by groups of participants by means of their own practical actions and by means of their own reflection upon the effects of those actions.
> Put simply action research is the way groups of people can organise the conditions under which they can learn from their own experience. (Kemmis)
> Action research is trying out an idea in practice with a view to improving or changing something, trying to have a real effect on the situation. (Kemmis)

The fourth is from John Elliott (1991: 69, original emphasis):

> Action-research might be defined as *'the study of a social situation with a view to improving the quality of action within it'*. It aims to feed practical judgement in concrete situations, and the validity of the 'theories' or hypotheses it generates depends not so much on 'scientific' tests of truth, as on their usefulness in helping people to act more intelligently and skillfully. In action-research 'theories' are not validated independently and then applied to practice. They are validated through practice.

The fifth and last is from Mills (2003: 1)

> Action research is any systematic inquiry conducted by teacher researchers to gather information about the ways that their particular school operates, how they teach, and how well their students learn. The information is gathered with the goals of gaining insight, developing reflective practice, effecting positive changes in the school environment and on educational practices in general, and improving student outcomes.

The development of the idea of action research is generally attributed to Kurt Lewin, who in the immediate post-war period used it as a methodology for intervening in and researching the major social problems of the day. Lewin maintained that through action research advances in theory and needed social changes might simultaneously be achieved. Action research, according to Lewin, 'consisted in analysis, fact-finding, conceptualisation, planning execution, more fact-finding or evaluation; and then a repetition of this whole circle of activities; indeed a spiral of such circles' (quoted in Kemmis 1988: 13).

Lewin's ideas on action research were almost immediately applied to education, as well as to social science more generally. It was the work of Stephen Corey at Teacher's College, Columbia University, however – in particular, his book *Action Research to Improve School Practice* (1953) – that spread the word about action research into 'main stream' American education.

More recently, action research has been seen as a methodology through which the aspirations of critical theory, which itself is regarded as an increasingly important trend in the philosophy of social science and the study of education, might be realized. Critical theory builds on the work of Marx, Freud and the traditions of the 'Frankfurt School' of philosophy, in particular the writings of Jurgen Habermas. Unfortunately, the outstanding characteristic of critical theory is its unintelligibility! This is a great pity as well as a paradox, because the central purpose of critical theory is emancipation – enabling people to take control and direction over their own lives. There are now, however, a number of books that admirably 'translate' critical theory and explore its educational implications. In one of them, my colleague at Cambridge, the late Rex Gibson (1986: 5–6) describes the central characteristic of critical theory like this:

> Critical theory acknowledges the sense of frustration and powerlessness that many feel as they see their personal destinies out of their control, and in the hands of (often unknown) others . . . Critical theory attempts to reveal those factors which prevent groups and individuals taking control of, or even influencing, those decisions which crucially affect their lives . . . In the exploration of the nature and limits of power, authority and freedom, critical theory claims to afford insight into how greater degrees of autonomy could be available.
>
> This characteristic marks out critical theory's true distinctiveness: its claim to be *emancipatory*. Not only does it provide enlightenment (deeper awareness of your true interests); more than that (indeed, because of that), it can set you free. Unlike scientific theory, it claims to provide guidance as to what to do.

If this all sounds too good to be true, Gibson (1986: 6) goes on to warn us that:

> There are clearly immense problems attaching to a theory which not only argues that it reveals the world more clearly, but also asserts that it can be used to change the world, to liberate from inequalities and unfair restrictions.

Obviously, neither critical theory nor action research are panaceas and they should not be regarded as such. We shall continue to see in this book, however, that their practical applications do provide a rationale and method for teachers who wish to take more control of their professional (and personal) lives.

From even this brief description, it can be seen how the method of action research with its twin emphasis on committed action and reflection is particularly suited to putting into practice such an emancipatory philosophy. There is also a pleasing symmetry between this more abstract discussion and the practical educational philosophy of Lawrence Stenhouse, and those who have followed his lead, as we see in the following section.

Models of action research

The combination of the action and the research components has a powerful appeal for teachers. In the UK, Lawrence Stenhouse was quick to point to the connection between action research and his concept of the teacher as researcher. Later, John Elliott popularized action research as a method for teachers doing research in their own classrooms through the Ford Teaching Project, and established the Classroom Action Research Network.

Subsequently, Stephen Kemmis refined and formalized the concept of action research and how it applies to education. His articles on action research (Kemmis 1983, 1988) are a useful review of how educational action research has developed from the work of Lewin and established its own character. Of more interest to us here is his 'Action Research Planner' (Kemmis and McTaggart 1988), where a sequential programme for teachers intending to engage in action research is outlined in some detail. He summarizes his approach to action research in the model shown in Figure 4.1.

John Elliott was quick to take up Kemmis's schema of the action research spiral and he, too, produced a similar but more elaborate model, as seen in Figure 4.2. Elliott (1991: 70) summarizes Kemmis's approach and then outlines his elaborations like this:

> Although I think Kemmis' model is an excellent basis for starting to think about what action research involves, it can allow those who use it to assume that 'The General Idea' can be fixed in advance, that 'Reconnaissance' is merely fact-finding and that 'Implementation' is a fairly straightforward process. But I would argue that:
>
> 'The General Idea' should be allowed to shift.
>
> 'Reconnaissance' should involve analysis as well as fact-finding, and should constantly recur in the spiral of activities, rather than occur only at the beginning.
>
> 'Implementation' of an action-step is not always easy, and one should not proceed to evaluate the effects of an action until one has monitored the extent to which it has been implemented.

Dave Ebbutt (1985), a colleague of Elliott, provides us with another variation on Kemmis's model and makes these comments about it:

> It seems clear to me that Elliott is wrong in one respect, in suggesting that Kemmis equates reconnaissance with fact finding only. The Kemmis diagram clearly shows reconnaissance to comprise discussing, negotiating, exploring opportunities, assessing possibilities and examining constraints – in short

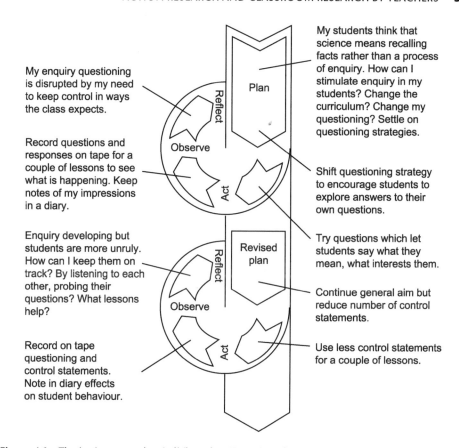

My students think that science means recalling facts rather than a process of enquiry. How can I stimulate enquiry in my students? Change the curriculum? Change my questioning? Settle on questioning strategies.

My enquiry questioning is disrupted by my need to keep control in ways the class expects.

Record questions and responses on tape for a couple of lessons to see what is happening. Keep notes of my impressions in a diary.

Shift questioning strategy to encourage students to explore answers to their own questions.

Enquiry developing but students are more unruly. How can I keep them on track? By listening to each other, probing their questions? What lessons help?

Try questions which let students say what they mean, what interests them.

Continue general aim but reduce number of control statements.

Record on tape questioning and control statements. Note in diary effects on student behaviour.

Use less control statements for a couple of lessons.

Figure 4.1   The 'action research spiral' (based on Kemmis and McTaggart 1988: 14).

there are elements of analysis in the Kemmis notion of reconnaissance. Never-theless I suggest that the thrust of Elliott's three statements is an attempt on the part of a person experienced in directing action research projects to recapture some of the 'messiness' of the action-research cycle which the Kem-mis version tends to gloss.

But Ebbutt (1985) claims that the spiral is not the most useful metaphor. Instead, the most

appropriate way to conceive of the process of action research is to think of it as comprising of a series of successive cycles, each incorporating the possibility for the feedback of information within and between cycles. Such a description is not nearly so neat as conceiving of the process as a spiral, neither does it lend itself quite so tidily to a diagrammatic representation. In my view the idealized process of educational action research can be more appropriately represented like this [as shown in Figure 4.3].

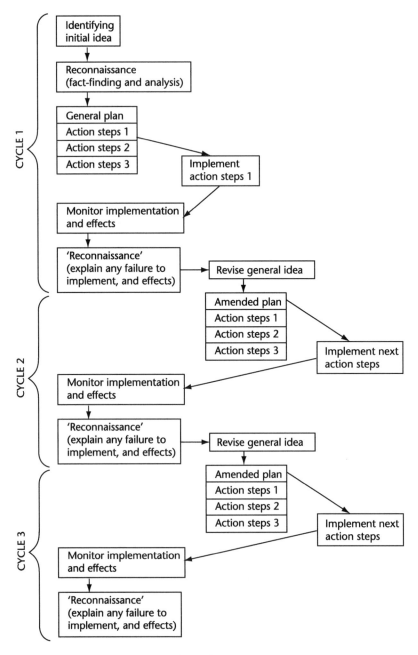

Figure 4.2 Elliott's action research model (from Elliott 1991: 71).

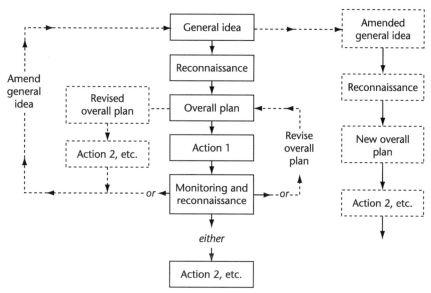

Idealized representation of the process of action research

Figure 4.3   Ebbutt's model (from Ebbutt 1985).

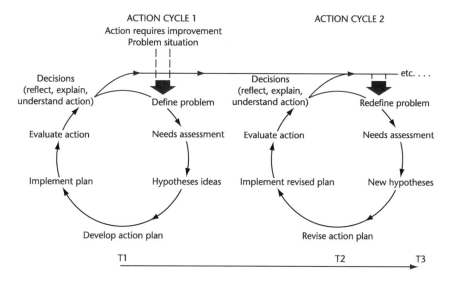

Figure 4.4   McKernan's action research model (from McKernan 1996: 29).

A number of other similar models have recently been developed, most of which build on Lewin's original idea or Kemmis's interpretation of it. For example, James McKernan (1996) has suggested a 'time process' model (see Figure 4.4) which emphasizes the importance of not allowing an action research 'problem' to become too rigidly fixed in time, and of rational problem solving and democratic ownership by the community of researchers.

More recently, the importance of students' participation in research and action research has been highlighted. Jean Rudduck's work has been particularly influential, as has been the importance given to the role of the student in the IQEA programme (Beresford 2003). This emphasis has led to the development of models where students are seen not only as 'data sources' or 'active respondents' but also as 'co-researchers' with teachers or as 'researchers' themselves (Fielding 2004). The work of Michael Fielding (2004) on student voice is relevant here (we explore student voice a bit further in Chapter 9). Fielding advocates that transformation is more likely to be realized through the active participation of students in the research process and believes that students can be radical agents of change. Although his work is not a step by step model of action research such as the ones described above, he provides a clear conceptual framework on how student participation in action research for transformation can occur.

Fielding sees 'students as co-researchers', as partners in the inquiry to be conducted and in the development of instruments and analysis. However, teachers are the driving force and the research lies predominantly with them. The following example explains the process:

> Thus, a primary school teacher keen to develop more independent learning with her Year 1 students asked them their view of independence in learning, what it meant, what it felt like, what it looked like. She and the class discussed these matters, developed an observation schedule, jointly videoed lessons, sat down and looked at the video data, discussed what it meant to them, and developed new learning and teaching practices together. Here the teacher learned things about independence in learning from her engagement and dialogue with her student co-researchers that she could not have done from traditional action research. Similarly, her students as co-researchers learned things about independence in learning, about their individual and collective agency that they could not have learned in other ways.
>
> (Fielding 2004: 306)

As implied, 'students as researchers' places students/pupils in the role of the researcher. Students are trained in research and attend the same training sessions as their teachers and are responsible for identifying the topic of the investigation and selecting the methods of data gathering and analysis. Teachers assist students in the process but 'student leadership is constitutive and distinctive of this approach' (Fielding 2004: 307). Fielding argues that the premise of this model is that students have a different standpoint from that of teachers and so different understandings of similar issues and their importance. This can result to innovation and renewal. Table 4.1 demonstrates the principles and values for this model.

My purpose in presenting these practical models of action research is twofold. First, my aim has been to provide an overview of action research to help the reader gain an understanding of the whole process. Second, it is to demonstrate that despite the proliferation of eponymous 'models', they do, in fact, share more similarities than differences. There is a high degree of consensus among those who write on the subject about overall method and purpose. There are, however, some problems inherent in these models and to these I now turn. In particular this critique will focus on the first four models.

Critique of educational action research

There are three main areas of concern that I have with the action research models developed by Kemmis, Elliott, Ebbutt, McKernan and others. Although this is not the place for a thoroughgoing critique, a brief discussion of these concerns is necessary because the problems may lead teacher researchers into possible confusion. Also, the critique will help explain the form and structure of the rest of the book.

My first concern is that there may be a misunderstanding of the nature of Lewinian action research. As I mentioned earlier, the term action research was coined as a useful label to describe what teacher-researchers were doing. Much energy has been devoted to setting out the intellectual basis for action research as it derived from Lewin. Lewin's conception of action research is, however, very different in some respects to what goes on in the name of teacher research. Lewin's concept of action research was (1) as an externally initiated intervention designed to assist a client system, (2) functionalist in orientation and (3) prescriptive in practice. None of these features apply to what I assume to be the nature of classroom research by teachers which is characterized by its practitioner, problem solving, and eclectic orientation.

We should take care that what began as a useful label to describe teacher research for professional development purposes does not assume a different character as a result of a quest for intellectual credibility.

My second concern relates to the specification of process in the action research models. There are three interrelated points. The first is that the tight specification of process steps and cycles may trap teachers within a framework which they may come to depend on and which will, consequently, inhibit independent action. The original purpose of teacher research was to free teachers from the constraints of prespecified research designs. It is useful to have a guide for action; my concern is when it becomes, or appears to become, prescriptive. Second, the models outline a process rather than a technology. They delineate a sequence of stages, but say little about the 'what' and the 'how' within these stages. Third, the models may appear daunting and confusing to practitioners. Ebbutt himself admits that Elliott's framework tends to 'mystification'.

Unfortunately, models and frameworks cannot mirror reality: they are one individual's interpretation of reality. Consequently, they impose upon the user a prespecified analysis of a process that the user may quite rightly interpret differently. At best, they provide a starting point, an initial guide to action. At worst, they trap the practitioners within a set of assumptions that bear little relationship to their reality and, consequently, constrain their freedom of action.

The line between specifying principles of procedure that encourage informed action, and prescribing activities that determine behaviour and limit outcomes, is a fine one indeed. There is a real danger that teacher research will assume the character of the objectives model, which 'is like a site-plan simplified so that people know exactly where to dig their trenches without having to know why' (Stenhouse 1980). To use Jean

Table 4.1 Levels of student (pupil) involvement in school self-review and school improvement (Fielding 2001: 136–7)

(a) rationale & engagement

	Students as DATA SOURCE	*Students as* ACTIVE RESPONDENTS	*Students as* CO-RESEARCHERS	*Students as* RESEARCHERS
Rationale	Teachers need to know about students' prior learning / perceptions of their learning in order to teach effectively	Teachers need to engage students in order to fully enhance both teaching and learning	Teachers need to engage students as partners in learning in order to deepen understanding and learning	Students need to engage with their teachers and peers in order to deepen understanding and learning
What Kind of Knowledge is Used	Knowing about student performance and attitudes towards learning	Knowing how students learn	Knowing what students might be able to contribute to deepen understanding	Knowing what teachers and peers might be able to contribute to deepen understanding
How Teachers Engage with Students	Acknowledging	Hearing	Listening in order to learn	Listening in order to contribute
Student Role	Recipients	Discussants	Co-Researchers	Initiators
How Meaning is Made	Dissemination	Discussion	Dialogue (teacher led)	Dialogue (student led)

(b) Classroom (pedagogy), Department / Team, School

Classroom
e.g.
• data about student past performance

Department / Team
e.g.
• looking at samples of student work

Classroom
e.g.
• shared lesson objectives
• explicit assessment criteria

Department / Team
e.g.
• department agenda based on student perception data / suggested by pupils
• teacher-led action research (ask students for feedback)
• pupils involved in evaluation of unit of work

Classroom
e.g.
• feedback techniques on pedagogy (teacher led)
• developing metacognition

Department / Team
e.g.
• students co-research aspects of pedagogy / learning with teacher

Classroom
e.g.
• feedback techniques on pedagogy (student led)
• developing metacognition & shared responsibility for learning

Department / Team
e.g.
• students run session for staff on how to engage with particular learning styles
• student suggestions for new units of work

Rudduck's felicitous phrase, it seems that already 'the elusive butterfly of teacher research has been caught and pinned'.

My third concern is a semantic one. There is a tendency for some 'action researchers' to overuse words and phrases like 'problem', 'improve', 'needs assessment' and so on. This could give the impression that action research is a deficit model of professional development. 'Something is wrong, so do this to make it better.' I know that this is not the intention, and I am as guilty of this as anyone in this regard, but it does behove all of us to talk (and write) about classroom research in as positive a way as we can. At the present time, the teaching profession in the UK is suffering from low morale largely as a result of ill-informed public and political criticism. Action research is one way of restoring and enhancing professional confidence.

These concerns notwithstanding, the importance of action research is not to be underestimated. Action research provides teachers with a more appropriate alternative to traditional research designs and one that is, in aspiration at least, emancipatory. We must, however, be aware of the problems associated with too prescriptive a framework for action and the values that are embedded within it. Consequently, I tend to use terms like 'classroom research by teachers' rather than action research. This is not a fundamental point of difference with those colleagues I have cited earlier. It does, however, serve to emphasize the importance of the acquisition of skills and techniques that become part of a teacher's repertoire and which are then subject to the exercise of their professional judgement.

Classroom research by teachers

My preference for the phrase 'classroom research by teachers' rather than 'action research' will not lead me to produce an alternative step-by-step model. Instead, I will present a series of methods and techniques that teachers can use in their classroom research efforts. In particular, I will discuss:

1   ways in which classroom research projects can be identified and initiated (Chapter 5);
2   principles and methods of classroom observation and of other ways of gathering data on classroom behaviours (Chapters 6–8);
3   ways of interpreting and analysing the data gathered from classroom research (Chapter 9);
4   ways in which classroom research can be reported (Chapter 10);
5   ways in which classroom research methods can be linked to a focus on teaching and learning (Chapter 11);
6   how staff development activities and networking can support teacher and school development (Chapter 12).

My purpose in tackling classroom research in this way is to give teachers an introduction to the variety of methods available to them as a means of extending their repertoire of professional practices and of encouraging flexibility in professional development. These are methods and approaches that teachers can put into use, that will

empower them, and make them increasingly competent and 'autonomous in professional judgement'.

Criteria for classroom research by teachers

The essence of what I am advocating is the development of a teacher's professional
expertise and judgement. Although many teachers are in broad agreement with this
general aim, some are quite rightly concerned about how far involvement in classroom
research activity will impinge upon their teaching and on their personal time. Concerns are also raised as to the utilitarian or practical value of classroom research. With
these concerns in mind, let me suggest the following six principles for classroom
research by teachers.

The first is that the teacher's primary job is to teach, and any research method
should not interfere with or disrupt the teaching commitment. This rule of thumb
should serve to quell immediate concerns, but it also points to certain ethical considerations. In some instances, it may be inevitable that the adoption of a new and barely
internalized teaching strategy is initially less effective than the way one previously
taught. Is it ethical, therefore, some may ask, for a teacher to subject students to an
inferior performance when the original behaviour was perfectly adequate? These are
questions which ultimately can only be answered by the individuals involved. For my
part, I am prepared to stand behind the teacher's judgement, particularly if the teachers
involved are so concerned about improving the teaching and the learning experience
of their students that they have broken the mould and are experimenting with new
models. In becoming a teacher-researcher, the individual teacher is deliberately and
consciously expanding their role to include a professional element. It is almost
inconceivable, then, that they would do this and at the same time ignore the primacy
of the teaching/learning process.

The second criterion is that the method of data collection must not be too demanding on the teacher's time. As a corollary, the teacher needs to be certain about the data
collection technique before using it. The reasons for this are obvious. Teachers already
consider themselves overworked and there are continuing demands for increased preparation and professional development time. It is naive to assume that the adoption of a
research role will make no inroads on a teacher's private time. This can be reduced,
however, by judicious use of specific data collection techniques, and the utilization of
easily analysed diagnostic methods. For example, the tape-recorder is widely regarded
as a very useful tool for the classroom researcher. It is, however, extremely expensive to
use both in terms of time and money. It takes approximately 50 per cent longer to listen
to a tape than to make it, and on top of that transcription (which is necessary if full use
is to be made of the method) is both time-consuming and expensive. Given this, it is
advisable to use another method for broad spectrum diagnosis and reserve such intensive techniques for specific and finely focused enquiries. A number of techniques for
classroom observation are discussed in Chapter 7 and a taxonomy of data collection
techniques is presented in Chapter 8.

The third principle is perhaps the most contentious. The methodology employed
must be reliable enough to allow teachers to formulate hypotheses confidently and

develop strategies applicable to their classroom situation. Traditional researchers hold a poor opinion of action research. In many cases, that opinion is well-founded, particularly if it is based on individual pieces of research. It behoves all researchers, be they psycho-statisticians engaged in large-scale research or a primary teacher testing Piaget's theoretical hypotheses, to be rigorous about their methodology. It is no excuse at all to claim that rigour is unnecessary because the research is practitioner-oriented, small-scale or used solely to improve individual practice. If a change in teaching strategy is to be made, then that decision needs to be based on reliable data. These issues form the substance of Chapter 9.

The fourth criterion is that the research focus undertaken by the teacher should be one to which he or she is committed. Although this sounds self-evident, it is difficult enough, given all the pressures on a teacher's time, to sustain energy in a project even if it is intrinsically interesting and important to the teacher's professional activities. As a corollary, the problem must in fact be a problem; that is, the problem must be capable of solution, else by definition it is not a problem. If a teacher chooses a topic that is too complex or amorphous, then frustration and disillusionment will soon set in.

The fifth criterion refers to the need for teacher-researchers to pay close attention to the ethical procedures surrounding their work. Ethical standards for classroom researchers were worked out during the 1970s and 1980s by researchers associated with the Centre for Applied Research in Education (e.g. MacDonald and Walker 1974; Simons 1982, 1987). A summary of ethical procedures for teacher-researchers can be found in the Appendix.

The sixth criterion is that as far as possible classroom research should adopt a 'classroom exceeding' perspective. What I mean by this is that all members of a school community actively build and share a common vision of their main purpose. Teachers are now increasingly relating the teaching and learning focus of their classroom research efforts to whole school priorities through the use of classroom observation techniques. They adapt educational ideas and policies to suit their own context and professional needs. The main focus for action is the teaching and learning in classrooms, in order that all students develop 'the intellectual and imaginative powers and competencies' that they need in as personalized a way as possible. Such classroom practice can only be sustained through ongoing staff development. These principles characterize an approach to teacher and school development that builds on the methods and philosophy of classroom research. In Chapters 11 and 12, we see how this can fit into an overall strategy for school improvement.

In the chapters that follow, these criteria will be dealt with in more detail. In the next chapter, the ways of developing a focus for classroom research projects are discussed.

Further reading

One of the earliest examples of teacher-based research was the Humanities Curriculum Project and the approach is still worth considering (Stenhouse 1970, 1983). Of similar interest are the accounts of the Ford Teaching Project (Elliott and Adelman 1976) and the materials from Deakin University, for example their *Action Research Reader* (1998). There are a number of well-known articles on Lewinian action research which, although rather technical and specialized, may be of interest (see Corey 1953; Lewin 1946; Rapoport 1970; Sandford 1970). The literature on action research and critical theory is growing. Carr and Kemmis's (1986) *Becoming Critical* provides an extensive rationale for action research. See also Carr and Kemmis's (2005) article 'Staying critical' where they revisit their book and identify the need that in any new edition of it they will have to demonstrate the possibility and desirability of 'staying critical' in the postmodern world (p.1). (Elliot's (2005) 'Becoming critical: The Failure to Connect' retrospective critique of their book is also of interest.) Rex Gibson's (1986) *Critical Theory and Education* provides an excellent introduction, while Young's (1989) *A Critical Theory of Education* is more theoretical. A discussion of how critical theory underpins school improvement is found in *School Improvement For Real* (Chapter 2, Hopkins 2001). Of much interest is the work of Stephen Kemmis. His articles on action research (Kemmis 1983, 1988, 2005, 2006) provide an excellent overview of the topic, and the revised *Action Research Planner* (Kemmis and McTaggart 1988) not only contains a step-by-step guide, but also has useful introductory essays on action research. Background reading on the teacher-researcher movement and its educational context is found in Stenhouse's (1975) *An Introduction to Curriculum Research and Development* and in John Elliott's (1991) *Action Research for Educational Change*.

5 Developing a focus

Engaging in classroom research is often initially an unnerving and occasionally threatening experience. Trying anything new involves uncertainty, and this is particularly true of teacher research. Increasingly, however, teachers are regarding the 'researching of practice' as part of their professional responsibilities. It is important therefore that the fourth criterion mentioned in the previous chapter – that of identifying and being committed to a topic for classroom research which is stated in workable terms – is adhered to. But even when this is the case, it is often difficult to establish a precise focus for the enquiry. For these reasons, in this chapter I review some ways in which teachers can develop a focus for classroom research, establish research questions and engage in theorizing. In short, this chapter deals with how to get started on classroom research.

Deriving to your research focus

Teacher research does not necessarily start with the setting of precise hypotheses! As Kemmis and McTaggart (1988: 18) point out in their first edition of *The Action Research Planner*:

> You do not have to begin with a 'problem'. All you need is a general idea that something might be improved. Your general idea may stem from a promising new idea or the recognition that existing practice falls short of aspiration. In either case you must centre attention on:
>
> - What is happening now?
> - In what sense is this problematic?
> - What can I do about it?
>
> General starting points will look like
>
> - I would like to improve the . . .
> - Some people are unhappy about . . .
> - What can I do to change the situation?
> - I am perplexed by . . .

- . . . is a source of irritation. What can I do about it?
- I have an idea I would like to try out in my class.
- How can the experience of . . . be applied to . . .?
- Just what do I do with respect to . . .?

As you read the extract, no doubt certain ideas or topics for classroom research come to mind. These ideas may also relate to the priorities on the school's development plan, or to the school's aims, targets or mission statement. More likely they will relate to practical and immediate concerns, such as a particular aspect of a scheme of work, or a troublesome individual or class. It is worth taking a few minutes to jot down these ideas. Don't worry about how well they are formed; at this stage it is more important to generate a list of topics from which you can work. Having produced a list, the next step is to evaluate the usefulness, viability and/or importance of the individual issue. There are a number of guidelines that can be of use here.

First, do not tackle issues that you cannot do anything about. For example, it may be impossible in the short or medium term to alter the banding or streaming system in your school or to change the textbook that you are using. Because you cannot do anything about it, either avoid the issue or rephrase it in a more solvable form. So, although you cannot change the textbook, it may be possible to experiment with different ways the text could be used as evidence in your classes.

Second, only take on, at least initially, small-scale and relatively limited issues. There are several reasons for this. It is important to build on success, and a small-scale project satisfactorily completed in a short space of time is reinforcing and encouraging. It is also very easy to underestimate the scale and amount of time a project will take. It is very discouraging to have found after the initial flush of enthusiasm that you have bitten off more than you can chew.

Third, choose an issue that is important to you or to your students, or one that you have to be involved with anyway in the course of your normal school activities. The topic that you focus on needs to be intrinsically motivating. If not, then again after the initial flush of enthusiasm and when the difficulties begin to build up, you will find that motivation will begin to evaporate.

Fourth, as far as possible try and work collaboratively on the focus of your classroom research. Professional partnerships, as is seen in the examples throughout the book, are a powerful form of staff development and personal support. It is also a way of reducing the isolation that some teachers work in.

Finally, make connections between your classroom research work, teaching and learning, and the school's development plan priorities or the school's aims. Although there need not be a direct relationship, it is important to relate one's individual professional enquiry to whole school initiatives and the direction in which the school is moving.

In summary, it is necessary to select an initial focus for classroom research that is viable, discrete, intrinsically interesting, involves collaboration and is related in some way to teaching and learning and whole school concerns.

Performance gap

A growing body of research suggests: (1) there is often incongruence between a teacher's publicly declared philosophy or beliefs about education and how they behave in the classroom; (2) there is often incongruence between the teacher's declared goals and objectives and the way in which the lesson is actually taught; and (3) there is often a discrepancy between a teacher's perceptions or account of a lesson, and the perceptions or account of other participants (e.g. pupils or observers) in the classroom (see Elbaz 1983). All of these discrepancies reflect a gap between behaviour and intention. The Ford Teaching Project also monitored the 'performance gap' between teachers' aspirations and their practice. These issues have more recently been commented on in contemporary reports on the state of primary education. The 'performance gap' therefore forms an important starting point for classroom research enquiries.

Dave Ebbutt (1985) writes about 'the performance gap' as follows:

> It is via the notion of a performance gap – a gap between espoused theory and theory in action – by which advocates of action research locate its niche as an appropriate mode of research in schools and classrooms. For instance Kemmis in his *Planner* uses this illustrative example:
>
>> There is a gap between the idea and the reality of inquiry teaching in my own classroom. Recognising this gap, I must develop a strategy of action if improvements in this kind of questioning are to be achieved . . .

If you now return to the list of possible classroom research topics that you have just generated, there is probably implicit in each of the topics a description of what is currently happening (that provides a basis for reflection) and an indication of some new action connected to the existing behaviour that will lead to improvement. So, for example, in the case studies in Chapter 2, the teachers identified an existing teaching behaviour and at the same time thought of ways in which this aspect of their teaching could be improved. It is this gap between what is and what could be that is an important source of motivation in classroom research by teachers.

Ebbutt (1985) also illustrates the notion of the performance gap by posing six simple questions to demonstrate the gap between the curriculum in action and the curriculum as intention:

1   What did the pupils actually do?
2   What were they learning?
3   How worthwhile was it?
4   What did I do?
5   What did I learn?
6   What do I intend to do now?

The concept of the performance gap is useful in refining your list of topics for classroom research. The identification of a gap between what is and what could be provides motivation for change and indicates a direction for improvement. Action leads out of existing behaviours towards a new articulated goal.

Open and closed questions

Implicit in much of what I have written so far is the idea that a research focus emerges out of a teacher's critical reflection on classroom experience, which is then explored through the use of the classroom research procedures.

In other words, both the formation and resolution of the research enquiry is grounded in the teacher's experience. The formation of a research focus or question occurs within either an open or closed context. Open questions take as their starting point a teacher's critical reflection on their teaching. This reflection culminates in a decision to utilize classroom research techniques to understand more fully and then develop their teaching (using the techniques discussed in the following four chapters). A number of the teacher-researchers whose work is cited in Chapter 2 started from an open position and developed hypotheses about their teaching by using classroom research procedures. Having identified a focus, they then developed a plan for action. The open approach, then, is one where teachers engage in classroom research as a reflective activity. From this reflection they derive questions that can be researched and that subsequently provide a basis for action.

The closed approach deviates from the open insofar as many teachers have already identified a specific issue or hypothesis before engaging in classroom research. In this instance, their classroom research begins with the testing of a hypothesis or exploring a specific activity. So with other examples in Chapter 2, teacher-researchers, having heard about a new teaching method that applied to their subject area, used classroom research to investigate the effectiveness of the approach. In this case, the focus on teaching strategies had immediate and direct relevance for classroom practice.

Later in this chapter, there is a more extensive discussion of formulating evaluation questions. Although the purpose there is specifically evaluation, rather than classroom research more generally, the same principles apply. The *open* approach is characterized as:

- take a broad area of enquiry
- carry out the initial enquiry
- gradually focus the enquiry.

By way of contrast, the *closed* approach typically follows this sequence:

- take a specific issue
- derive research questions
- choose an appropriate methodology.

The difference between open and closed reflects the derivation of the focus. In the first instance, the hypothesis or question emerges as a result of critical reflection; in the second, it is a given, and the teacher having refined it proceeds to the enquiry. Both approaches reflect classroom research as it is defined in this book, because in both instances the research is controlled by the teacher for the purpose of improving practice. The contrast between open and closed questions or hypotheses can also be represented in diagrammatic form as in Figure 5.1.

Dillon (1983) has produced a similar (if rather more academic) schema for conceptualizing 'problem formation'. He writes:

> Three existential levels of problem and three corresponding psychological activities can be identified as forming part of those events which may be appropriately designated as problem finding. In existential terms, a problem can be existent, emergent or potential. An existent problem has fully-developed being and appearance in the phenomenological field of events facing the observer. In psychological terms, the problem is evident and the observer perceives, recognizes, and identifies it. At a second, less developed level an emergent problem exists which is implicit rather than evident. After probing the data – nosing about in the field of events, so to speak – the observer discovers or 'finds it'. At a still less developed level, a potential problem exists. No problem in an ontological sense exists *qua* problem, but constituent elements are present, striking the observer as an inchoate problem. By combining these and other elements in some way, the observer creates, produces or invents a problem. These descriptive terms relate the existential and psychological dimensions of problem finding activity at three levels, as follows [see Figure 5.2].

My purpose in going into such detail about developing research questions, or what others call 'problem formation', is simply to legitimize the position of teachers who want to engage in classroom research just to find out about their teaching. Classroom research is not solely about exploring specific 'problems' or testing explicit hypotheses. It is appropriate for teachers to use classroom research as a means of critically reflecting on their teaching and developing hypotheses about it.

Formulating hypotheses

Whether or not teachers are initially involved in open or closed problems, they will have to formulate hypotheses or questions at some stage. As I suggested in Chapter 4, the teacher-researcher, either as an individual or as a member of a group, needs to

Type	Hypothesis
Open	Generating
Closed	Testing

Figure 5.1

Problem level (existential/ psychological)	Problem ———	Activity ———	Solution
1 existing/evident	. . . as problematic	Perceiving the situation (Recognition)	. . . as resolved
2 emergent/implicit	. . . for elements of a problem	Probing the data (Discovery)	. . . for elements of a solution
3 potential/inchoate	. . . a defined problem	Producing the problem-event (Invention)	. . . a defined solution

Figure 5.2   A conceptual scheme for comparing levels of problem finding and solving.

define their problem clearly, for it is this definition that determines what data are collected and analysed. It is inevitable that our observations tend to be theory-laden, so consequently it is important to formulate as explicitly as one can the hypotheses that are being tested or the research questions one wishes to explore. If, for example, a group of teachers are concerned about the problem of initiating classroom discussion, they may first hypothesize that asking more open-ended questions would encourage freer responses; a number of different hypotheses could be developed and tested around this contingency. The hypotheses, however, need to be extremely clear and precise. Because there are so many variables in the complex art of teaching, even a carefully worded hypothesis can sometimes only be reported as tentative and provisional. Pring (1978) gives some examples of classroom research hypotheses taken from the Ford Teaching project:

> In order to cut out 'the guessing game' and move from a formal to an informal pattern, teachers may have to refrain from the following acts:
>
> 1 Changing topic
> Hypothesis. When teachers change the topic under discussion, they may prevent pupils from expressing and developing their own ideas, since pupils tend to interpret such interventions as attempts to get conformity to a particular line of reasoning.
>
> 2 Positive reinforcers
> Hypothesis. Utterances like 'good', 'interesting', 'right', in response to ideas expressed can prevent the expression and discussion of alternative ideas, since pupils tend to interpret them as attempts to legitimate the development of some ideas rather than others.

Following Popper's answer to the problem of induction (see Magee 1973: Chapter 2), it is more appropriate to formulate hypotheses as unambiguously as we can, so as to expose them as clearly as possible to refutation. For as Popper pointed out, although empirical generalizations are in principle not verifiable, they are falsifiable and, consequently, they can be tested by systematic attempts to refute them.

The case of curriculum evaluation

Many of the issues related to 'developing a focus' for classroom research have been paralleled in recent years by developments in curriculum evaluation. Although many curriculum evaluations were initially 'externally funded', increasingly much of this evaluation activity became school-based. Unfortunately, this approach to evaluation, instead of building on the traditions of classroom research, has remained wedded to an academic view of evaluation that is based on the ubiquitous evaluation report. Yet evaluations that have an improvement perspective, provide a structure for teachers and others to subject a particular curriculum change to their own professional judgement and, in so doing, to improve the programme and make further plans for implementation. In this way, an evaluation can, like classroom research, provide a means for translating an educational idea into practice as well as monitoring and enhancing curriculum development. This was the central theme of my book *Evaluation for School Development* (Hopkins 1989), where I tried to outline an approach to evaluation that was:

- built on the best practice of classroom research insofar as it supported development and was linked to classroom practice;
- sufficiently pragmatic to serve the decision-making purposes of evaluation; and
- as far as possible fitted into the day-to-day life of the school.

The reason for discussing curriculum evaluation at this point is twofold. The first is that one of the approaches to school-focused evaluation described in the book was based around the use of the evaluation or research question that is one of the themes of this chapter. The second is that the structure of curriculum evaluation provides another model or format for conducting whole school, teacher research. In the following example, I describe two approaches to the formulation of questions in an evaluation we did of 'technology across the curriculum' (TAC; see Figure 5.3).

An evaluation question is, simply, a question that can be answered by some form of structured investigation or research. In this context, it is important to:

- avoid grandiose questions outside the scope of formative evaluation, such as: 'Is TAC a "Good Thing"?';
- avoid long-term questions outside the time frame: 'Are this year's students getting a better experience of technology?';
- avoid questions that are only answerable by large-scale or very technical research;
- aim for suitably defined questions that can be addressed through the limited quantity of data you can be expected to collect.

1 *A linear approach*

Take a specific evaluation issue

'To what extent is TAC awareness shared by all staff in the establishment?'

Derive evaluation questions that can be used

'Does technology feature in the schemes of work in all subjects?' 'What definitions of technology are used by heads of department?'
'What is the students' experience of technology in other core subjects?'

Choose an appropriate evaluation methodology

This might include, respectively: document search; interview; student questionnaire.

2 *An evolutionary approach*

Take a broad area for investigation

Gender issues in the provision of TAC.

Carry out initial investigation and analyse data

Analysis of enrolment data and exam results.
Classroom observation of some technology lessons.
Unstructured interviews with teachers/students.

Derive evaluation questions that can be used

'Why did more boys than girls enrol for this course this year?'
'Are the practical activities appropriate or interesting to girls?'

Choose an appropriate evaluation methodology

This might include, respectively: student interview; structured observation and interview.

Figure 5.3 Formulating evaluation questions.

Although the formulation of questions is often quite challenging, this should not deter us from confronting tough 'bottom line' issues that reflect the various stages in the change process. Obviously, not all the following questions will apply to every evaluation, but the following examples are the types of questions that will help us assess the impact of a curriculum change on student achievement and the process of school improvement:

- What changes have occurred in teachers' or students' knowledge base?
- What changes have occurred in teachers' or students' skill level and use?
- What changes have occurred in teachers' or students' opinions and feelings?
- What changes have occurred in the culture or organization of the school?
- What changes have occurred in student tests or examinations?

This general approach to evaluation includes four major activities:

1   *Agree on evaluation questions*. Generating questions helps focus the evaluation. Often the questions will relate to the school development plan priorities. It is important not to be too ambitious about the number and scope of the questions asked.

2   *Determine information needs and collection methods*. Once the questions are generated, clarified and prioritized, some way of answering them has to be devised. Potential information sources and collection methods should be identified for each evaluation question. The more sources and methods used, the greater the likelihood that the information will be valid. One way of structuring this important stage in the design of the evaluation is to use a simple worksheet as outlined in Figure 5.4. As you begin to formulate your evaluation question(s) and devise appropriate data-gathering methods, it is helpful to 'cost' them in terms of (1) the time it will take to complete the work and (2) the time and people available to you. The plan shown in Figure 5.4 is an example of an evaluation schedule for Technology Across the Curriculum (TAC).

3   *Collect and analyse information*. This activity should co-exist with data collection. Early checks allow evaluators to seek new information sources if necessary and to identify emerging and unanticipated outcomes.

4   *Reports*. Feedback should normally occur as soon as possible, be tailored to its audience and include follow-up activities if required. This may include reporting to governors and parents and providing information for the school's next development plan. The reports need not be written; they may be given orally with handouts containing summaries of data as 'back-up' material. Often, reduced data are sufficient to act as a basis for discussion. When reports are written they should be short; usually data summaries can be prepared on one side of A4. They should also distinguish clearly between the presentation of data and any interpretation that may be made of the results.

An overview of this evaluation process is given in Figure 5.5. This figure is of course far more linear than the action research cycle described in the previous chapter, in reality, a number of these steps co-exist and time-lines tend to merge. It may also be that questions have to be refined and unanticipated logistical problems may occur during the evaluation. An obvious precaution is to ensure that time-lines are realistic, that one is not expecting too much too soon, and that as many problems as possible are anticipated.

Two further points need to be made about this process. The first is that there needs to be a logic or flow between the evaluation question, the data collected, analysis, feedback and the resulting action. In that way, the evaluation develops a power of its own because each stage builds on the other. The second is to make certain that the evaluation questions are important to the school and staff concerned. Evaluation is so time-consuming that its results should not be gratuitous, but feed real need and be able to provide useful and pertinent information.

Question	Source	Collection method	Responsibility	Time-line
How was the plan for the delivery of TAC formulated? Was the process effective?	TAC co-ordinator; school co-ordinator	Interviews	Evaluator	Oct.–Dec.
What is the plan? Why was this method of delivery chosen?	TAC/school co-ordinators; staff	Review documents; question-naires; interviews	TAC co-ordinator; evaluator	Jan.–Mar.
Have students received 10% balanced TAC? Does the reality reflect the plan?	Staff; students	Interviews; question-naires	Co-ordinator; evaluator	Easter onward

Figure 5.4   A practical evaluation schedule.

Figure 5.5   The evaluation process.

Theory and theorizing

Finally a word about theory. So far, I have used the word in two distinct senses. The first refers to a set of personal assumptions, beliefs or presuppositions that individuals hold. Our view of the world, our individual construction of reality is at one level essentially theoretical. The second use of the word is in the more traditional or 'grand' sense, where theory refers to a coherent set of assumptions which purport to explain, predict and be used as a guide to practice. This is the sense in which the word was used when the teacher-researchers in Chapter 2 turn to theory in order to inform their classroom research problem.

Unfortunately, all too often educational theory in this second sense is not all that useful in telling us in a practical way how to behave in the classroom. In many instances, the gap between theory and practice is so large that it prevents any useful connection. This occurs because our theories are often not specific enough, or the propositions they contain are not easily generalized to individual situations. This, of course, is an unsatisfactory situation, and one that argues for a different approach to educational theory.

A viable alternative is to theorize about practice, and theorizing is a third way in which we can understand theory. Theorizing approaches theory through practice (the reverse of grand theory, which goes from theory to practice), much in the same way as the hypotheses, assumptions and constructs we develop from classroom research procedures emerge from data gathered from actual classroom experiences. The discussion of grounded theory in Chapter 9 illustrates how theory can be generated from data gathered in a substantive situation. When we are engaged in classroom research, we can be said to be engaged in educational theorizing because we are reflecting systematically and critically on practice. As Richard Pring (1978: 244–5) writes:

> Such systematic and critical examination will involve philosophizing, appeal-ing to evidence, reference to . . . theories. But there is no reason for saying that it will add up to a theory. [Classroom research is about] helping the prac-titioner to theorize, i.e. think more systematically, critically and intelligently about his or her practice.

You will remember that Stenhouse (1975) in his discussion of the teacher-researcher illustrates this attitude when he suggested that the teacher, instead of accept-ing uncritically what a particular theory claims, implements it in the form of a working hypothesis or curriculum proposal. This thought captures two of the fundamental aspects of what Donald Schön (1991) has called the 'reflective practitioner'. In educational terms, such professional teachers (a) stand in control of knowledge rather than being subservient to it; and (b) by doing this they are engaged in the process of theorizing and achieving self-knowledge.

The idea of 'self-knowledge' is an important one in this context. It refers to the individual internalization of ideas that empowers the person. It refers to those moments of clarity and power that occur when we understand a concept and see how we can use it in our personal or professional lives. It is an exciting and exhilarating moment and one which, for teachers and pupils alike, is too rare in our schools. This, as I understand it, is the basis of Polanyi's (1973) writing on *Personal Knowledge*. Personal knowledge is that which is mediated through subjective experience and subsequently owned by the individual. The most pertinent feature of Polanyi's work is the concept of tacit knowledge, the knowledge we cannot articulate. He suggests that we know a great deal more than we can put into words, and that we sense and understand more than we can describe or explain. An aspiration of the approach to classroom research adopted in this book is for teachers to gain more clarity on their 'tacit knowledge' and to incorporate this in their teaching.

Walt Whitman (1855/1959) captures a similar thought in this evocative passage from *Leaves of Grass*:

> You shall no longer take things at second or third hand . . . nor look through the eyes of the dead . . . nor feed on the spectres in books, You shall not look through my eyes either, nor take things from me, You shall listen to all sides and filter them from yourself.

In this chapter, I have discussed the challenges involved in developing a focus for classroom research by teachers. I have been at pains to point out that the focus of an enquiry can be either open or closed insofar as the teacher is engaged in hypothesis generation or testing. I have also pointed to some ways in which the focus of classroom research can be clarified and made more specific, and then linked the whole discussion to a notion of theorizing and self-knowledge. The underlying theme is that through developing a focus for their research, teachers gain more control over their professional lives.

The advice in this chapter obviously applies to both teachers working alone or in collaboration. For reasons already rehearsed in previous chapters, I believe that collaborative efforts at teacher research are to be preferred. Talking to others, for example, is an excellent way of clarifying the focus of a research enquiry. In the next three chapters, we discuss practical ways in which data about the focus of a classroom research enquiry can be gathered.

Further reading

The third edition of *The Action Research Planner* by Stephen Kemmis and Robin McTaggart (1988) contains detailed and helpful advice on 'finding a theme' for classroom research. Other helpful sources for 'getting started' are Judith Bell's (2005) *Doing Your Research Project* and Jean McNiff's (2002) *Action Research: Principles and Practice* and McNiff and Whitehead's (2006) *All You Need to Know about Action Research*. More specific foci for classroom research enquiries are comprehensively illustrated in Good and Brophy's (2003) *Looking in Class-rooms*. A description of evaluation techniques and approaches similar in aspiration and application to the strategies described in this book is found in *Evaluation for School Development* (Hopkins 1989). For a discussion of hypothesis generation, it is useful to look at some of the Ford Teaching Project materials (see Elliott 1976). The article by Dillon (1983) on problem finding is very informative. Bryan Magee's (1973) monograph on Popper is a paragon of clarity and neatly summarizes Popper's solution to the problem of induction. Donald Schön's (1991) *The Reflective Practitioner*, although not specifically about education, echoes many of the themes of this book, particularly in regard to how professionals develop and learn through reflection and action.

6 Principles of classroom observation

Observation plays a crucial role not only in classroom research, but also more generally in supporting the professional growth of teachers and in the process of school development. In my experience, it seems to be the pivotal activity that links together reflection for the individual teacher and collaborative enquiry for pairs or groups of teachers. It also encourages the development of a language for talking about teaching and provides a means for working on developmental priorities for the staff as a whole. This chapter is therefore of central importance. I begin by outlining five criteria crucial to the successful practice of classroom observation, then describe the generic three-stage cycle of classroom observation and its specific application to partnership teaching and conclude by making some suggestions for training activities. In discussing the principles underlying observation, the emphasis is not just on classroom research, but also more generally on teacher and school development. The following chapter is devoted to a description of four methods of undertaking classroom observation: *open, focused, structured* and *systematic* observation.

Key features of classroom observation

Although I believe that, in general, classroom observation is a 'good thing', there are a number of specific skills associated with it which, if not acquired, can have disastrous results for the morale of individuals and the whole staff. The main problem, it seems to me, is that often we jump too quickly to conclusions about the behaviour of others. As I note in Chapter 9, the philosopher Karl Popper claims that, 'observations . . . are [always] interpretations in the light of theories' (Magee 1973: 107). Although we constantly need to use our personal theories to construct our worlds (and without doing so would not survive long in the classroom!), this uniquely human intuition is not the greatest asset during classroom observation. Moving to judgement too quickly is one of the main characteristics of poor observation. There are at least five key features of classroom observation that need to characterize our approach if the process is to lead to professional growth.

Joint planning

A joint planning meeting is of crucial importance, especially if it precedes the first in a series of observations. There is a need to establish at the outset a climate of trust between observer and observed, to agree on a focus that both regard as worthwhile, to discuss the context of the lesson, to sort out the 'ground rules' – time and place of the observation, where to sit, how to interact with the pupils, how long to spend in the classroom, etc. The more specific and focused the observation, the more there is a need for joint planning. Once the observer and the observed become familiar with each other's style and the roles are reversed, then the time spent in the initial meeting can be reduced. It may also be possible during an ongoing cycle of observations to combine feedback and planning meetings.

Focus

There are two broad ways of categorizing the focus of classroom observation activities: general or specific. The terms are self-explanatory: the former indicating an approach where 'everything counts' and therefore could be commented on; and the latter where the observation is confined to a particular or well-defined classroom activity or teaching practice. When the focus is broad, the more likely it is that the observer, who having no criteria to turn to, will rely on 'subjective' judgements to interpret what is going on in the classroom. Although these judgements may be perfectly valid, they most probably will be of little use to the teacher being observed unless the basis for them has been discussed and agreed on in advance. The danger in this situation is that the teacher being observed is subject to a series of 'mini-judgements' on their teaching that tell you more about the educational values of the observer than the teacher whose classroom practice is under scrutiny. The more specific and negotiated the focus of the classroom observation, the more likely it is that the 'data' so gathered will be useful for developmental purposes. If the focus for classroom observation relates to the development plan, then the observation could contribute both to teacher and school development.

Establishing criteria

The contribution of classroom observation to professional development is greatly enhanced if, during the initial discussion, criteria for the observation are established. I remember vividly during an interview on our evaluation of the 'School Teacher Appraisal' project, asking an appraiser, the head of a primary school, what criteria she used when observing her colleagues. 'We don't use checklists in this school', she replied angrily. 'Come on', I said, 'What were you looking for when you went into the classroom?' 'Oh', she said, 'Were the children smiling and engaged in their work? Was the classroom environment attractive? Was the work they were doing appropriate for their ability?', and so on. Before too long she had given me a fairly sophisticated description of 'good primary practice'. What a pity I thought that the staff of that primary school had not had that discussion before the start of the appraisal process. Criteria are nothing to be frightened of, particularly if they are negotiated and agreed *before* the start of an observation. It may be helpful for the staff as a whole to agree and develop criteria on a particular classroom observation before the cycle of observation begins. It is also important that such criteria are subject to ongoing review as those involved refine their definitions of good practice. When viewed in this way, the discussion of criteria can act as a 'road map' for development as well as providing standards by which to discuss the outcomes of an observation.

Observation skills

There are three main 'skills' involved here. The first is guarding against the natural tendency to move too quickly into judgement. This can be achieved to some extent, as we have seen already, by having a clear focus for the observation and agreeing the ground rules beforehand. Second, there are the interpersonal skills involved when 'invading another person's space'; this includes creating a sense of trust and being supportive in situations where the other person may feel threatened. The third skill area is more technical. It is knowing how to design schedules that will allow the observer to gather appropriate information on classroom behaviour or transactions, or of knowing which are the most appropriate checklists or *aide-mémoires* to use in a particular situation. This latter point is especially important, as one obviously wishes to avoid having the values underlying an observation schedule imposing themselves on the outcomes of the feedback discussion.

Feedback

The benefits of classroom observation will only be realized if appropriate feedback is given. Put another way, poor feedback is characterized by being rushed, judgemental, one-way and impressionistic. As has already been implied, feedback appears to work best if:

- it is given within 24 hours of the observation;
- it is based on careful and systematic recording;
- it is based on factual data;
- the factual data are interpreted with reference to known and agreed criteria;
- the interpretation comes in the first instance from the teacher who has been observed;
- it is given as part of a two-way discussion; and
- it leads to the development of strategies for building on what has been learnt.

The three-phase observation cycle

These key features lay the basis for a professional development approach to classroom observation. The 'three-phase observation cycle', originally called 'clinical supervision', was initially developed in North America as a method of supervising student teachers, but it is well suited for use in classroom research situations.

The three essential phases of this classroom observation process are a planning meeting, the classroom observation itself and a feedback discussion. The *planning meeting* provides the observer and teacher with an opportunity to reflect on the proposed lesson, and this leads to a mutual decision to collect observational data on an aspect of the teacher's classroom practice. During the *classroom observation* phase, the observer observes the teacher in the classroom and collects objective data on that aspect of the teaching or learning they agreed upon earlier. It is during the *feedback discussion* that the observer and teacher share the information gathered during the observation, decide on appropriate action, agree a record of the discussion, and often plan another round of observation. An outline of the process is given in Figure 6.1. It is important to realize that to be effective, all three phases of the process need to be gone through systematically.

There are a number of principles that are important to consider in this approach to classroom observation. First, the climate of interaction between teacher and observer needs to be non-threatening, helping and one of mutual trust. Second, the focus of the activity should be on improving classroom practice and the reinforcing of successful strategies, rather than on criticism of unsuccessful patterns of behaviour, or changing the teacher's personality. Third, the process depends on the collection and use of objective observational data, not unsubstantiated value judgements. Fourth, teachers are encouraged to make inferences about their teaching from the data, and to use the data to construct 'hypotheses' that can be tested out in the future. Next, each cycle of observation is part of an ongoing process that builds on the other. Finally, both observer and teacher are engaged in a mutual process of professional development that can lead to improvement in teaching and observational skills for both. In all these ways, classroom observation can support both specific purposes, as well as the more general aspirations of teacher and school development.

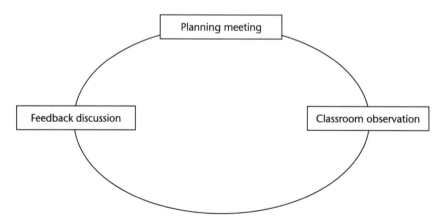

Figure 6.1   The three-phase observation cycle.

CASE STUDY

An example of the three-phase approach to classroom observation is given by Marsha and George.

Marsha had already observed several of George's Year 8 History classes. During a planning conference, they went over George's lesson plan. George identified his objectives, one of which was to involve as many pupils as possible in discussing a particular historical event. They decided to focus the observation on the type of questions George asked and the pupils' responses. Marsha suggested she use a seating plan on which to 'tally' the voluntary and solicited comments from the pupils. George agreed and also requested that she jot down his questions verbatim.

During the lesson, Marsha recorded information for the 20 minutes George had planned for the discussion. Afterwards, as they went over the data, patterns began to emerge. George noticed that, although the discussion had been lively, only 12 out of the 28 pupils had participated (he had thought during the lesson that more were involved). Also, certain types of questions tended to elicit more complete responses.

They both decided that it might be useful if George sequenced his questions from factual types (to establish a common knowledge base) to more open-ended, opinion questions. Also, now that he knew which pupils were reticent, George would attempt to involve them more in class discussions. Marsha suggested a couple of techniques that worked for her, and George was excited about trying them out. The feedback conference ended with both agreeing to use the same observation focus in the near future to compare the results of George's new strategies.

Partnership observation

The three-phase cycle provides a general framework for classroom observation which is particularly relevant to 'partnership' teaching or collaborative observation. I try to encourage teachers to engage in classroom research in pairs or small groups for a number of reasons. Among them is the emotional support they gain from each other, particularly as this activity is initially threatening. It is now fairly well established that teachers learn best from other teachers, and take criticism most easily from this source. It is ideal if teachers in cross-hierarchical groups can act as observers for each other, and this mutual exchange of roles quickly breaks down barriers which otherwise may be monolithic.

The observer in the partnership can play any number of differing roles. They can observe a lesson in general, focus on specific aspects of the teaching and talk to pupils all during one observation period. This lightens the teacher's problem of analysis and tends to increase the objectivity of the data gathered. In addition, the observer may also be able to note incidents that the teacher would ordinarily miss.

Colleagues involved in the University of Cambridge Institute of Education and Bedfordshire Education Service 'Developing Successful Learning Project' refined an approach to classroom observation that emphasizes the partnership role. The following description is taken from their work.

This approach to partnership observation assumes that:

- all teachers can develop their practice; and
- all students can learn successfully.

It is based on the following principles:

- Practice can only be improved in the contexts in which it normally occurs.
- Individuals need the support of colleagues as they seek to develop their practice.

The central strategy is to create partnerships of teachers who are committed to helping one another develop their classroom practice. These partnerships usually involve two or three colleagues who, for the purposes of this work, regard one another as equals. A partner must be somebody with whom you can work comfortably.

Before the observation, a number of issues have to be considered and decisions made by the partners:

- the role of the observer in the classroom;
- the confidentiality of discussions;
- commitment to the programme;
- date/time place of observation;
- date/time place of *review* – this should be set as near to the observation as possible (within 24 hours); the place must be one without interruptions, on or off site, and needs to be non-threatening; it is best to allow a minimum of 40 minutes for the review;
- how often observation is to take place – this is dependent on the timetable and the availability of cover;
- which classes and lessons are to be observed;
- whether this is to be a focused or unfocused observation; and
- methods of observation to be used.

During the observation, the observer should only record what is seen or heard and not be judgemental or intrusive. Time should also be found for one or two minutes of positive discussion at the end of the observation period. This will allow the observed teacher to release any tension that may have developed during the lesson. The observer may also give the class teacher a copy of the observation notes.

During the review discussion, feedback should be non-threatening, supportive and based on the information gathered during the observation. *Target setting* evolves from feedback, and once this has been given it is time to identify one area of learning to be developed. Targets must be realistic and attainable within the designated time-span. This does not, however, preclude the developments continuing over an extended period. If successful, these changes often become an integral part of effective class teaching, thus enhancing the learning experience of students.

Action planning for development is based on the answers to a series of questions that need to be addressed before modifying teaching practice:

- What do I want to achieve?
- How am I going to achieve this?
- How will this improve the quality of learning?
- How will this development be evaluated?
- Will I involve the pupils in the process of monitoring and evaluation?
- Are there adequate resources to implement the proposed development?

If, after carrying out the *action plan*, the outcomes were not successful, do not be discouraged! Try to discover why. This is where assistance and advice from a 'third person' could be invaluable. Perhaps you were too ambitious in your objectives; if so, return to target setting. If the objective was realistic, it may have been the way in which it was developed in the class; if this was the case, return to the *action plan*. If the outcomes were successful, why were they? Always reflect on practice. The partnership may now wish to continue with the original target, or a new target may be set.

CASE STUDY

This is an example of partnership observation from the work of the 'Developing Successful Learning Project', prepared by Pamela Hughes of Sharnbrook Upper School. It focuses on involving students in the observation process.

This classroom project placed particular emphasis on the idea of student involvement. There are 29 students in the class. The project included the following steps:

1   Initially the students in the two classes involved were given letters to take home, to explain their involvement and to give parents an opportunity to contact us if they wished.
2   The students, working in groups, discussed and then listed things which (a) helped their learning and (b) hindered their learning within the class. (This took 10 minutes in one class and 30 in the other where it was used as an oral exercise.)
3   After the observation, the students in my class were very keen to be involved further. They knew that the focus would be evaluating group work, but they did not know the specific areas.

We discussed ways of evaluating our learning, but not in those terms! The outcomes, from the students, were recorded by further observation, videotaping and by questionnaire (testing was not mentioned). I explained that I had already designed a questionnaire. Somebody asked if the class could compile their own – we debated time, costs, what it would include, how to go about it, etc.

I decided to let them try during the following lesson. I was able to do this because they were Year 9 and the task was suitable for an English lesson. I think this would have been more difficult to organize in other areas of the curriculum. They were also keen to video the lesson and one student was made responsible for setting it up in the corner of the room before the beginning of the lesson.

I began to think of my action plan when they undertook the task, i.e. using the board for key points and ensuring a better mix within groups.

The lesson

The video: It was difficult to decide where to focus as we did not want it to be intrusive. The students decided that they would focus the camera on one side of the room and that halfway through a designated person would change its direction. The lesson followed after-noon registration and so there was no difficulty in setting the camera up prior to the class arriving.

The observation: This was unscheduled. We were just about to begin the lesson when a member of the class asked if one of them could observe as the other teacher had. I 'thought on my feet' and could not see any objection. I asked for a volunteer and chose the first hand that shot up. I knew that I did not have time to explain about how to do observation, so placed him in a position from where he could see most of the class and told him to write down anything that he thought might be affecting our learning. This would by nature be judgemental and for 'my eyes only'.

The task: The aim was for each group to produce a questionnaire which would be used by a group, not an individual. Whole class discussion (using the board for key points), followed by paired friendship groups. Further brainstorming as a class, followed by each pair joining another. I chose the groupings.

Follow-up

I used the student observation notes and the video with my teaching partner, Christine. We were both surprised at the candid nature of the observation notes. Groups of students have also seen extracts from the video (during lunchtimes) and this has led to further discussion. One 'spin-off' from the student involvement has been greater tolerance of individuals within the class and the building of a more positive class identity.

Notes made by the class member

(The comments in brackets have been added by Pamela Hughes.)

Beginning of lesson: everybody is chatting quietly. Then group task is explained. Groups are scattered around the room. (Group task in pairs.)
Same groups (pairs) as they are sitting in. They begin the group discussion. One pair mess-ing around.
Everybody works with somebody of the same sex.
Groups talking.
People at the back of the class are working more than the people towards the front.

Another member of staff enters – pupils cease to work and then get back to what they were doing before they entered.

Class discussion: Most people are contributing to the questions.
Some people had very good questions.
Some doodling in their notebooks while class discussion.
Nobody talked between themselves during this part of class discussion.
A couple of people are chewing pencils, pens.
Some people seem to be getting bored.

Groups combine: People only joined in a mixed group when there was no other choice.
Once the groups had been rearranged there was new discussion.
People who did not want to really work together in groups are working better than groups made up of just friends.
The people working best are the people with the camera directed towards them.
Most of the groups seem to have forgotten about the camera.
People who are messing around at the beginning seem to have calmed down a bit.
When the camera was moved for a second time people who had been fairly quiet up until now suddenly started moving and talking.
The people who are not in the picture now relax and start playing the fool to the camera. (I collated the group tasks some had not finished. Those who finished quickly began designing the layout.)
Quick response from all to correct teacher. (I cannot remember what this was – it may have been homework.)
Bell goes, chattering began and people started to pack away, but Mrs Hughes stopped them straight away.

Training for observation

Classroom observation can be a sensitive issue for teachers unused to regular or systematic observation since their teacher training and early days in the profession. It is also associated in many teachers' minds with accountability procedures such as inspection, appraisal, evaluation and performance management. As I am arguing in this book however, observation is something that can be valuable in its own right and used for a variety of staff development and school improvement purposes. Experience suggests that initial apprehension disappears once the process of observation is under way, providing appropriate procedures are used. I have already discussed some of the main principles of classroom observation, and it may be useful in concluding this chapter to briefly describe some training activities that can be used to promote good practice.

The first activity is designed to acquaint participants with the three phase cycle of classroom observation. The activity utilizes video examples to provide 'action images' which participants can relate to their own experience. The session could be divided into five parts:

1 Overview of benefits of the three-phase cycle.
2 Video example of the planning meeting. In discussing the video, participants may wish to consider:
   • How important is negotiation in the whole process?
   • What skills are involved?
   • What is the relationship between the participants?
   • How realistic is the agreed focus?
3 Video example of the classroom observation. During the video, participants should be encouraged to keep in mind the agreed focus of the observation and make notes on it as if they were in the classroom. In discussing the video, participants may wish to consider:
   • What other areas of focus could have been identified?
   • How feasible was it to obtain information on the agreed focus?
   • What skills are needed by the observer?
   • What are the relative benefits of open or focused observation?
4 Video example of the feedback discussion. In discussing the video, participants may wish to consider:
   • How far do you agree with the points raised in the discussion?
   • What is the balance between judgement and reflection in the discussion?
   • How far can this discussion lay the basis for professional growth?
   • What skills are required by an observer in promoting the developmental nature of such a discussion?
5 Review the classroom observation process in relation to the five key issues discussed earlier.

The second activity is designed to aid thinking about which areas to focus on in classroom observation and suitable data collection methods. Each group member should in turn select an aspect of their work as a possible focus for classroom observation and outline it to the group. The remainder of the group should then discuss the following questions:

• What information could be gathered through classroom observation?
• How would the observer collect it?
• How would the observer record it?
• What are the criteria that could most helpfully be applied to this particular aspect of the teacher's work?

As each member of the group presents an example and the others respond to it, the group should build up an *aide-mémoire* using the box below. The *aide-mémoire* may then be helpful in designing appropriate observation instruments or schedules and for identifying the most appropriate criteria to inform the feedback discussion.

If possible, back in school, participants should ask a colleague to use the approach devised during this exercise in their classroom and then to report back to other colleagues on how well it worked. Experience suggests that 'dry runs' such as this assist enormously in the process of acquiring the skills of, and allaying fears about, classroom observation.

Area of focus	Information needs	How to collect	How to record	Criteria

As the examples in this chapter demonstrate, classroom observation can provide powerful insights into classroom practice, as well as being a means of professional development and a major tool for the classroom researcher. In the chapter, I have described some of the main principles involved in doing classroom observation as well as providing a series of examples which hopefully give a feel of the method in practice and some suggestions for training activities. I have emphasized the partnership approach to observation because I feel that it is here where the link between teacher and school development lies, especially if the focus of the observation is related to whole school issues. In the following chapter, we look more closely at the methods available to the classroom observer committed to enhancing classroom practice.

Further reading

The 'clinical supervision' approach to classroom observation, on which this three-phase approach was based, is described in a practical way by Acheson and Gall (1997) in their *Techniques in the Clinical Supervision of Teachers*. The other classic texts on clinical supervision are by Goldhammer *et al.* (1993) and Cogan (1973). The work of Jean Rudduck contains a number of examples of teachers in partnership (Rudduck 1982, 1991; Rudduck and Sigsworth 1985). Colin Hook's (1995) *Studying Classrooms* contains a detailed discussion of the place of classroom observation in teacher research, and Judith Bell's (2005) helpful book on research in general contains a rationale for a more traditional approach to classroom observation.

7 Methods of observation in classroom research

Within the general framework of the three-phase classroom observation or partnership teaching approach, there is no one best method to use. When teachers observe each other teach, all they often require are simple ways of gathering information on basic topics, such as questioning techniques, on- or off-task behaviour, and classroom management. It is usually preferable for teachers to devise their own observation schedules, to invent them for a specific purpose. By doing this, there is usually more ownership developed over the subject of the observation and a better fit between the focus of the observation and the data-gathering method.

Before devising the observation checklist, it is often useful to ask some organizing questions in order to clarify the purpose of the observation. These questions are illustrative:

- What is the purpose of the observation?
- What is the focus of the observation?
- What teacher/student behaviours are important to observe?
- What data-gathering methods will best serve the purpose?
- How will the data be used?

These and similar questions should help the teachers involved clarify how easy it is to use the chosen approach, how much the observer looks at and how far the observer makes judgements.

The next step is to decide on the observation method. Although there are many approaches, it is possible to categorize them into four main groups. Each of them could involve the use of 'pencil and paper', audio- or video-recording. They are open observation, focused observation, structured observation and systematic observation.

Open observation

In this approach, the observer literally uses a blank sheet of paper to record the lesson. The observer either notes down key points about the lesson or uses a personal form of shorthand for making a verbatim recording of classroom transactions. For example:

Teacher: Turn 2 p. 46. Mary give us y. ans. to q. 1.

Mary: WW II was partly t. result of unresolved conflicts of WW I.

Teacher: That's 1 pt. of the ans. John give us y. ans.

The aim is usually to enable subsequent reconstruction of the lesson. A variation of this approach is to agree to record only those events that fit into certain broad categories or under certain headings, as shown in Figure 7.1.

The observer should aim to record factual and descriptive information.

Teaching skills

(i)	Presentation	
(ii)	Indirect teaching	
(iii)	Direct teaching	
(iv)	Voice	
(v)	Questioning strategies	
(vi)	Feedback	
(vii)	Subject matter	
(viii)	Expectations	

Figure 7.1   An example of open observation (from Bollington and Bradley 1990).

A problem with this approach is that it is often unfocused and can lead to premature judgements. The best way to handle this approach is to make open recording as factual as possible and leave interpretation until a discussion after the lesson. Because of its general nature, it is important to stick closely to each component of the three-phase cycle; otherwise what began as a mutual approach to observation could result in a one-way monologue!

CASE STUDY

In this extended example, Heather Lockhart describes how she went about observing her colleague Maureen's teaching.

Maureen has recently begun to doubt the effectiveness of her questioning techniques. She asked me to observe a review lesson on a 'Plants and Seeds' unit she had recently completed. We decided to concentrate on observing the effectiveness of her questioning techniques rather than the lesson content.

We also decided that I would be in the classroom strictly as an observer. I would not participate in the lesson in any way. We felt that, as many of the children in the room had been former students of mine and because I work with her class two periods every week, the children were familiar with me and comfortable in my presence.

We also decided not to use a tape-recorder or videotape so that the children would not be inhibited by them. Maureen and I discussed the most effective way of monitoring and decided on a checklist. I made a checklist and showed it to Maureen. Maureen agreed that it should give us the information we needed.

I positioned myself in the room within the children's immediate sight but slightly separated from the group. As I was within the field of their vision, I would not be causing distraction through children turning to check to see what I was doing. By separating myself slightly from the group, I was implying that I was not participating in the lesson. Maureen reinforced this by telling the children that I was going to watch because I didn't believe that they knew anything about plants and seeds. As we had predicted, outside of an occasional quick glance or smile, the children tended to ignore my presence.

When we first sat down, Maureen allowed the class about a minute of 'wriggle time' before she began to speak. She quickly explained my presence, then went directly into the lesson. She began by giving the children 'fact' questions that they could answer directly from the pictures. The responses were slow to come. Few children volunteered to answer the first few questions. As Maureen continued with the 'fact' questions, the children became more excited and eager to answer.

Maureen then began to inject 'inference questions'. The children were experiencing such success with 'fact questions' that they experienced no trouble in making inferences from the pictures. She then interspersed questions which required the children to form opinions. Again, the children responded freely and confidently. The children began to get restless after about 15 minutes and their attention began to wander. Maureen realized what was happening and quickly ended the lesson.

Looking at the checklist after the observation, my reactions to Maureen's questioning techniques were confirmed. The questions were asked clearly and concisely. The children had full understanding of the type of response that was being elicited. As they understood the questions, they were comfortable and eager to respond.

Maureen's interaction with the children was warm and caring. She listened carefully and respectfully to each response whether the response was correct or incorrect. She encouraged hesitant children by smiling at them, giving verbal encouragement or nodding while the child was speaking. She was careful to ensure that each child had the opportunity to respond at least once during the lesson.

I feel that Maureen has excellent questioning techniques. This includes the variety in the type of questions she asks, the manner in which she uses her voice, the positive reinforcement she employs, the pace of the lesson and the warmth she shows towards the children.

I feel that Maureen's main problem with questioning techniques is that she doesn't recognize her expertise in this area. I would suggest she tape the lessons that use intensive questioning methods and analyse the results for her own benefit.

Focused observation

When a pair of teachers have decided on a focus for an observation (e.g. questioning technique), they are often at a loss as to exactly what to look at or for. They may not know, for example, the range of higher-order/lower-order questions. In another situation, they may have decided to look at 'praise' in their classrooms, but when they think more about it they may have some difficulty in describing all the different possible forms of praise. Or again even with a phrase as commonplace as 'effective teaching', what exactly is it that we are looking for? In these situations, it may be helpful to draw on some external resources to help focus the observation. It may be that the teachers who were focusing on 'questioning' would find a form like that illustrated in Figure 7.2 of some help; or the teachers interested in praise may find the lists of effective and ineffective praise illuminating (see Table 7.1). Similarly, the teachers who were discussing effective teaching may find the observation schedule, distilled from four works on the subject, a useful research tool (see Table 7.2).

All of these forms, *aide-mémoires* and summaries of research can be of help as long as they are subject to the teacher's own judgement. Problems arise when the checklist controls the focus of the observation, or encourages the observer to become judgemental. This is another situation when Lawrence Stenhouse's (1975: 142) warning that such specifications are to be regarded as intelligent, but not necessarily correct, is apposite. They are there to help focus and refine the teacher's judgement, not supplant it. It should also go without saying that such 'prompts' should be agreed and negotiated beforehand. If the use of criteria are implied in the observation, then they also should be negotiated, shared and understood by all those involved.

Structured observation

Although the *aide-mémoires* described in the previous section are helpful in some situations, often all that an observer requires is fairly simple information that can be collected by either using a *tally system* or a *diagram*. I call this approach 'structured observation'.

With a tally system, an observer puts down a tally or tick *every time* a particular event occurs, e.g. every time the teacher asks a question or gives praise. The resulting record is factual rather than judgemental and can be made more detailed by basing them on *aide-mémoires* such as those described earlier. The aim of a diagram is to produce a record of what happens in the classroom. It records in diagrammatic form a series of classroom interactions. This approach lends itself to a factual or a descriptive record. It should be noted that all of these approaches can fit a wide range of concerns. They can focus on aspects of the teacher's work, pupil-teacher interaction or the work of one or more pupils.

The following examples of structured observation involve both tally systems and diagrams. They were developed by teachers who were interested in gathering data on questioning techniques and on- or off-task behaviour.

Observing questioning techniques

1   *Question distribution*: in Box 7.1 the circles represent pupils. When they answer a question, the number of the question is entered into their circle; blank circles indicate pupils who have not answered a question.
2   *Volunteered and solicited answers*: in Box 7.2 the circles again represent pupils. Use a 'V' for pupils who volunteer answers and an 'A' for those who are asked to answer. Placing a number beside the 'V' or 'A' will indicate the sequence of the questioning (e.g. V1, A2, V3, V4, A5, A6, etc.).

FORM 10.6 Questioning techniques

Use: When teacher is asking class or group questions
Purpose: To see if teacher is following principles for good questioning practices

For each question, code the following categories:

Behaviour categories

A *Type of question asked*
  1 Academic: Factual. Seeks specific correct response
  2 Academic: Opinion. Seeks opinion on a complex issue where there is no clear-cut response
  3 Non-academic: Question deals with personal, procedural, or disciplinary matters rather than curriculum

B *Type of response required*
  1 Thought question. Student must reason through to a conclusion or explain something at length
  2 Fact question. Student must provide fact(s) from memory
  3 Choice question. Requires only a yes–no or either–or response

C *Selection of respondent*
  1 Names child before asking question
  2 Calls on volunteer (after asking question)
  3 Calls on non-volunteer (after asking question)

D *Pause (after asking question)*
  1 Paused a few seconds before calling on student
  2 Failed to pause before calling on student
  3 Not applicable; teacher named student before asking question

E *Tone and manner in presenting question*
  1 Question presented as challenge or stimulation
  2 Question presented matter-of-factly
  3 Question presented as threat or test

Record any information relevant to the following:
Multiple Questions. Tally the number of times the teacher:
1 Repeats or rephrases question before calling on anyone 11
2 Asks two or more questions at the same time 0

Sequence. Were questions integrated into an orderly sequence or did they seem to be random or unrelated?

Teacher seemed to be following sequence given in manual (led up to next history unit).

Did students themselves pose questions? No

Was there student–student interaction?
How much? None

When appropriate, did the teacher redirect questions to several students or ask students to evaluate their own or others' responses? No

Codes

	A	B	C	D	E
1	1	2	2	1	2
2	1	2	2	1	2
3	1	3	2	1	2
4	1	2	2	1	2
5	1	2	2	1	2
6	1	3	2	1	2
7	1	2	2	1	2
8	2	1	2	1	1
9	1	2	2	1	2
10	1	2	2	1	2
11	1	2	2	1	2
12	1	2	2	1	2
13					
14					
15					
16					
17					
18					
19					
20					
21					
22					
23					
24					
25					
26					
27					
28					
29					
30					
31					
32					
33					
34					
35					
36					
37					
38					
39					
40					

Figure 7.2 Questioning techniques (from Good and Brophy 1997).

Table 7.1   Guidelines for effective praise

Effective praise	Ineffective praise
1 Is delivered contingently	1 Is delivered randomly or unsystematically
2 Specifies the particulars of the accomplishment	2 Is restricted to global positive reactions
3 Shows spontaneity, variety and other signs of credibility; suggests clear attention to the student's accomplishment	3 Shows a bland uniformity that suggests a conditioned response made with minimal attention
4 Rewards attainment of specified performance criteria (which can include effort criteria, however)	4 Rewards mere participation, without consideration of performance processes or outcomes
5 Provides information to students about their competence or the value of their accomplishments	5 Provides no information at all or gives students information about their status
6 Orients students towards better appreciation of their own task-related behaviour and thinking about problem-solving	6 Orients students towards comparing themselves with others and thinking about competing
7 Uses students' own prior accomplishments as the context for describing present accomplishments	7 Uses the accomplishments of peers as the context for describing students' present accomplishments
8 Is given in recognition of noteworthy effort or success at difficult (for *this* student) tasks	8 Is given without regard to the effort expended or the meaning of the accomplishment
9 Attributes success to effort and ability, implying that similar successes can be expected in the future	9 Attributes success to ability alone or to external factors such as luck or low task difficulty
10 Fosters endogenous attributions (students believe that they expend effort on the task because they enjoy the task and/or want to develop task-relevant skills)	10 Fosters exogenous attributions (students believe that they expend effort on the task for external reasons – to please the teacher, win a competition or reward, etc.)
11 Focuses students' attention on their own task-relevant behaviour	11 Focuses students' attention on the teacher as an external authority figure who is manipulating them
12 Fosters appreciation of, and desirable attributions about, task-relevant behaviour after the process is completed	12 Intrudes into the ongoing process, distracting attention from task-relevant behaviour

Source: Reproduced with permission from Brophy (1981).

Table 7.2   IQEA Observation schedule relating to features of effective teaching

An effective teacher	Check when observed
achieves eye contact with pupils during lessons	
allows pupil practice after each learning step	
allows short breaks where pupils move about	
allows pupils thinking time	
asks a large number of questions	
attributes ownership of ideas to initiating pupils	
attributes pupils' successes to their efforts	
avoids digressions/ambiguous phrases	
calls pupils by first names	
checks for pupil understanding	
conveys sense of enthusiasm in presentation of tasks	
discourages pupil–pupil verbal abuse	
gets high percentage of correct answers from pupils	
gets pupils to restate answers	
gives clear/detailed instructions/explanations	
gives concrete, varied examples	
gives hints, clues	
gives moderate amount of praise	
gives short review of previous learning	
guides pupils during initial practice	
has brief contacts with individual pupils (maximum 30 seconds)	
has pupils asking questions/initiating verbal interactions	
highlights main points of lesson	
is knowledgeable about subject matter	
monitors pupils' work when necessary	
moves around class and approaches all pupils	
obtains responses from all pupils	
organizes break when pupils' energy wanes	
organizes short transitions between activities	
presents new material in short steps	

An effective teacher	Check when observed
provides answers, asking pupils to restate in own words/give other examples	
provides systematic feedback/corrections	
rephrases questions	
responds positively to incorrect answers, identifying correct parts	
restates questions	
specifies expected pupil performance on tasks	
specifies what pupils did to achieve success	
teaches with pace	
uses anecdotes, asides relating to task	
uses humour	

Source: Beresford (1998: 85–6).

3   *Teacher response to questions answered*: indicate how the teacher responds to answers by using the following abbreviations. Tally scores as in Box 7.3.

V = verbal response
NV = non-verbal response
+ = indicated positive response
0 = indicated no response
– = indicated negative response.

Observing on-task/off-task behaviours

- Identify, by scanning the classroom, all of the students who appear to be off-task every two minutes. Number each scan, using the same number for all pupils who appear to be off-task during that scan. For example, during scan 7, five pupils appeared to be off-task as in Box 7.4.
- Tally on-task/off-task behaviour: list in the off-task column the number of pupils off-task at each scan (say every two minutes). Subtract the off-task from the class total to determine on-task pupils. Work out the percentages as in Box 7.5.
- Tally observable off-task behaviour by using the following code:
    1   talking not related to task assigned;
    2   doodling;
    3   daydreaming;
    4   wandering around;

Box 7.1

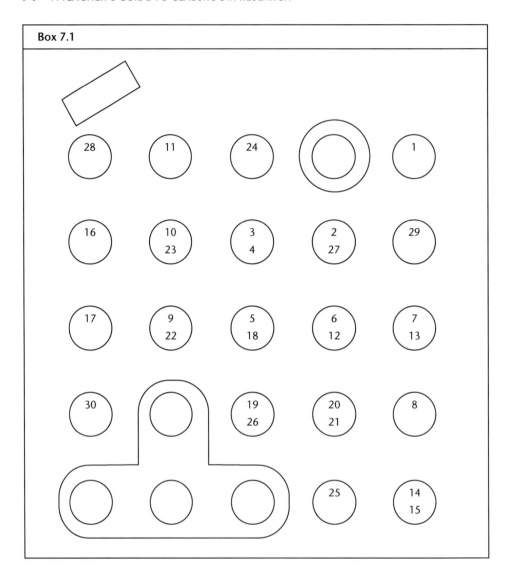

5 working at other tasks;
6 physically bothering other pupils;
7 attempting to draw attention;
8 pencil-sharpener, fountain, washroom;
9 other.

This observation is easiest to do if you concentrate on a small number of pupils over an extended period of time, rather than trying to observe a whole class at once. During each scan (say every two minutes), observe the off-task behaviour and place the appropriate number in the space. If the student is on-task during the scan, the space is left blank as seen in Box 7.6.

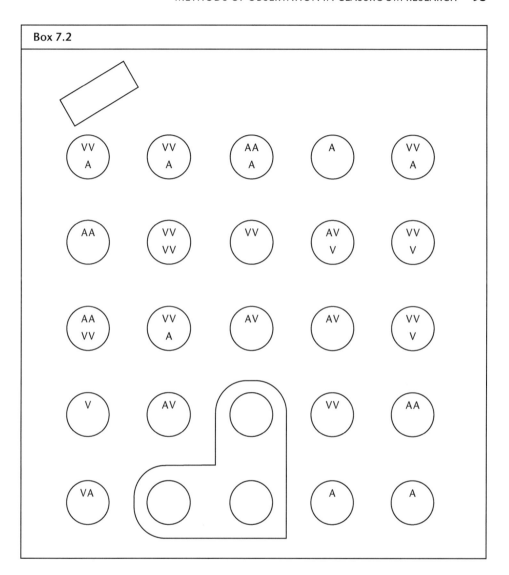

Systematic observation

Classroom observations using coding scales are generally appropriate where a range of behaviours, too numerous to record in an open observation and too complex to collect in a structured observation, need to be mapped. Recording the on-task and off-task behaviour of students, *along with their causes*, would require such an approach, as would an audit and categorization of teaching strategies used in a range of lessons.

Although it may be preferable for teacher-researchers to devise their own observation scales, sometimes they may not have the time, or they may already be familiar

Box 7.3					
Question	Response				
	V	NV	+	0	–
1	✓		✓		
2	✓		✓		
3		✓	✓		
4	✓				✓
5		✓		✓	
6	✓		✓		
7	✓		✓		
8	✓			✓	
9		✓	✓		
10		✓		✓	
Totals	6	4	6	3	1

with an existing coding scale previously invented. In this section, I will discuss a variety of coding scales that can be utilized in specific situations by teachers, and give a more detailed illustration of one interaction scale – the Flanders Interaction Analysis Categories.

The research approach that relies entirely on the use of observation scales is known as 'systematic classroom observation'. The impetus for coding scales and checklists has come from North America where there is, and has been for some time, a concern for 'scientific' approaches to teaching (Gage 1978). But there is also a strong British tradition of systematic classroom observation; for example, the Oracle Project in primary education, which was the first large-scale study of classroom inter-action in Britain (Galton *et al.* 1980). I appreciate that I am drawing on somewhat dated sources here, but am doing this because the principles and procedures they demonstrate still have a contemporary application to the practice of observation in teacher research.

There are some potential problems in the use of coding or interaction scales. The first problem is that most scales were not designed for use by teachers. Their original intent was as research tools for analysing classrooms. Given the aspirations of this book, however, it is important to stress that these are tools teachers can use to enhance their practice. The teacher-researcher's orientation is always action.

The second difficulty is that each scale represents the author's concept of a situation. One is looking at classrooms through someone else's eyes: their purposes and perceptions could be very different from one's own. It is easy, therefore, to get trapped within the intentions of the researcher who designed the scale. Consequently, it is important for the teacher-researcher to match his or her needs closely to the intent and

Box 7.4

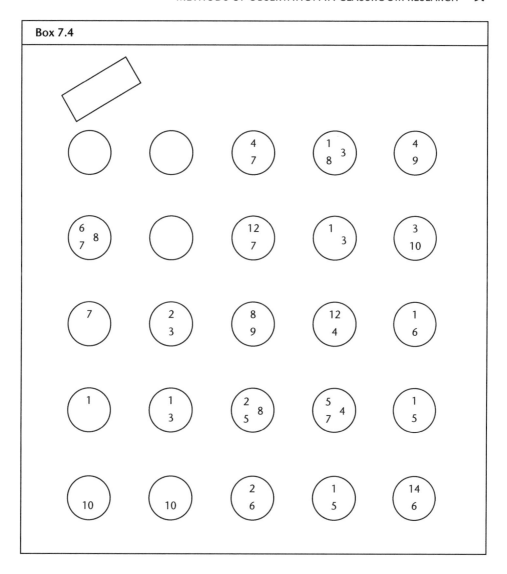

focus of the scale. In that way, the teacher-researcher can maintain control over the situation.

Third, there is a heavy emphasis on quantitative methods in systematic observation. This frequently results in a conflict between statistical rigour and analytical richness. In my opinion, this inevitably leads to abstraction rather than reflection on (or in) action. This approach often leads away from the classroom rather than into it. To misquote T.S. Eliot, systematic observers may well have the experience, but in so doing they are in danger of losing the meaning.

Because of the 'scientific' bias in this approach it is unsurprising to find that most coding scales available are American in origin. As Galton (1978) comments:

The obvious starting point for any classification of interaction analysis systems must be *Mirrors for Behaviour* (Simon and Boyer, 1975). The current edition of this anthology contains some 200 observation schedules. Most are American and only two are British. In their collection the observation instruments are classified under eight main headings:

1   the subject of observation (teacher, pupil),
2   the setting under which the instrument is used (subject area),
3   the number of targets observed,

Box 7.5

Scan	Off-task		On-task	
	Number	%	Number	%
1	4	16	21	84
2	6	24	19	76
3	1	4	24	96
4	0	0	25	100
5	3	12	22	88
6	3	12	22	88
7	6	24	19	76
8	5	20	20	80
9	4	16	21	84
10	4	16	21	84
Total	36		214	
Average		15		85

Box 7.6

Student	Scan										
	1	2	3	4	5	6	7	8	9	10	%
Jeroen	3	4				3		8			40
Jessica	2	2		3	3		4	2	3	2	80
Marloes	6	7			6	6		7			40
David		5	5			5	5		5		50
Dylan	1	1	1	8				8	1		70

4   the coding unit used,
5   the collecting method employed,
6   the number of observers required,
7   the dimensions of the system (affective, cognitive), and
8   the uses reported by the author.

One of the problems with many of the American scales is that they are overly concerned with the formal teaching situation. British researchers have also been developing their own coding scales which, in general, stand in contrast to the American models. Galton (1978) comments again:

> A feature of British research has been the wide variety of different organisational contexts within which classroom observation has been carried out. Much criticism has been directed at American systems because they often seem appropriate only to the more formal type of teaching situation. One of the most interesting features of the British research is the emphasis on observation in informal settings at one extreme and the variety of schedules suitable for use in the microteaching setting for the purpose of evaluating performance in questioning and lecturing skills at the other.

These quotations from Galton (1978) are taken from his book *British Mirrors*, which is a collection of 41 classroom observation systems that are British in origin. The majority of these instruments are junior and secondary school oriented but some are specifically designed for infant or higher education settings. Their target is almost exclusively teachers and pupils, most require only one observer and they are almost exclusively concerned with descriptions of classroom practice. The four major foci of the instruments are: classroom climate, organizational learning, the management and control of routine activities, and knowledge content. In general, they are applicable across all curriculum areas.

One of the earliest coding systems is the Flanders Interaction Analysis Categories (FIAC). Although it may not necessarily be the most effective of the systems available, it is probably the best known. It is widely used and has influenced the design of many other category systems.

FIAC is based on ten analytical categories that reflects Flanders' conceptualization of teacher–pupil verbal interaction (see Table 7.3). Each of the categories has a number, but no scale is implied. In his book *Analysing Teaching Behaviour*, Flanders (1970) described the ten categories in detail, but for our purposes the descriptions given are sufficient. In order to help memorize the categories and make coding easier, one can shorten the descriptions of the categories as shown in Box 7.7.

The procedures for using the Flanders system are quite straightforward. Observers are first trained until they show a high level of agreement with other trained observers. Once they have been trained, they watch a lesson and apply the technique as follows using a coding sheet such as that illustrated in Figure 7.3.

1   Every three seconds the observer writes down the category best describing the verbal behaviour of the teacher and class.

Table 7.3 Flanders interaction analysis categories

Teacher talk Indirect influence	1	*Accepts feelings*: accepts and clarifies the feeling tone of the student in a non-threatening manner. Feelings may be positive or negative. Predicting and recalling feelings are included.
	2	*Praises or encourages*: praises or encourages student action or behaviour. Jokes that release tension, not at the expense of another individual, nodding head or saying 'uh huh?' or 'go on' are included.
	3	*Accepts or uses ideas of student*: clarifying, building or developing ideas or suggestions by a student. As teacher brings more of his own ideas into play, shift to category 5.
	4	*Asks questions*: asking a question about content or procedure with the intent that a student answers.
Direct *influence*	5	*Lectures*: giving facts or opinions about content or procedures, expressing his own idea; asking rhetorical questions.
	6	*Gives directions*: directions, commands or orders with which a student is expected to comply.
	7	*Criticizes or justifies authority*: statements, intended to change student behaviour from non-acceptable to acceptable pattern; bawling someone out; stating why the teacher is doing what he is doing; extreme self-reference.
Student talk	8	*Student talk-response*: talk by students in response to teacher. Teacher initiates the contact or solicits student statement.
	9	*Student talk-initiation*: talk by students, which they initiate. If 'calling on' student is only to indicate who may talk next, observer must decide whether student wanted to talk. If he did, use this category.
	10	*Silence or confusion*: pauses, short periods of silence, and periods of confusion in which communication cannot be understood by the observer.

Source: Open University (1976).

Box 7.7		
Teacher talk	1 2 3 4 5 6 7	accepts feelings praise accepts ideas question lecture command criticism
Pupil talk	8 9	solicited unsolicited
	10	silence

Source: Open University (1976).

School _____   Teacher_____
Class _____   Subject _____
Date _____   Observer _____
Lesson (1st, 2nd, etc.) _____

TALLY ACROSS

01																							
02																							
03																							
04																							
05																							
06																							
07																							
08																							
09																							
10																							
11																							
12																							
13																							
14																							
15																							
16																							
17																							
18																							
19																							
20																							
21																							
22																							
23																							
24																							
25																							
26																							
27																							
28																							
29																							
30																							

Figure 7.3   FIAC lesson observation sheet (Open University 1976).

2   The numbers are written in sequence across the data sheet.
3   Each line of the data sheet contains 20 squares, thus representing approximately one minute of time.
4   Separate 'episodes' can be identified by scribbled margin notes, and a new line commenced for a new 'episode'.
5   In a research project, the observer would have a pocket timer designed to give a signal every three seconds, thus reminding them to record a tally (a mobile phone or a pager can be used).

Two main advantages of the Flanders system are that it is fairly easy to learn and apply, and that the ten categories describe a number of behaviours which many would agree are important, such as the teacher's use of praise and criticism and the pupil's solicited and unsolicited talk. Also, the tallying of events every three seconds enables considerable information to be collected and analysed. There is usually a high agreement between trained observers.

On the other hand, much information is lost, especially non-verbal aspects of communication. In particular, some categories are too broad (e.g. category 4) and others discriminate insufficiently. For example, category 5 does not discriminate between giving information which is correct and that which is incorrect. Category 10 can represent both the silence achieved by an autocrat and the chaos which occurs when a teacher has lost control. Also, there are too few pupil categories, and it is difficult to use in informal classrooms, where two or more members may be talking at once.

For our purposes, FIAC is most appropriately used as a means for gathering classroom data that can then be used as a basis for action. So, for example, if after using FIAC a teacher discovered that they were talking too much, then that becomes an identifiable problem upon which action can be taken and monitored by classroom research procedures.

CASE STUDY

A simple example illustrates the first few seconds of an exchange occurring in the twelfth minute of a lesson.

The teacher tells children to look at a map on page 60 of their books and asks the name of the country coloured green. There is a short pause and then a child replies. The text of this exchange and the data sheet would look like that shown in Box 7.8.

```
┌─────────────────────────────────────────────────────────────────┐
│  Box 7.8                                                          │
│  ┌─────────────────────────────────────────────────────────────┐│
│  │                                          Category number      ││
│  │                                          tallied by observer  ││
│  │                                                               ││
│  │  Teacher:  'Look at the map on page 60'    6  (command)       ││
│  │  Teacher:  'What is the country coloured   4  (question)      ││
│  │            green?'                                            ││
│  │            three second pause            10  (silence)        ││
│  │  Pupil:    'I think it's Finland, but I'm not  8 (solicited   ││
│  │            sure.'                               pupil talk)   ││
│  │                                                               ││
│  │  Data sheet entry                                             ││
│  │  (minute 12 of the lesson)       ┌────┬┬────┬────┬────┬────┐  ││
│  │                                  │ 12 ││ 6  │ 4  │ 10 │ 8  │  ││
│  │                                  └────┴┴────┴────┴────┴────┘  ││
│  └─────────────────────────────────────────────────────────────┘│
└─────────────────────────────────────────────────────────────────┘
```

Source: Open University (1976).

Further reading

Rob Walker's (1989) *Doing Research* and Colin Hook's (1995) *Studying Classrooms* both contain exemplary and sound advice on methods of classroom observation that are sympathetic to the theme of this book. Walker and Adelman (1990), Wragg's (1999) *An Introduction to Classroom Observation*, Daniels *et al.*'s (2001) *Understanding Children: Interview and Observation Guide for Educators* and Reed and Bergemann's (2004) CD-ROM *Guide to Observation, Participation and Reflection in the Classroom with Forms for Field Use* also provide useful information on classroom observation. Hitchcock and Hughes (1995), in their *Research and the Teacher*, provide extensive advice but from a more traditional perspective. Good and Brophy's (2003) *Looking in Classrooms* contains many schedules for assessing classroom behaviour; this book is an important resource for teacher-researchers as it provides a range of material on teaching skills and ways of measuring their impact in the classroom. Sara Delamont's (1983) *Interaction in the Classroom* is a balanced and introductory account of the domain of classroom observation research. Paul Croll's (2000) second edition of his book *Systematic Classroom Observation* contains a fairly sustained argument for the centrality of systematic observation in quantitative research. This book also provides a detailed introduction to the large-scale 'Oracle' and 'One in Five' classroom interaction research studies. The approach taken in this book, however, tends to lead away from the classroom rather than into it, and Croll overemphasizes, in my opinion, the distinction between teachers and researchers rather than the benefits of collaboration between them. In the same tradition, the two collections of classroom observation scales by Simon and Boyer (1975) and Galton (1978) are primary resources for teacher-researchers wanting examples of coding scales. Critiques of these various approaches to classroom interaction and observation are to be found in Sara Delamont's (1984) *Readings on Interaction in the Classroom* and Martin Hammersley's (1993) *Controversies in Classroom Research*. John Beresford (1998), in his *Collecting Information for School Improvement*, provides a range of instruments for school-based and classroom research, as well as useful hints on how to administer them.

8   Data gathering

In this chapter, I discuss a variety of techniques other than observation that teachers can use to gather information about their teaching. I will observe a similar format in discussing each of the approaches: the technique will briefly be described, advantages and disadvantages will be considered, appropriate uses will be stated and an example of the technique in practice will be given. At the end of the chapter, I will present a taxonomy of teacher research methods.

The Ford Teaching Project (Elliott and Adelman 1976) in general, and the booklet *Ways of Doing Research in One's Own Classroom* (Bowen *et al.* n.d.) in particular, provided the inspiration for this chapter. The idea for the boxes illustrating the advantages/ disadvantages of the data collection methods came from the appendix of *Ways of Doing Research in One's Own Classroom* and a number of the points made there are reproduced here verbatim. Also, all the methods of data collection mentioned below, with the exception of sociometry, were used by the Ford Teaching Project. Once again I am very grateful to the Ford Teaching Project for allowing me to use their material in this chapter.

Before describing these methods in more detail, two caveats have to be entered. The first is that describing the techniques individually may give a false impression of orderliness and discreteness. In practice, these techniques are more often than not used eclectically and in combination. Second, we need to remember the criteria established earlier which cautioned that the method employed should not be too demanding on the teacher's time.

Field notes

Keeping field notes is a way of reporting observations, reflections and reactions to classroom problems. Ideally, they should be written as soon as possible after a lesson, but can be based on impressionistic jottings made during a lesson. The greater the time-lapse between the event and recording it, the more difficult it becomes to reconstruct problems and responses accurately and retain conscious awareness of one's original thinking. Many teachers I know keep a notebook open on their desk or keep a space in their daybooks for jotting down notes as the lesson and the day progresses. Keeping a record in this way is not very time-consuming and provides surprisingly frank information that is built up over time. They also provide a fascinating biographical record of our development as teachers.

Field notes can be of a number of different types. They can be 'issue-oriented' insofar as the observations focus on a particular aspect of one's teaching or classroom behaviour and constitute an ongoing record. On the other hand, they can reflect general impressions of the classroom, its climate or incidental events. Field notes can also be used to provide case study material of a particular child. This information should be descriptive rather than speculative, so that a broad picture amenable to interpretation can be built up.

The main advantages and disadvantages of field notes are listed in point form in Box 8.1.

Four uses of field notes in classroom research are:

1   They can focus on a particular issue or teaching behaviour over a period of time.
2   They can reflect general impressions of the classroom and its climate.
3   They can provide an ongoing description of an individual child that is amenable to interpretation and use in case study.
4   They can record our development as teachers.

Box 8.1	
Advantages	**Disadvantages**
• Very simple to keep; no outsider needed • Provide good ongoing record; used as a diary they give good continuity • First-hand information can be studied conveniently in teacher's own time • Act as an *aide-mémoire* • Help to relate incidents, explore emerging trends • Very useful if teacher intends to write a case study	• Need to fall back on aids such as question analysis sheets, tapes and transcripts for specific information • Conversation impossible to record by field notes • Notebook works with small groups but not with a full class • Initially time-consuming • Can be highly subjective

CASE STUDY

In this example Ian uses field notes to build up a picture of the work ethic in a low academic set of 12–13-year-olds.

I started making observations, keeping a note pad on the desk. I chose not to take a particular focus. After making initial observations on movement, posture and seating arrangements, and after some interviews of a general nature concerning the pupil's attitudes to the teaching of language and the organization into sets that the pupils had to submit to, a picture of the work ethic of a low academic set was gradually built up.

For each distinct activity that goes on in the English language lesson (story writing, grammar skills, etc.), the working environments and climates are different. In language work, for example, there is always an initial rush to complete one card – the minimum requirement. When this is completed, although another card is often collected, intensive work ceases and chatting about the weekend, with some desultory work, is the norm (the lesson is first period Monday). This ritualized behaviour has the function of reaffirming certain social groups, and talk is, interestingly enough, voluntarily kept to quite a quiet level. The various friendship groups have distinct topics of conversation which don't vary much over the year. Changes to the seating, which I have tried, cause a much higher level of noise. All the other English activities – each one has one lesson a week – have different structures and patterns of social interaction, attitudes and noise levels which have built up over time.

I noted that the pattern of work throughout the term – and the year – is affected by traditional school rituals. The arrangement of pupils into sets is reviewed at the end of each term and this ritual always influences work rate and conversation:

> *Girl:* You 'eard about moving up yet, sir?
> *Teacher:* No, I've been asked to make three recommendations to go up and down. Mr . . . will make the decision. [chorus of inquiries]
> *Girl:* Shut up you – you're thick. If you move, it'll be down. I hope I move up – we do no work in 'ere. 'Alf of 'em can't even write (looking at the boys). (Cheers from boys)

The low status of the set is always a factor in the pupils' perceptions of their ability and in their attitude to work.

[This example is taken from a series of teacher-researcher reports on children's thinking in Hull *et al.* (1985). At a later date, the teacher could have used notes like this as 'evidence' in discussions with his students about their progress and aspirations.]

Audiotape recording

Audiotape recording is one of the most popular teacher research methods. Transcripts are excellent for those situations where teachers require a very specific and accurate record of a limited aspect of their teaching, or of a particular interaction, say between a specific teacher and child or between two children. An increasing number of teachers are using audiotape as one further way of gathering data to support other forms of assessment, albeit on an incidental basis. Also, simply playing back tapes of one's teaching can be very illuminating and provide useful starting points for further investigation. Having a tape deck in one's car is a great asset for doing this.

Playing back tapes or making transcripts can be very time-consuming and expensive, however, unless the method is used judiciously. The Ford Teaching Project teachers and staff were very enthusiastic about this method, but they did have secretarial support for making transcripts. Most teachers do not, and for that reason I advise against it as a broad-spectrum diagnostic tool.

On the practical side, the use of the tape-recorder requires some technical knowledge, so make certain you can use it before taking it into class and that the batteries are charged! It is important when recording to ensure that the microphone is picking up what is intended, and this also may require practice. Pupils often find the presence of a tape-recorder in the class disturbing and have to be introduced to the technique over time. Always check with the pupils and other teachers or adults that they do not mind you recording the conversation or discussion.

The main advantages and disadvantages of the audiotape recorder are listed in point form in Box 8.2. Three uses of the tape-recorder in classroom research are:

1   as a general diagnostic tool for identifying aspects of one's teaching;
2   for providing detailed evidence on specific aspects of teaching through the use of transcripts;
3   as an additional source of evidence for classroom assessment.

Box 8.2	
Advantages	**Disadvantages**
• Very successfully monitors all conversations within range of the recorder • Provides ample material with great ease • Versatility – can be transported or left with a group • Records personality developments • Can trace development of a group's activities • Can support classroom assessment	• Nothing visual – does not record silent activities • Transcription largely prohibitive because of expense and time involved • Masses of material may provide little relevant information • Can disturb pupils because of its novelty; can be inhibiting • Continuity can be disturbed by the practical problems of operating

CASE STUDY

In this example Val uses an audiotape-recorder as an aid to understanding children's thinking in relation to sketch maps in geography.

The class (of very bright 11-year-olds) was arranged in groups of four or five pupils and each group was given copies of the four maps and asked to discuss them and decide which they thought was 'best'. I only had access to one tape-recorder and was only able therefore to record one discussion. When I listened to the tape, I realized that discussion clearly had potential as a research tool and that this strategy for gaining access to pupils' critical thinking was worth repeating. Pupils were realistic in their criticisms and were to some extent impersonal. The discussion helped me to see what criteria they were using and how the range of their considerations might be extended.

In my next attempt . . . (there was only one tape-recorder available), there were several groups responding to the maps, so each group chose a leader and he or she gave a report to the class at the end of the discussion and it was the final reports that were taped. Some of the spontaneity of the original discussion was lost, but nevertheless some interesting points emerged.

It seemed that the brighter pupils were more methodical and precise in their criticism:

Simon:	Our verdict on map 1 was that a ruler could have been used and some of the buildings had doors missing and that there wasn't any scale . . . title, key or north direction.
	Map 3 – it's a drawing, it's not a map.
	Map 4 – that's quite good, that's more of a map, they have got a key and direction and a suitable title.
Sarah:	We thought map 1 wasn't very good because the writing is too small.
	Map 3 wasn't very good – too artistic.
Valerie:	Map 2 was the best because it showed all the roads and railways and bridges.

[This example is taken from a series of teacher-researcher reports on children's thinking in Hull *et al.* (1985). The teacher was subsequently able to use this information to revise the sketch maps; the discussions also helped her adapt her teaching style with more able pupils.]

Pupil diaries

It is common practice in many schools for pupils to keep a daily log. This is also a quick way of obtaining information, as teachers normally check pupil diaries as a matter of course. Also, pupil diaries provide an interesting contrast to the field notes kept by the teacher on the same topic. Once the pupils have been taken into the teacher's confidence and are aware of the teacher's concern to research their teaching, then these diaries are an excellent way of obtaining honest feedback, particularly when the pupils retain the right to decide whether the teacher has access to the diary. The teacher can use pupil diaries as feedback on a particular teaching episode, to gain an indication of the general class climate or to assess the progress of an individual pupil. When pupils feel comfortable with the approach, they may feel free to write about other teachers and aspects of the school. Sometimes the ethical issues raised by this may be difficult to resolve, particularly when the use of pupil diaries is not commonplace in the school.

The main advantages and disadvantages of pupil diaries are listed in point form in Box 8.3. Three uses of pupil diaries in classroom research are:

Box 8.3	
Advantages	Disadvantages
• Provides feedback from pupil's perspective • Can be either focused on a specific training episode or related to the general classroom climate • Can be part of a lesson • Can help in identifying individual pupil problems • Involves pupil in improving the quality of the class • Provides a basis for triangulation	• May not be an established practice in the school • Difficult for younger children to record their thoughts and feelings • Pupils may be inhibited in discussing their feelings with the teacher • Pupil's accounts are obviously subjective • May raise ethical dilemmas

1   to provide a pupil perspective on a teaching episode;
2   to provide data on the general climate of the classroom; and
3   to provide information for triangulation.

CASE STUDY

In this example Judy is using pupil diaries as part of her strategy for reorganizing her maths class.

I used the diaries mainly as immediate feedback for myself and as an aid in monitoring the daily progress of the students. The following are samples of information that I gathered from the various student diaries during a four-week period:

1 There were explanations as to why they hadn't completed a number of assignments for my substitute while I was at a convention.
2 Throughout the four weeks the students used the logs to tell me when they were having trouble with an assignment and to ask to see me the next day for help.
3 A number of students suggested that I put in a centre containing mazes and logic puzzles that they could go to when they had completed all their assignments.
4 Occasionally, a pupil would ask me to change their seating arrangement as they weren't able to work near a certain person.
5 Many of them began to use the log to establish a private conversation between us.
6 I used the logs to indicate when I was disappointed in a student's performance or behaviour and to question them about it. I found that they were more open since they weren't put on the spot in front of their classmates.
7 Some of them mentioned when they felt I had let the noise level get too high or

when they had been able to do more than usual because it had been exceptionally quiet.

8   They pointed out when they had wasted time waiting for me to get their books marked so they could finish off their corrections.

9   I found it especially helped me monitor the progress of my less assertive students.

10   The students would indicate when they felt I had given too heavy a workload for the week.

11   Students twice pointed out that they had come to me for assistance and I had been too busy to help them.

I felt that these logs were one of the most valuable aspects of my research project. They weren't always relevant to my actual research, but the personal contact I managed to establish with each of my students was of more importance to me than keeping them on target concerning their work in the maths programme.

Interviews

Interviewing in classroom research can take four forms: it can occur between teacher and pupil, observer and pupil, pupil and pupil and, occasionally, teacher and observer. This latter activity, however, normally occurs as a consequence of peer observation (see Chapters 6 and 7). Because teacher–pupil interviews are very time-consuming, it may be more profitable to devote that time to general classroom meetings, and only talk individually with pupils (for research purposes) when a specific instance warrants it. On the other hand, individual interviews are often very productive sources of information for a participant observer who wants to verify observations they have previously made. Like other researchers, however, I increasingly find group interviews with three or four students the most productive. Far from inhibiting each other, the individuals 'spark' themselves into sensitive and perceptive discussion. I also find it helpful to tape-record my summary of the discussion with the students at the end of the interview. This enables them to correct or amplify my interpretation and provides me with a brief and succinct account of the interview that can easily be transcribed.

Pupil–pupil interviews can provide rich sources of data, particularly if the pupil interviewer keeps to an interview schedule prepared by the teacher. It is a good idea to tape-record these individual interviews for future reference, particularly if the encounters are relatively short.

Walker and Adelman (1990) make a number of points about effective interviewing:

1   Be a sympathetic, interested and attentive listener, without taking an active conservative role; this is a way of conveying that you value and appreciate the child's opinion.

2   Be neutral with respect to subject matter. Do not express your own opinions either on the subjects being discussed by the children or on the children's ideas about these subjects, and be especially careful not to betray feelings of surprise or disapproval at what the child knows.

3 Your own sense of ease is also important. If you feel hesitant or hurried, the students will sense this feeling and behave accordingly.
4 The students may also be fearful that they will expose an attitude or idea that you don't think is correct. Reassure along the lines of 'Your opinions are important to me. All I want to know is what you think – this isn't a test and there isn't any one answer to the questions I want to ask.'
5 Specifically we suggest that you:
   • phrase questions similarly each time,
   • keep the outline of interview questions before you, and
   • be prepared to reword a question if it is not understood or if the answer is vague and too general. Sometimes it is hard not to give an 'answer' to the question in the process of rewording it.

The main advantages and disadvantages of interviewing are listed in point form in Boxes 8.4 (a–c).

Box 8.4(a) Teacher/pupil (individually or in groups of three or four)	
Advantages	**Disadvantages**
• Teacher in direct contact with pupil • Pupil(s) familiar with teacher, therefore more at ease • Teacher able to seek information they want directly and not through a ream of irrelevant information • Can be done in lesson time or outside the class • Can follow up problems immediately when they arise and get information while minds are still fresh	• Time-consuming • May be carried out with some form of recording equipment, with attendant disadvantages • Frequently difficult to get younger children to explain their thoughts and feelings

Box 8.4(b) Observer/pupil (individually or in groups of three or four)

Advantages	Disadvantages
• Leaves teacher free as the interviewer discovers initial information from the pupil(s) • Pupil(s) frequently more candid with the outsider than with class teacher or teacher from within the school • Outsider is likely to be more objective • Outsider can focus the information provided along predetermined lines of investigation • Outsider can focus the information provided along predetermined lines of investigation	• Pupil(s) unfamiliar with observer may be reluctant to divulge relevant information • Mutual uncertainty • If the teacher is the primary agent in the research, then they will get their information secondhand and subject to the biases of the interviewer • The whole set up is time-consuming as information goes from pupil(s) to interviewer to teacher • Difficult to obtain a skilled outsider

Box 8.4(c) Pupil/pupil

Advantages	Disadvantages
• Pupils may be more candid with each other • Leaves teacher free • Can occur during lesson time • May produce unanticipated/unusual perspectives	• Pupils may find the activity too unfamiliar • May encourage disruption • Has to be recorded and played to teacher

Three uses of the interview in classroom research are:

- to focus on a specific aspect of teaching or classroom life in detail;
- to provide general diagnostic information through teacher–pupil classroom discussion; and
- to improve the classroom climate.

CASE STUDY

This example contains extracts from a conversation between three Year 9 students (S) at the Sanders Draper School, Havering, Mel Ainscow (MA), David Hargreaves (DHH) and myself (DH). Sanders Draper was involved in the 'Improving the Quality of Education for All' school improvement project. The purpose of the discussion was to assess how far the school's development priority 'Resource Based Learning' had affected students' perceptions of the way they were taught and learned. We used this information in feedback to staff, who in turn incorporated it in their own developmental work. I have included such an extended illustration partly for its intrinsic interest, but also to show how classroom research can support whole school development and to illustrate the power of the group interview.

DH: What is it like to learn in this school?

S: It's changed now that we are able to use the library more, we are now using more visual/audio type stuff, videos, rather than just learning out of a textbook.

S: Also teachers tell you to get on with it, rather than them telling you what to do. You can come in here (the library), you find out all the information and you can say to a teacher I want to do this and that, and they say alright then.

S: Well we are more tending to get into things like, in maths for example, we tend to go into our own investigations where we can take a problem and we investigate it in our own way.

DH: Tell me a bit about how you actually find the information.

S: Well, if you find a book, look through the subject index, or there is a disk thing on the computer, it's got all newspaper things, you put the disk in and you say what subjects you want to find out about, type it in and it comes up with all the different things in the subjects. You choose what you want. There is also an encyclopaedia list on the computer.

DH: What happens when you've done all this and got some information on the subject you are dealing with, say four or five bits of information – what do you do then?

S: We either make it into like a folder of work, put it into graphs, or sometimes we get the chance to make a play out of it, but there is still a certain amount of written work to record it all. Things like – they'll tell a certain amount of detail. Like in science they were telling us about disease and then we had to write a newspaper report about it, so used the pictures.

DH: What happens if you get into the situation where you find that one bit of information disagrees with another piece of information. How do you make a decision?

S: Usually you put both of the arguments, both for and against, or you decide which you think, but explain that there are other sides to the idea. Put down what you thought what was right and what was wrong. Put both sides down.

MA: That's quite demanding, do some students struggle with that?

S: It depends if you are looking through hundreds of encyclopaedias for the one thing you are looking for; otherwise you might as well watch it on the video if you are looking for something about the Third Reich, see if they've got a video about it. That's easier. There will always be people who work at different speeds, are capable of different things. When we do learning in our own way, then it is better because they are not trying to keep up with the top students in the class.

DHH: You have given me the impression that this new style of learning, your relationship with the teacher is different.

S: Well it is in some ways because there are some teachers who are sitting there and want to teach you everything on the line, but there are others who think it best for us to work down here (in the library).

DHH: But is it? Is it best for you?

S: Yes, I think it is. I prefer it anyway. You are at your own pace. Not like a teacher dictating to you and you just sitting there with your mouth open.

DH: Some people say that the real way to be taught is to write down lots of notes, do exercises from the book.

S: But the two ways compensate each other. You learn at your own pace and then answer the questions from the book. Then you remember it, take it in rather than just taking notes. You sort of construct it your own way. No real way of learning, different people find it easier to do different things, so I don't think anyone can say it is a lot better to work out of a textbook or it is a lot better to watch a video.

DHH: If I understand you correctly when you take notes, you are not really learning anything.

S: You learn about half of it but if you are in control of your own learning, you are doing it the way you want to do it, you actually want to learn about it, you are taking it in, and remembering more because you are doing it your way.

[*The students then showed us some examples of work.*]

MA: Who produced this?

S: I decided to do it on a computer at home, then it would be easier to read.

MA: So this in a sense summarizes all the research that you did, you've put it into your own words and made an information sheet.

S: Yes, that's what they said, do it like a magazine article, then it comes out in your own words. More likely to remember something that way.

DH: You have been in the school now for three years, do you think there has been a change in the way that teachers teach over those three years?

S: (Since the new Head arrived) the school has got more disciplined.

DH: More disciplined in the school, but at the same time a more open approach to teaching and learning?

S: Well we've been given the chance to like express ourselves, but because of that we've had to go by their rules.

DH: So there is a good response to this more open way.

S: Yes, you've got the responsibility of getting on with what you want to do, you've got to do it even if the teacher isn't watching you. It sort of works two ways, you respect the school rules and they'll respect you, they are trusting you to work on your own.

DHH: Somebody might say, from outside, that you might choose a very slow pace for yourself and the job of the teacher is to make you go at a faster pace. What do you say to that?

S: Well the teachers would like say to you, I don't think you have done enough work. If you have only done a couple of sentences of work for your whole project, they will like give you a detention, or a series of detentions, or something like that. That will teach you to work more rather than at a faster pace.

S: You will always have to do a certain amount of work, you will never give in one sheet of work for a project and it will be OK. That's never going to be told OK so that's your pace then.

DHH: So you are not going to get away with that sort of thing.

S: No.

DH: So that is an example of the rules on the one hand and the flexibility on the other.

S: Yes.

DHH: So it is tough in some ways but not in others.

S: Yes.

S: It's like the correct balance between lenience and strictness.
No good coming in one day and doing a little work and then saying that's enough, then coming in the next day and doing nothing, you have to try to do as much work as possible on both days.

[*We were then shown another piece of work.*]

DHH: Did you change your mind on anything when you were writing.

S: Yeah I did actually. At first I thought the approach was all wrong and it should never be allowed. When I started researching into it and found out things, there are fors and against. I really decided that it was a matter of individuals really, so I put that in there. For and against, and then my own views.

DHH: It has a terrific ending to it. You went through the arguments, then you made your own mind up personally at the end, and then it ends 'then I hope you've decided what you think' – the reader is asked to decide for himself, or herself.

S: Well really you've got to decide for yourself. There is no one who can say that one thing is right and one thing is wrong, it's a matter of your own decision.

Videotape recorder and digital camera

The videotape recorder is increasingly being used by teachers as a means of gathering general information about their teaching. It allows the teacher to observe many facets of their teaching quickly, and provides heuristic and accurate information for diagnosis. After this, the teacher may wish to use a different method to examine specific aspects of their teaching.

Many of the teacher-researchers I know use the video on an intermittent but regular basis to enable them to keep in touch with their teaching. If an observer or student can be used to operate the videotape recorder, then more attention can be paid to specific teaching episodes (identified beforehand) or the reaction of particular students.

The main advantages and disadvantages of the videotape recorder are listed in point form in Box 8.5a. Three uses of videotape recorders in classroom research are:

1   for obtaining visual material of the total teaching situation;
2   acting as an aid to diagnosis; and
3   as a means of examining in detail a specific teaching episode.

Photographs, and the more recent use of the digital camera, are useful ways of recording critical incidents in classrooms or of illustrating particular teaching episodes. They can also be used to support other forms of data gathering (e.g. interviews or field notes) or as a means for providing reference points for interviews or discussions.

The main advantages and disadvantages of photographs and digital photography are listed in point form in Box 8.5b.

Box 8.5(a) (Videotape recorder)	
Advantages	**Disadvantages**
• Enables all situations to be constantly reviewed • Origin of problems can be diagnosed • Behavioural patterns of teacher and pupils can be seen • Patterns of progress over long periods can be clearly charted	• Can be very conspicuous and distracting • If camera is directed by operator, it will only record that which they deem to be of importance; operator acts as editor

Box 8.5(b) (Digital camera)	
Advantages	**Disadvantages**
• Advantage may be obtained by looking at images of kids working, or at end products of their work, and as a stimulus for discussion • As an instrument which helps you get observation and comment from other teachers who were not present at the time	• Shows isolated situations; difficulty of being in the right place at the right time; concentrates on small groups and individuals, not classes; records nothing in depth • Images may not truly depict activities of the children, if photographer is selective

CASE STUDY

In this example I describe the first experience Geoff, a student on one of my in-service courses, had with the videotape recorder.

Geoff is a deputy headteacher in a special school. His pupils face many learning challenges, but the expectation is that they will eventually be able to cope by themselves in some limited way. To give his pupils that basic level of life-skill is Geoff's main goal. Geoff used the videotape recorder to examine his teaching and to try and find an answer to the question 'why is everything so time-consuming?'.

Geoff decided to video the morning session from 9:30 to 10:15, which was the most structured and high energy time of the day. During the lesson, the nursery nurse was also involved in the class. Before videoing, Geoff identified a series of topics on which he wanted to get information:

- maximum time worked by each pupil;
- time wasted by each pupil;
- time unavoidably lost;
- time to be spent with each pupil; and
- number of tasks accomplished in the 45-minute session by each pupil.

The videotaping session went well. Geoff had had the camera in his room for a few days, so the pupils were used to having it around. With a wide-angle lens he was able to capture all the activity in the class. Geoff then began reviewing the tape. Besides gathering data on the points above, he also detailed the following:

- amount of time he spent out of the class on administrative duties;
- the number of times he praised/reprimanded a pupil;
- how long the pupils were left unsupervised;
- time spent by nursery nurse with each pupil; and
- pupil's reaction to attention.

Geoff then analysed the tape for each pupil and produced a detailed analysis of how individual lessons were spent. From this information Geoff was able to derive a number of hypotheses concerning the class and set up a programme for utilizing the time more effectively.

Questionnaires

Questionnaires that ask specific questions about aspects of the classroom, curriculum or teaching method are a quick and simple way of obtaining broad and rich information from pupils. It is important, however, particularly in the primary grades, to be relatively unsophisticated in the structuring of the questions. Condense the usual 5-point scale to two or three responses, keep the questions simple, and use the basic 'what did you like best?', 'what did you like least?', 'what would you do differently?' type of open-ended question.

With younger (and older) pupils it is often more profitable to use a happy face as the criterion response to questions as in Figure 8.1. More imaginatively, cartoon pictures can be used, as in Figure 8.2 – the possibilities are endless!

The main advantages and disadvantages of the questionnaire are listed in point form in Box 8.6. The main use of the questionnaire in classroom research is to obtain quantitative responses to specific predetermined questions. Examples of questionnaires are given in Figures 8.2 and 8.3.

Sociometry

Sociometric analysis or sociometry is a technique used to measure the emotional structure of a group. As a diagnostic instrument, sociometry's purpose is to highlight the feelings of attraction, indifference and rejection that occur within a group and between its members. The approach has obvious applications to classrooms where teachers want to discover the social structure of the class for research and other purposes. The most important 'other purpose' is to identify pupils who are socially isolated in order to take remedial action.

Before administering a sociometric test, it is important to ensure that the pupils know each other fairly well, that confidentiality is established, and that action be taken as a consequence. Sociometry in this sense is a dynamic process that can lead to improvement in children's attitudes and relationships and the general enhancement of a classroom climate.

Congdon (1978: 6) describes a method for administering the sociometric test:

> Each child is handed a slip of blank paper and told to write his name at the top. Some teachers prefer to have the names of all pupils in the class written on the blackboard. It is always advisable to write up the names of any pupils who are

Figure 8.1

NAME _____ ROOM _____ TEACHER _____

1 How do you feel when your teacher reads a story aloud?

2 How do you feel when someone gives you a book for a present?

3 How do you feel about reading books for fun at home?

4 How do you feel when you are asked to read aloud to your group?

5 How do you feel when you are asked to read aloud to your teacher?

Figure 8.2 Reading attitude survey.

Box 8.6

Advantages	Disadvantages

• Easy to administer; quick to fill in
 • Easy to follow up
 • Provides direct comparison of groups and individuals
 • Provides feedback on:
 	
   – attitudes
   – adequacy of resources
   – adequacy of teacher help
   – preparation for next session
   – conclusions at end of term
 	
 • Data are quantifiable
	• Analysis is time-consuming
	 • Extensive preparation to get clear and relevant questions
	 • Difficult to get questions that explore in depth
	 • Effectiveness depends very much on reading ability and comprehension of the child
	 • Children may be fearful of answering candidly
	 • Children will try to produce 'right' answers

Inquiry/discovery follow-up questionnaire
Please put a ring round the answer you wish to give to each question. If you are not sure ring the nearest to what you think.

1 How much of the lesson did you enjoy?   All of it/Some of it/None
2 How much do you think you learnt?   Nothing/Something/A lot
3 How much did you understand?   Most of it/Some of it/Nothing
4 Could you find the books, information,   None/Some of it/Most of it
   equipment you needed?
5 Did other people help you?   A lot/A little/Not at all
6 Did other people stop you working?   A lot/Sometimes/Not at all
7 Did the teacher help you   Enough/Not enough
8 Did the lesson last   Long enough/Too long/Not long
                         enough
9 Was the lesson   Boring/Interesting
10 Did you need anything you could   Yes/No
    not find?
11 Where did you get help from?   Teacher/Group/Someone else
12 Did you find this work   Easy/Hard/Just about right
13 Write down anything which made it hard for you to learn
14 Write down anything you particularly enjoyed about this lesson

Figure 8.3 A sample questionnaire designed by Roger Pols. Reproduced with permission from Bowen *et al.* (n.d.).

absent. The test should be meaningful to the pupils. So, for example, the context of the test could be a project. After deciding on a project the pupils could be told that they will be allowed to work in groups and that the groups would be made up according to their own choices.

On the left hand side of the sheet the pupils are asked to write the name of the person with whom they would most like to work in a group. Underneath they are asked to write the name of the one they would like next best, then the next and so on. They can be told to write as many names as they wish or none at all. The pupil is then asked to turn over the sheet and again down the left hand side of the page to write the names of any children with whom they do not wish to work. The teacher again tells them that they may write as many names as they wish or none at all. And what is more important she tells them that the names will be known only to herself, i.e. the choices are made privately and no pupil should be told either who chose him or how many choices he received. In this way no one's feelings are hurt.

After the test has been administered, the pupil choices are analysed to establish the structure of relationships within the class. The best known and easiest understood method of doing this is the sociogram. Congdon (1978: 7) continues to describe how a sociogram is constructed:

> In drawing a sociogram it is often useful to begin with the most chosen pupil and add the symbols for any pupils who reciprocate his or her choices. Next, pupils who have mutual choices with this group can be added. When these have been exhausted then a fresh group can be drawn up starting with the next most highly-chosen pupil and so on. The sociogram can be completed by filling in the unreciprocated choices.

Figure 8.4 is an example of a sociogram for a group of eight individuals with the symbols most commonly used marked on it.

Clearly in Figure 8.4 pupils E, F and H are unpopular and this information encourages the teacher to act to remedy this situation; action that can also be monitored through other classroom research techniques. The sociogram is a useful method for teacher-researchers who wish to explore the social structure of their class and the relationships between pupils. It also provides a starting point for action and further research. As sociometry emphasizes the class as a group, parallel efforts could focus on the perspectives of individual children, using, for example, self-concept inventories.

The major advantages and disadvantages of sociometry are listed in point form in

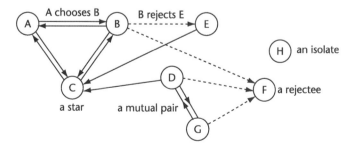

Figure 8.4   Example of a sociogram.

Box 8.7	
Advantages	Disadvantages
• Simple way to discover social relationships in class • Provides guide to action • Can be integrated into class activity	• Possibility of compounding the isolation of some pupils

Box 8.7. The main use of sociometry in classroom research is to disclose the social structure of the class.

CASE STUDY

In this example Ann was using a behaviour modification 'game' to improve the level of assignment completion in her maths class.

Since I had scruples about such a game causing social rejection of the target pupils, a sociogram was done before and after the experiment. Pupils were each asked to name three children they would like to sit next to during art lessons or storytime. It was stressed that this would be a non-academic, non-competitive time. The first choices were assigned three points, the second two points and the third one point. Points were totalled and the results entered on a graph.

Pre- and post-use of the sociogram showed that the popularity of the target pupils was not detrimentally affected by the game. None of them were social isolates but they all fell into the lower half of the class.

Documentary evidence

Documents (memos, letters, position papers, examination papers, newspaper clippings, etc.) surrounding a curriculum or other educational concern can illuminate rationale and purpose in interesting ways. The use of such material can provide background information and understanding of issues that would not otherwise be available.

The main advantages and disadvantages of documentary evidence are listed in point form in Box 8.8. The main use of documents in classroom research is that they provide a context for understanding a particular curriculum or teaching method.

Box 8.8	
Advantages	Disadvantages
• Illuminate issues surrounding a curriculum or teaching method • Provide context, background and understanding • Provide an easy way of obtaining other people's perceptions	• Obtaining documents can be time-consuming • Certain documents may be difficult to obtain • Certain persons may be unwilling to share 'confidential' documents

CASE STUDY

In this example Gill used documents to understand the nature of the art curriculum.

During her work for a postgraduate degree, Gill, an art teacher, examined some of the influences on the art curriculum. Her reason for doing this was largely personal: increasingly she was feeling a tension between her aspirations for art teaching and the general approach to the art curriculum that she was being encouraged to adopt. Gill's approach to the teaching of art was essentially child-centred. She has a commitment to developing a pupil's artistic talents and her teaching style and the activities she set her pupils were designed to achieve this goal. Her investigation involved examining a range of past papers and examiners' comments. To her chagrin, she found that the art curriculum in general was influenced not by pupil achievement or aspirations but more by the examiners' (rather traditional) comments. This discovery served at least to explain her tension. It also encouraged her to develop a scheme of work in painting for younger pupils and propose alternative syllabi for examination pupils that integrated her own ideas on art teaching with the more traditional approach.

Case study

The case study is a relatively formal analysis of an aspect of classroom life. Some teachers may wish to produce case studies for a university course they are taking or as research towards a higher degree. These situations apart, it is unlikely that teachers will devote time to producing a formal case report of their teacher-researcher efforts every time they undertake a project. (For a more detailed discussion of case study research see Stake 1995.)

The main advantages and disadvantages of the case study are listed in point form in Box 8.9. The main use of the case study in classroom research is that it provides a relatively formal and fairly definitive analysis of a specific aspect of teaching behaviour or classroom life. Examples of teacher research case studies are given in Chapters 2 and 6.

Box 8.9	
Advantages	**Disadvantages**
• A relatively simple way of plotting the progress of a course or a pupil's or group's reaction to teaching methods • Information yielded by case studies will tend to give a more accurate and representative picture than will any one of the research methods detailed above; case studies draw on data gathered by many methods	• In order for the case study to be of value it must be fairly exhaustive; this means that it will be time-consuming in its preparation and its writing • Feedback available to teacher only after considerable lapse of time

Box 8.10	
Advantages	**Disadvantages**
• An easy, fun and quick approach to gathering pupils' views and reactions to teaching and to life within the school • Information can be informative and could depict accurately students' views and experiences	• Analysis of the drawings could be challenging • Children that do not see this medium as their preferred way of expressing themselves could feel threatened and provide invalid data • Children could provide the 'right' answers

Pupil drawings

Pupil drawings are a method of collecting students' perceptions and experiences on teaching and on their educational experience. This method is a fun activity, and one that students respond to, that can provide rich and informative data. Many researchers conduct follow up interviews with the children and ask them to deconstruct their pictures. The advantages and the disadvantages of this method are illustrated in Box 8.10.

In this example, a student that participated in the *Working with Disaffected Students*[1] research project describes his experience in the classroom through the drawing in Figure 8.5. He portrays himself as a mushroom. He explains that whilst at school he hid in the background and as a result grew very little. He continues by stating that teachers had to look hard to find him in the classroom.

---

[1] This example is reproduced with the permission of Prof Kathryn Riley and is taken from Riley and Rustique-Forrester with Fuller *et al.*

Figure 8.5   Riley and Rustique-Forrester with Fuller *et al.* (2002: 35).

Mapping the 'process of change' in schools

The final data-gathering method refers to a battery of techniques rather than a single approach, so will therefore be described a little differently from the others. During our programme of research and development into school improvement, we have come to recognize that traditional research methods are sometimes too cumbersome and time-consuming in disclosing the intricacies of the change process. We felt that there was room for new, more user-friendly yet penetrating techniques for investigating and measuring the complex processes and relationships involved in school change. With a grant from the ESRC we developed six new techniques for mapping the process of change in schools. A comprehensive description, with advice on administration, of the techniques is found in the manual produced as a result of the research *Mapping Change in Schools: The Cambridge Manual of Research Techniques* (Cambridge University 1994) and in a paper by Ainscow, Hargreaves and Hopkins (1995).

The six techniques in the series cluster around two key elements in the change process: the individual teacher and the school as an institution. Despite the proliferation of externally mandated changes, the success of many change initiatives remains attributable to the commitment of individual teachers. Certainly the impact of any change on student outcomes is heavily affected by behaviour in the classroom. At the same time, it is claimed that the school as a whole, especially its climate/ethos/culture, makes an important contribution to development and change. Three of the techniques focus on the *individual teacher* and tap data at that level. The other three focus on the *school as an institution*. Data from both levels are essential if the interaction between individual and institution in processes of change is to be better understood. The manual of techniques is accordingly divided into two series.

Series 1: Individual (teacher) level

- *Technique 1: The time line of change* The aim of this technique is to record how individuals within a school perceive their experience of a particular change over a period of time.
- *Technique 2: The experience of change* The purpose of this technique is to gather information about the feelings of individuals towards changes in their school.
- *Technique 3: The initiation of change* This technique taps teachers' commitment to change and their sense of control over it. It differs from the previous two techniques in that it is concerned with change in general rather than a specific change.

Series 2: Institutional (school) level

- *Technique 4: The culture of the school* The purpose of this technique is to generate data on teachers' perceptions of the culture of their school, the direction in which the culture is moving and their ideal culture (see Hargreaves 1995).
- *Technique 5: The structures of the school* The purpose of this technique is to generate data on some of the basic social structures underlying school cultures.
- *Technique 6: The conditions of school* This technique consists of a scale for measuring a school's internal conditions and potential for innovation. The 24 items are grouped under six headings that represent the key conditions necessary for school improvement.

There are a number of ways in which teacher-researchers can use the data generated by the techniques, and feed the data back to schools.

First, because the techniques are amenable to rapid analysis and presentation, virtually immediate feedback can be given in some cases. This is especially true of the culture game, school structures and responses to change techniques. When used with teachers as part of a training day or staff meeting, it is possible to give aggregate responses to the whole staff during the same session. This feedback has often aroused great interest and animated discussion.

The second method of feedback is to talk through the results from the administration of the whole battery with the senior staff of the school involved. There is a method for reducing the data onto one side of A4, and this makes the conveying of information much easier to handle. Our approach is to present the data in a sequential and descriptive way, and then on the basis of this to encourage discussion and interpretation of the results from the senior staff. This proves at times to be a delicate process. Occasionally our ethic of confidentiality is challenged particularly when we are encouraged to be judgemental rather than descriptive. In these discussions it is vital to maintain confidentiality and to not go beyond the data.

The third approach to giving feedback is where the data are used as part of a school improvement process within a school. The techniques are now routinely used in IQEA schools as a basis for action planning. The experience we have had convinces us that the data emerging from the techniques have great heuristic power.

To summarize, when taken together the techniques provide a map of the process of change in a school. They can be used individually to investigate particular aspects of change processes or in combination for a more comprehensive analysis. The techniques can also be used to map changes in the school's conditions over time, and facilitate the process of change and improvement in schools.

In this chapter, I have described a variety of ways in which data can be gathered for the purpose of classroom research. The techniques described in this chapter are basically open-ended insofar as they are used most effectively for diagnostic purposes. Although I have described these techniques individually, it is important to realize that they can and are most often used eclectically and in combination. But each has a specific purpose and is best suited to a particular situation. A taxonomy of the main advantages, disadvantages and uses of the various techniques is given in Table 8.1.

Table 8.1 Taxonomy of classroom research techniques

Technique	Advantage(s)	Disadvantage(s)	Use(s)
Field notes	simple; ongoing; personal; *aide-mémoire*	subjective; needs practice	• specific issue • case study • general impression
Audiotape recording Pupil diaries	versatile; accurate; provides ample data provides pupils' perspective	transcription difficult; time-consuming; often inhibiting subjective	• detailed evidence • diagnostic • triangulation • specific in-depth information
Interviews and discussions Videotape recorder and Digital photography	can be teacher–pupil, observer–pupil, pupil–pupil visual and comprehensive	time-consuming awkward and expensive; can be distracting	• visual and diagnostic • illustrates critical incidents
Questionnaires Sociometry Documentary evidence	highly specific; easy to administer; comparative easy to administer; provides guide to action illuminative accurate; representative; uses range of techniques	time-consuming to analyse; problem of 'right' answers can threaten isolated pupils difficult to obtain; time-consuming	• specific information and feedback • analyses social relationships • provides context and information
Case study Mapping techniques	comprehensive; easy to administer and analyse simple; quick accurate;	time-consuming requires whole staff response; can be threatening; confidentiality sometimes challenged	• comprehensive overview of an issue • publishable format • provides a map of the process of change in a school • can be used to promote development
Pupil drawings		analysis can be challenging; can provide invalid data from some pupils; can encourage children to give the 'right' answer	• specific issue • diagnostic • specific in-depth information • can be used to promote development

Further reading

Additional information about the techniques of classroom research can be found in the publications associated with the Ford Teaching Project. Elliott and Adelman's (1976) case study of the Ford Teaching Project in the Open University curriculum course 'Innovation at the Classroom Level' is informative and useful, as is the Ford Teaching Project booklet *Ways of Doing Research in One's Own Classroom* (Bowen *et al*. n.d.). Walker and Adelman's (1990) book *A Guide to Classroom Observation* is similarly helpful and contains advice on, and examples of, the use of photography in classroom research. Rob Walker's (1989) book *Doing Research* and Cohen, Manion and Morrison's (2007) *Research Methods in Education* (6th edn) contains detailed advice about methods, as does James McKernan's (1996) *Curriculum Action Research*. Colin Hook's (1995) *Studying Classrooms* is extensive and practical and also contains a useful taxonomy of approaches similar to Table 8.1. Kemmis and McTaggart's (1988) third edition of *The Action Research Planner*, John Elliott's (1991) *Action Research for Educational Change*, Alan Bryman's (2004) second edition, *Social Research Methods*, John Beresford's (1998) *Collecting Information for School Improvement*, Sagor's (2007) *The Action Research Guidebook*, Briggs and Coleman's (2007) second edition of *Research Methods in Educational Leadership and Management* and my *Evaluation for School Development* (Hopkins 1989) also contain helpful advice on data collection methods. For more details on case study as a data gathering method I recommend Yin's (2003) third edition *Case Study Research: Design and Methods*.

9   Analysing classroom research data

The third criterion for teacher research outlined in Chapter 4 was that the methodology employed must be reliable enough to allow teachers confidently to formulate hypotheses and develop strategies applicable to their own classroom situations. This is an area where teacher research in particular, and qualitative research in general, has not been conspicuously successful. Qualitative research procedures (i.e. where the emphasis is on expressing one's data and conclusions in the form of words) seem often to be shrouded in mystery. The findings of such studies are arrived at by usually unannounced procedures and techniques, thus creating methodologies which can be neither fully scrutinized nor usefully emulated. Consequently, it is important to establish a coherent methodology for analysing classroom research data. In this chapter, I first outline the problem in a little more detail, then suggest a framework for analysis and describe the four stages that comprise the process.

The problem

Action research, like most practitioner-oriented methodologies, has been widely criticized, but mainly by those who implicitly denigrate the method by criticizing individual research projects that have adopted classroom research techniques. It is illogical – not to say unfair – to judge the quality of a Shakespeare play by observing a performance by amateur actors. And so it is with classroom research.

It is true though that classroom research has often been done badly, mainly because of unarticulated procedures for analysis. By way of contrast, the rules for quasi-experimental research have been cogently articulated notably some time ago by Campbell and Stanley (1963) and have a long and distinguished tradition. This tradition is so prevalent that research in education is commonly equated with studies carried out within this paradigm. This should not be surprising, for the rules are simple to apply and are consistent with the ubiquitous psycho-statistical research tradition. It is unfortunate, as we have seen, that this approach is ill-suited to the research needs of the classroom teacher.

In classroom research, the concern is more with cases than samples. This implies a methodology more applicable to understanding a problematic situation than one based on predicting outcomes within the parameters of an existing and tacitly accepted social system. The skills required of classroom researchers are, as Strauss and Corbin (1998) claim, 'The ability to step back and critically analyze situations, to recognize and avoid bias, to obtain valid and reliable data, and to think abstractly'.

Unfortunately, as Miles and Huberman (1984: 20) note in their paper 'Drawing valid meaning from qualitative data', there is an Achilles heel here: there are few agreed canons for the analysis of qualitative data, and therefore the truth claims and validity underlying such work are uncertain. They describe the problem like this (1984: 20):

> Despite a growing interest in qualitative studies, we lack a body of clearly defined methods for drawing valid meaning from qualitative data. We need methods that are practical, communicable, and not self deluding: scientific in the positivist's sense of the word, and aimed toward interpretive understanding in the best sense of that term.

What follows is an attempt to rectify this situation, at least with regards to teacher-based classroom research.

A framework for analysis

Making sense of social situations has long been the task of sociologists and it is from their (and anthropologists') methodological canons that much avant-garde work on educational evaluation was initially drawn (see Hamilton *et al.* 1977). It is this research tradition that provides a framework within which to consider teacher-based classroom research. Classrooms are also complex social situations that require understanding. We need to produce theory that is applicable to classrooms as well as within them.

Two of the classic statements on sociological fieldwork were made by Becker (1958) and Glaser and Strauss (1967). In his paper 'Problems of inference and proof in participant observation', Becker (1958: 653) described four stages in the analysis of fieldwork data:

> We can distinguish three distinct stages of analysis conducted in the field itself, and a fourth stage, carried on after completion of the field work. These stages are differentiated, first, by their logical sequence: each succeeding stage depends on some analysis in the preceding stage. They are further differentiated by the fact that different kinds of conclusions are arrived at in each stage and that these conclusions are put to different uses in the continuing research. Finally, they are differentiated by the different criteria that are used to assess evidence and to reach conclusions in each stage. The three stages of field analysis are: the selection and definition of problems, concepts, and indices; the check on the frequency and distribution of phenomena; and the incorporation of individual findings into a model of the organisation under study. The fourth stage of final analysis involves problems of presentation of evidence and proof.

In a similar way, in *The Discovery of Grounded Theory*, Glaser and Strauss (1967: 105) describe the concept of the constant comparative method as a means of analysing sociological data:

> We shall describe in four stages the constant comparative method; 1. comparing incidents applicable to each category, 2. integrating categories and their properties, 3. delimiting the theory, and 4. writing the theory. Although this method of generating theory is a continuously growing process – each stage after a time is transformed into the next – earlier stages do remain in operation simultaneously throughout the analysis and each provides continuous development to its successive stage until the analysis is terminated.

Although Glaser and Strauss's notion of the constant comparative method is a more dynamic concept than Becker's linear sequence of stages, there are basic similarities in their approaches to the analysis of field data. Each envisage the analytical process as having four distinct generic stages: (1) data collection and the initial generation of categories, (2) validation of categories, (3) interpretation of categories and (4) action. These various stages are summarized in Table 9.1 and represent standard practice for the analysis of qualitative field data. My major point is that this same process can be used by teachers to analyse data emerging from their own classroom research efforts.

Table 9.1 Fieldwork methodology

Classroom research	Becker	Glaser and Strauss
• Data collection	• Selection and definition of concepts	• Compare incidents applicable to each category
• Validation	• Frequency and distribution of concepts	• Integrate categories and their phenomena
• Interpretation	• Incorporation of findings into model	• Delimit theory
• Action	• Presentation of evidence and proof	• Write theory

CASE STUDY

Jane: an example

As part of the requirements for a course I taught on the 'Analysis of Teaching', Jane made a videotape of herself experimenting with various models of teaching. After reviewing the videotape, Jane felt that among other observations she had been rather abrupt in her questioning technique and had given the pupils little time to formulate responses to her questions. I suggested to Jane that she explore this observation a little further and ascertain whether this was a consistent behaviour or an aberration. She did this by taking a further videotape of her teaching, and by asking a colleague to observe her teaching. Jane also developed a short questionnaire on her questioning technique, which she administered to her pupils and subsequently analysed. As a result of this endeavour, Jane realized that she did in fact interject very quickly after asking a question, and quite often answered her own questions. All well and good, Jane thought, but what does this mean? Thinking that recent research on teaching might help, Jane did some reading and came across an article on think-time. The article reviewed a number of studies on the relationship between the amount of time that elapsed after questioning and the quality of pupil response. Jane felt that she was not allowing her pupils enough time to think after she had asked a question to the detriment perhaps of their level of cognitive functioning. So she developed a plan to change and monitor her questioning technique. It took Jane some six months to complete these tasks (teaching is a time-consuming job!), but there was no pressure on her to complete the research. In fact, the longer time-frame allowed for more valid data, and she was pleased with the results. Not only did she find evidence of higher-level responses from her pupils, but also, by involving them in the evaluation of her teaching, the climate of her class was enhanced by the mutual and overt commitment of both teacher and pupils to the learning process.

Data collection

In the classroom research process, the first step is collecting data. With the use of, say, a videotape recorder, or any other of a range of methods (methods of data gathering were discussed in Chapter 8), the teacher gathers information about their teaching. Having collected the data, a substage follows immediately or co-exists with the collection of data – the generation of hypotheses. We are always generating ideas to explain class-room events. Even at the earliest stages of research, we are interpreting and explaining to ourselves 'why this is happening' and 'what caused that'. It is inevitable that as individuals we bring our experience and beliefs to bear upon situations that we wish to understand better. As Popper says, 'observations . . . are always interpretations of the facts observed . . . they are interpretations in the light of theories' (quoted in Magee 1973: 107). Popper's use of the word theory implies, of course, not only 'grand' theory, but also personal theory – the presuppositions, assumptions and beliefs that guide our actions.

At the end of the data collection stage, not only have we collected our data, but we have also established a number of hypotheses, constructs or categories that begin to explain what is happening in the classroom.

These hypotheses (I am using the word broadly) usually emerge quite naturally from the data-gathering process. Jane, in the previous example, generated a number of ideas about her teaching from viewing the videotape. Among these was an observation that she was too abrupt in her questioning technique and had given her pupils too little time to answer questions. These hypotheses not only reflect the data but are also an interpretation of them. At this stage, the more ideas the better. The richer and more creative our thoughts, the more likely it is that the research will result in a coherent and complete interpretation of the problem. It is in the following stage that we begin to evaluate the hypotheses, so initially one should be as creative and as suggestive as possible.

Validation

The second stage in the process concerns the validation of the hypotheses. I will suggest a number of techniques for establishing the validity of a category or hypothesis. Of all these 'tests for trustworthiness', triangulation is most probably the best known, and so I describe it first.

The technique of *triangulation* was popularized by John Elliott and Clem Adelman during their work with the Ford Teaching Project. It involves contrasting the perceptions of one actor in a specific situation against those of other actors in the same situation. By doing this, an initial subjective observation or perception is fleshed out and given a degree of authenticity. Elliott and Adelman (1976: 74) describe the technique thus:

> Triangulation involves gathering accounts of a teaching situation from three quite different points of view; namely those of the teacher, his pupils, and a participant observer. Who in the 'triangle' gathers the accounts, how they are elicited, and who compares them, depends largely on the context. The process of gathering accounts from three distinct standpoints has an epistemological justification. Each point of the triangle stands in a unique epistemological position with respect to access to relevant data about a teaching situation. The teacher is in the best position to gain access via introspection to his own intentions and aims in the situation. The students are in the best position to explain how the teacher's actions influence the way they respond in the situation. The participant observer is in the best position to collect data about the observable features of the interaction between teachers and pupils. By comparing his own account with accounts from the other two standpoints a person at one point of the triangle has an opportunity to test and perhaps revise it on the basis of more sufficient data.

Jane, in the example, validated her observations through triangulation. She had another teacher observe her teaching and she also gave her pupils a questionnaire on her questioning technique. From this evidence, she was able to validate and refine the observation from three different sources.

It must be admitted that triangulation is not always an easy process to engage in. Initially, it may be threatening for a teacher to involve students in the evaluation of their teaching, or it may prove difficult to obtain the services of a peer to act as a participant observer. Teachers with the personal openness and interest in their teaching needed to initiate such research will, however, eventually overcome these difficulties. As mentioned earlier, I believe that it is important for the teacher to involve their pupils in the research process as soon as their confidence allows. Rudduck *et al.* (2000) point out that the consultation of pupils about things that matter in school can provide a rich and powerful source of data that could be used by teachers to enhance pupil efforts and attainment. In England, 'pupil voice' – that requires pupils to play an active role in their schooling and has been a result of schools becoming more responsive to pupils' views (Hargreaves 2004) – is now considered one of the most powerful approaches for improving classroom practice. McIntyre *et al.*'s (2005) study on how teachers use data that pupils offer when consulted concluded that pupils commented – almost without exception – in polite, serious, thoughtful and constructive ways (p. 166). They did point out, however, the difficulty some students have in articulating their thoughts and providing feedback, which results in the voice of those students being silenced. They advocate that the students teachers find most difficult to consult are those who they most need to hear.

Another well-known technique is *saturation*. Becker (1958) and Glaser and Strauss (1967) point to a similar process: Becker refers to 'the check on the frequency and distribution of phenomenon' (p. 653) and Glaser and Strauss to 'saturation', a situation where 'no additional data are being found . . . [to] develop properties of the category' (p. 67). When applied to the classroom research situation, this implies that the hypothesis or category generated from observation is tested repeatedly against the data in an attempt to modify or falsify it.

It is difficult and perhaps reckless to suggest a frequency that ensures the validity of a category, for that will vary from case to case, but during this process a number of predictable events can occur. First, if on repeated testing the category is found wanting it is then discarded. Second, the category may have been conceptualized crudely and, through testing, the concept is modified, refined and amplified. Third, although the process of falsification (in the Popperian sense) is never complete, there comes a time when repeated observation leads neither to refutation nor amplification and only serves to support the hypothesis. At this point, when the utility of observation decreases, saturation can be said to have occurred and the hypothesis has been validated.

Referring to the example of Jane, having decided to explore her questioning technique further, she videotaped herself again and found that, in fact, she was quite abrupt in her questioning and interjected far too quickly. In this way, she firmly validated the observation by saturating it.

There are a number of other techniques for establishing validity which I will describe more briefly.

In the same way as one triangulates the perception of various individuals, so too must we triangulate our *sources of data*. There are, as we have seen, many data sources open to the classroom researcher, e.g. surveys, questionnaires, observation, interviews and documents. The matrix shown in Figure 9.1 helps illustrate the range of data sources available at different levels of analysis. Although not every cell should be completed, a wide scatter should usually be employed. Each data source gives information of a different type which usually serves to complement and provide a check on the others.

Two other common techniques used at this stage of analysis are *rival explanations* and the search for *negative cases*. Michael Patton (1990: 327–8) describes these techniques like this:

> When considering rival hypotheses and competing explanations the strategy to be employed is not one of attempting to disprove the alternatives; rather,

Analysis	Information source				
	Surveys	Questionnaires	Observations	Interviews	Documents
1 Data collection and the generation of categories or hypotheses					
2 Validation of categories or hypotheses					
3 Interpretation by reference to theory, agreed criteria, established practice or teacher judgement					
4 Plan action for development					

Figure 9.1   A matrix for analysing classroom research data.

the analyst looks for data that *support* alternative explanations. Failure to find strong supporting evidence for alternative explanations helps increase confidence in the original, principal explanation.

Closely related to the testing of alternative explanations is the search for negative cases. Where patterns and trends have been identified, our understanding of those patterns and trends is increased by considering the instances and cases that do not fit within the pattern.

I use the phrase 'call things by their right name' to describe the next technique, which is nicely illustrated by Humpty Dumpty when he says: 'When I use a word it means just what I choose it to mean – neither more or less.' The point is an obvious one – we need to know what we are looking for. As classroom researchers, we have to do our conceptual work properly. We should be aware, for example, of suggesting that a child who is looking intently at a teacher is in fact paying attention; or of dictionary definitions that define intelligence as mental ability; or of operational definitions that regard paying attention as not looking out of the window. None of these help us very much. Conceptualization involves articulating a full, clear and coherent account of what constitutes being an instance of something; that is to say, it necessitates elaborating the criteria that have to be met if, for example, a pupil is legitimately to be described as engaging in enquiry/discovery learning (Barrow 1986). This may be difficult to do at the outset, but the clarification of concepts should always be a major concern throughout the research process.

An *audit trail* is a technique used to increase the validity of one's data and which borrows its name from the concept of a financial audit. Schwandt and Halpern (1988: 73) describe the usefulness of an audit trail, or of establishing a chain of evidence, in this way:

> Preparing an audit trail is important for two reasons. First, it documents the inquiry in a fashion that facilitates a third-party examination. The audit trail contains information that describes the methods used to control error and to reach justifiable conclusions ... Second, an audit trail helps [classroom researchers] manage their record keeping. They find an organized trail useful when they need to retrieve information easily and when they prepare their final reports ... [it helps them] become more thoughtful, critical, and reflective.

Another widely used strategy for ensuring validity is having *key respondents* review drafts of one's research reports. This can either be the people involved in the research (one's colleagues or students), or those knowledgeable about the situation you are enquiring into. To the extent that those involved in the research do not recognize the description and analysis in the report, then its validity is suspect. Involving others in the research is also a worthwhile activity in itself.

Let me now restate the important methodological point. I am arguing that by employing analytical techniques such as triangulation and the other methods just described, teacher-researchers can produce hypotheses and concepts that are methodologically sound and to an extent generalizable.

By engaging in this process of hypothesis generation, teacher researchers are producing what Glaser and Strauss have called grounded theory, because it is theory grounded in data gathered from and applicable to a specific social situation. By utilizing this methodology, we can have confidence in our subsequent actions for, as Dunn and Swierczek (1977: 137) comment:

> The application of grounded theories promises to contribute to improvements in the degree to which findings
>
> 1   reflect conditions actually present in particular change efforts (internal validity);
> 2   typify conditions actually present in other change efforts (external validity);
> 3   contribute to the generation of new concepts by constantly comparing information obtained by different methods (reflexivity); and
> 4   promote understanding among groups with conflicting frames of reference.

Interpretation

The third stage in the research process is interpretation. This involves taking a validated hypothesis and fitting it into a frame of reference that gives it meaning. For the classroom researcher, this means taking a hypothesis and relating it either to theory, the norms of accepted practice or the teacher's own intuition as to what comprises good teaching. This allows the teacher-researcher to give meaning to a particular observation or series of observations that can lead profitably to action. In doing this, the classroom researcher is creating meaning out of hitherto discrete observations and constructs. Jane gave meaning to her hypothesis by reading about 'thinktime'. That information not only helped her understand the implications of her behaviour but also suggested a direction for action.

Action

The final step in the process is action. Having created meaning out of the research data, the teacher-researcher is in a position to plan for future action. Building on the evidence gathered during the research, the teacher is able to plan realistic strategies which are themselves monitored by classroom research procedures. Jane did just that. The interpretation stage gave her information on how to change her questioning technique, which after some planning she attempted to monitor and evaluate.

The ongoing process of data analysis

The analysis of data is a very important part of the classroom research process. It is only at this stage that the teacher can be certain that the results obtained are valid and trustworthy. When teacher-researchers fail to analyse their data adequately, they lack a secure platform for action. The four stages of classroom research are outlined in Box 9.1.

The four stages of classroom research, although based on sociological research methods, are, in fact, only organized common sense. These stages are also far more interactive than the linear description given so far in this chapter would imply. In fact, the whole process is in reality a very dynamic one. There are two aspects of this 'dynamism' that I want to mention in particular.

In Figure 9.1, the matrix illustrates the range of data sources available at each stage of analysis. As noted earlier, not every cell of the matrix needs to be completed. The point to be made here is that in the initial phase, one analyses the questionnaire or interview schedules, then uses the analysed data from a number of different sources to generate the categories or hypotheses. Having done that, one validates them in the

---

Box 9.1 Four stages of classroom research
1 *Data collection* and the generation of categories or hypotheses.
2 *Validation* of categories or hypotheses using the techniques for trustworthiness, such as triangulation.
3 *Interpretation* by reference to theory, agreed criteria, established practice or teacher judgement.
4 *Action* for development that is also monitored by classroom research techniques.

second phase and then returns to phase one to collect more data. This ongoing process of data collection and verification is a characteristic of the analysis of qualitative or naturalistic research data.

The second point is that the *whole* process is interactive. Matthew Miles and Michael Huberman, whose concern about the lack of agreement on methods for analysis we have already noted, have written a very practical and detailed book called *Qualitative Data Analysis*. In it they describe the interactive model of data analysis like this (Miles and Huberman 1994: 21–2):

> *Data reduction*: Data reduction refers to the process of selecting, focusing, sim-
> plifying, abstracting and transforming the 'raw' data that appear in written up
> field notes. As data collection proceeds, there are further episodes of data
> reduction (doing summaries, coding, teasing out themes, making clusters,
> making partitions, writing memos). And the data reduction/transforming
> process continues after fieldwork, until a final report is complete.

> *Data display*: The second major flow of analysis activity is data display. We
> define a 'display' as an organised assembly of information that permits conclu-
> sion drawing and action taking. Looking at displays helps us to understand
> what is happening and to do something – further analysis or action – based on
> that understanding.

> *Conclusion drawing/verification*: The third stream of analytic activity is conclu-
> sion drawing and verification. From the beginning of data collection, the
> [classroom researcher] is beginning to decide what things mean, is noting
> regularities, patterns, explanations, possible configurations, causal flows and
> propositions. The competent researcher holds these conclusions lightly, main-
> taining openness and scepticism, but the conclusions are still there, inchoate
> and vague at first, then increasingly explicit and grounded.

In this sense, qualitative data analysis is a continuous, iterative enterprise as seen in Figure 9.2. Issues of data reduction of display, and of conclusion drawing/verification come into the process successfully as analysis episodes follow each other.

Enhancing validity

In the final section of this chapter, I wish to bring the discussion together by looking at the process of analysing data in a different way, using the concept of validity as the advanced organizer. Concepts of validity are of great importance to both quantitative and qualitative researchers. However, the latter has historically been charged as employing non-scientific methods in its analysis and thus, some would argue, as not being valid. Certainly this has been an argument made by policy-makers for many years and most recently concerns about validity have increased internationally (see for example Bradbury and Reason 2001). On the one hand, quantitative research has elab-orate statistical techniques at its disposal to ensure the trustworthiness of its data

Figure 9.2 Components of data analysis: Miles and Huberman's flow and interactive models.

although there is always a measure of standard error that is inbuilt and needs to be recognized. Qualitative research on the other hand might address issues of validity through the honesty and richness of the data achieved. In general, most classroom researchers and those who use qualitative methods are concerned with validity rather than reliability, insofar as their focus is a particular case rather than a sample.

Validity is usually regarded as the degree to which the researcher has measured what they have set out to measure. I take a catholic view of the word 'valid'. My dictionary defines it as 'sound, defensible, well grounded ... executed with proper formalities', and these are the general sense in which to use the term. Although there is a range of definitions and so of meanings of validity (Hammersley 1987; Patton 1990) one of the most useful and cited ones is that of Hammersley, who after reviewing a number of definitions of both reliability and validity asserted that there is an inconsistency in the usage of the terms. He defined validity as 'An account is valid or true if it represents accurately those features of the phenomena, that it is intended to describe, explain or theorise' (1987: 79). McCormick and James (1989) give us a more traditional definition of validity, but in my opinion also a very useful one:

> Researchers are expected to demonstrate that the observations they actually record and analyze, match what they purport to be recording and analyzing. This is the concept of validity ... Validity is concerned with errors that may occur in the research ... the validity of a method is basically the extent to which the observations recorded are those that the researcher set out to record.

Although other authors identify a number of other types of validity (Cohen *et al.* (2007), for example, identify 21 types of validity), McCormick and James's (1989) six different types fit our purposes:

1   *face validity:* requires that a measure looks as if it measures what it purports to measure;

2   *content validity:* requires that data produced covers all relevant subject matter;
3   *criterion related validity:* refers to the agreement between, for example, scores on a test and some other criterion such as teacher's estimates of ability;
4   *construct validity:* measurement must reflect the construct in which researchers are interested;
5   *internal validity:* the soundness of an explanation; whether that is interpreted as the cause produces the effect;
6   *external validity:* the generalizability of results to the whole population.

However, this book is mainly concerned with the general notion of validity and with the threats to internal validity. Internal validity is the basic minimum without which classroom research is uninterpretable. If the various threats to validity are not taken into account, then one cannot claim that one's interpretation is correct. The existence of possible sources of invalidity potentially offer plausible, rival interpretations to our findings when we do not account for them.

Campbell and Stanley (1963) carefully documented the major threats to validity. Although their monograph was written some time ago for those concerned with experimental and quasi-experimental research, many of their threats to validity still apply. The original discussion of the these threats has been expanded in Cook and Campbell (1979) and in Campbell and Russo (1999) in their book *Social Experimentation*. Although it is probably impossible to take account of each of the variables, they do serve as a useful checklist and guide to good practice. Those that cannot be accounted for should at least be recognized and, if necessary, a rival explanation discussed. Although a discussion of each of these variables is redundant, some key examples may be of interest.

1   *History:* Over the time-span of data collection many events occur in addition to the study's independent variable. The history factor refers to the possibility that any one of these events rather than the hypothesized variable.
2   *Instrumentation:* Changes in the measurement process may be spuriously attributed to the dependent variable. For instance, where interviews or observations become increasing sloppy, fatigued, or more competent and experienced, results may subtly change.
3   *Differential mortality:* On any occasion that non-random subsets of subjects drop out of a study, comparison of the dependent variable across groups might be accounted for by these differential 'mortality' rates rather than by actual effects of the independent variable.

Although space precludes, Miles and Huberman (1994) have two sections in their chapter on 'Making good sense. Drawing and verifying conclusions' that are so pertinent to this discussion they need to be reported briefly here. They comment that a general analysis strategy is a necessary but not sufficient condition and that there is also a flow of specific analytic tactics, ways of drawing and verifying conclusions that need to be employed during the analytic process. They distinguish between 'tactics for generating meaning' (pp. 245–6) and 'tactics for testing or confirming findings' (p. 263).

A quick overview of the tactics for generating meaning, numbered from 1 to 13, and roughly arranged from the descriptive to the explanatory, and from the concrete to the more conceptual and abstract, includes: *noting patterns, themes* (tactic 1), *seeing plausibility* (2) and *clustering* (3), which help the analyst see 'what goes with what'. *Making metaphors* (4) like the preceding three tactics, is a way to achieve more integration among diverse pieces of data. *Counting* (5) is also a familiar way to see 'what's there'. *Making contrasts/comparisons* (6) is a pervasive tactic that sharpens understanding. Differentiation sometimes is needed, too, as in *partitioning variables* (7). We also need tactics for seeing things and their relationships more abstractly. These tactics include *subsuming particulars into the general* (8) and *factoring* (9), an analogue of a familiar quantitative technique, *noting relations between variables* (10); and *finding intervening variables* (11). Finally, how can we systematically assemble a coherent understanding of data? The tactics discussed are *building a logical chain of evidence* (12) and *making conceptual/theoretical coherence* (13).

After generating meaning we are confronted with issue of validity. Miles and Huberman (1994) identify 13 tactics for testing or confirming findings. These are numbered as before and begin with ones aimed at ensuring the basic quality of the data, then move to those that check findings by examining exceptions to early patterns, and conclude with tactics that take a sceptical, demanding approach to emerging explanations.

Data quality can be assessed through *checking for representativeness* (1); *checking for researcher effects* (2) on the case, and vice-versa; and *triangulating* (3) across data sources and methods. These checks also may involve *weighting the evidence* (4), deciding which kinds of data are most trustable. Looking at 'unpatterns' can tell us a lot. *Checking the meaning of outliers* (5), *using extreme cases* (6), *following up surprises* (7), and *looking for negative evidence* (8) are all tactics that test a conclusion about a 'pattern' by saying what it is not like. How can we really test our explanations? *Making if-then tests* (9), *ruling out spurious relations* (10), *replicating a finding* (11), and *checking out rival explanations* (12) are all ways of submitting our beautiful theories to the assault of brute facts, or to a race with someone else's beautiful theory. Finally, a good explanation deserves attention from the very people whose behaviour it is about – informants who supply the original data. The tactic of *getting feedback from informants* (13) concludes the list.

Some of these tactics have been described earlier, but this economical list of tactics provides a useful overview of the techniques in linking broad analytical strategies to more specific activities.

Although the style of research discussed in this book is, as noted earlier, inevitably concerned with validity, concerns about reliability should not be ignored. Reliability is concerned with consistency and generalizability and the use of standardized instruments. McCormick and James (1989: 188) describe it thus:

> Basically reliability is concerned with consistency in the production of results and refers to the requirement that, at least in principle, another researcher, or the same researcher on the same occasion, should be able to replicate the same piece of research and achieve comparable evidence and results.

In concluding this discussion I have attempted to draw together the various analytic techniques described in this chapter and link them to particular tests of validity

Box 9.2   Enhancing validity in qualitative research

Test	Analytic technique
Construct validity (i.e. the research must focus on the operational issues it purports to reflect)	• use multiple sources of evidence • call things by their right name • establish a chain of evidence • know what you are looking for • have key informants review drafts • use tactics for verifying conclusions
Internal validity (i.e. the integrity of the evaluation; that what is interpreted as cause produces the effect)	• collect data at different points in time (time series design) • seek for alternative or rival explanations • be clear and rigorous over all stages of analysis • triangulation • use tactics for generating meaning
External validity (i.e. the generalizability of findings from one case to others)	• try and collect data from more than one site • replicate the focus of evaluation during the period of the evaluation
Reliability (i.e. minimizing the errors and biases in a study so that another researcher could conduct the same evaluation study to arrive at the same conclusions)	• protocol • construct an audit trail • Huberman and Miles' (1994) Interactive model of Data Analysis

Source: Adapted from Yin (1984: 36).

and reliability (see Box 9.2). This is inevitably a somewhat arbitrary exercise as the various techniques overlap from category to category. The exercise does, however, demonstrate that just because one's data is qualitative does not mean that one's results need to be based on any less rigorous analysis than more traditional quantitative approaches.

Further reading

The territory covered in this chapter is complex, which I have tried to present as simply as I can. Since the mid-1970s, there has been a growing interest in illuminative, anthropological and ethnographic research approaches. Much of this literature is technical and not ideally suited for our purposes however it is of interest: although the references in this section appear to be dated, they are by far the most important ones in qualitative analysis. The book by Hammersley and Atkinson (1995), *Ethnography: Principles in Practice*, provides an excellent overview of the field and an introduction to the literature. Lincoln and Guba's (1985)

Naturalistic Inquiry is also a useful source, as is Patton's (1990) *Qualitative Evaluation Methods*. *Beyond the Numbers Game* (Hamilton *et al*. 1977) is a comprehensive statement but somewhat historical on the illuminative (or new wave) tradition in educational evaluation and research, mainly from the UK perspective. One of the most helpful sections in this collection is the discussion of alternative methodology, especially the work of Louis Smith. Clem Adelman's book, *Uttering, Muttering* (1981), on linguistic research in classrooms contains a helpful chapter on triangulation. McCormick and James's (1989) book *Curriculum Evaluation in Schools*, besides being an excellent general source, contains some very helpful sections on validity and reliability.

The references mentioned in the text should also be consulted, especially Becker (1958) and Glaser and Strauss (1967), although the latter may prove to be a little hard going. Fortunately, two books by Strauss (1987) and Strauss and Corbin (1998) are more accessible. The first chapter of Strauss's *Qualitative Analysis for Social Scientists* provides an exemplary introduction to grounded theory. Anyone seriously interested in educational research should also be familiar with Campbell and Stanley's (1963) classic 'Experimental and quasi-experimental designs for research on teaching'. Although written from a different perspective from this book, its discussion of research designs and the concepts of internal and external validity are essential knowledge for those involved in educational research. Cohen *et al.*'s (2007) sixth edition of *Research Methods in Education* also offers a useful source on qualitative data analysis as well as on reliability and validity. This is also the case with Colin Robson's (2002) second edition of his exemplary *Real World Research*. It should be noted however that Miles and Huberman's (1994) *Qualitative Data Analysis* is the essential source book for anyone interested in the ideas and themes touched on in this chapter. Denzin and Lincoln's (2003) *Collecting and Interpreting Qualitative Methods Volume* 3 and Weinberg's (2002) *Qualitative Research Methods* complement the above reading.

10 Reporting classroom research

The link between research and action has been an implicit theme throughout this book. To teacher-researchers, research alone is a necessary but not sufficient condition: research has to feed action and development. The classroom research process described in previous chapters has as its goal professional development and the enhancement of classroom performance. The fourth stage in the analytical framework discussed in this chapter is action, which itself is monitored and researched using classroom research procedures. This is the crowning achievement of the research process. In this concluding section, I want to look at some of the ways in which the action and information generated by the research process can be reported.

A classroom research report can in itself have significant impact. Technology in particular has provided the opportunity to teachers from all over the world to come closer together. This has opened up the prospect for substantive and sustained professional dialogues and the global exchange of ideas and good practice. These activities, in my opinion, are invaluable, as I believe that classroom researchers should not only feel responsible for improving their own classrooms but be concerned about the improvement of all classrooms and all schools in their own country and, yes, in the world. Hence, when classroom research reports are shared across a school, across a system and across systems they hold the potential to transform classroom practices around the globe and for the better.

In this chapter I will illustrate the various ways in which classroom research can be reported: first, by exploring literature on report writing; second, by discussing how one could write a report; third, by outlining other formats for reporting research; fourth, by identifying appropriate questions for evaluating your research report; fifth, by setting out criteria on how research can inform action; and sixth, by considering different approaches to the dissemination of results, before suggesting further reading for this chapter.

Reporting research

Producing accounts of research could never be a literal representation of events. Denscombe (2007: 285) provides us with a useful list of why envisioning a literal depiction is impossible:

- There are always limitations to the space available to provide the account of what happened, which means the researcher needs to provide an edited version of the totality. Decisions need to be made about what can be missed out of the account.
- The editorial decisions taken by the researcher are likely to be shaped by the researcher's need to present the methods in their best possible light. Quite rationally, the researcher will wish to put a positive spin on events and to bring out the best in the process. Without resorting to deceit or untruths, the account of research will almost certainly entail some upbeat positive filtering. The point, after all, is to justify the procedures as 'good' research.
- Although research notes will be used to anchor the description of what happened during the course of the research, the writing up of the research is inevitably a retrospective vision. Situations and data are likely to have a different meaning when viewed from the end of the research process from that at the time they occurred. They will be interpreted with the vision of hindsight.
- The impact of social norms and personal values on the way we interpret events pretty well guarantees that, to a greater or lesser extent, any account of research should be regarded as a version of the truth rather than a literal depiction of what happened. Within the social sciences, the idea of a purely objective position is controversial and a researcher would be naïve to presume that her/his account can stand, without careful considerations, as an 'objective' description of what actually occurred.

The end product, therefore, no matter how scrupulous it attempts to be, must always be recognized for what it is – an account of the research.

Bearing this cautious word in mind, we shall also see there are a number of different ways of reporting teacher research efforts. I have seen them range from loose anecdotal accounts to highly 'scientific' and formal research reports submitted for a higher degree. Brooker and MacPherson (1999) confirm my argument in the previous chapter when they suggest that much published practitioner research isn't rigorous in research terms but comes across as 'little more than picturesque journeys of self-indulgent descriptions of "this is what I did" . . .' (p. 210). They continue:

Although 'insider accounts' focusing on personal experience are interesting, they have less meaning for the wider audience who aren't familiar with the context in which research took place. If such reports are to become more useful they must become more than exercises in self-indulgence where more is learned about the researcher than is learned about their interactions in the field . . . Practitioner researchers have a professional responsibility to ensure that sound precepts and practices inform their research efforts, and that these are clearly articulated in the reports of their research.

(Brooker and MacPherson 1999: 209)

To avoid 'self-indulgent' descriptions and capitalize on the power of a research report, teacher-researchers need to put their data together in such a way that:

- the research could be replicated on another occasion;
- the evidence used to generate hypotheses and consequent action is clearly documented;
- action taken as a result of the research is monitored;
- the reader finds the research accessible and that it resonates with his or her own experience.

The process of setting a clear purpose, of using a methodology which provides valid results, and then using these as a basis for action, can be assisted if the researcher keeps a loose-leaf log or diary as the research progresses. An ongoing research diary like this also provides an invaluable basis for reflection and is great fun to look at with the wisdom of hindsight. It provides an excellent record of how one's views and attitudes evolve over time. The diary can also reveal the researcher's biases and how these impacted on decisions taken during the research and on the interpretation of events. Such information is invaluable when writing a report where personal biases should be highlighted and attempts to address them indicated, and their possible impact on the research results accounted for.

Writing a report

One of the first things one has to consider when preparing a research report is the intended audience. Teacher-researchers have to decide in advance who they are writing for and choose the most effective format and style to address their audience. The British Educational Research Association's (2000) *Good Practice in Educational Research*, identifies three major audiences for research writing: researchers, policy-makers and practitioners, and asserts that 'it is good practice in all research writing to aim for lucid prose which communicates effectively to the intended audience and avoids what that audience may perceive as jargon or obscurantism' (p. 2).

The length of the report is also something that needs to be taken into account. Most people that read reports say that they are either too long to read or so short that there is insufficient evidence to be believable. The best bet is a report as short and condensed as you can make it (with detailed justification tucked away in appendices). The biggest temptation is to display your productivity in too many pages.

Formulating the report comes next. There are a number of guidelines and criteria available that are helpful at this stage. To begin with, there is the somewhat traditional approach that uses as a guide, points similar to the following:

1 *Statement of intent*
   - clarify purpose
   - rationale
2 *Procedures and process*
   - research design

- techniques of data collection
- verification of concepts
- what actually occurred
3 *Results and implementation*
   - outcomes of research
   - theoretical implications
   - action taken as a result
   - evaluation of action
4 *Meta-analysis*
   - review whole process
   - conclusions as to the usefulness of the research
   - what would you do differently next time?

A checklist of areas that need to be covered in such a conventional research report is illustrated in Box 10.1.

The purpose of both the outline and the checklist is to provide teacher researchers with a framework for their report. While this is important, what perhaps is even more critical is that the format of a report encourages the teacher to stand back and to examine the process systematically by reflecting on or making a meta-analysis of the research.

Evaluating your research report

As most classroom research data will probably be presented in a written form, it is helpful to identify a set of questions that could provide the basis of evaluating them. Judith Bell, in her book *Doing your Research Project* (2005: 244–5), provides us with an extensive and helpful list of such questions:

1 Is the meaning clear? Are there any obscure passages?
2 Is the report well written? Check tenses, grammar, spelling, overlapping passages, punctuations, jargon.
3 Is the referencing well done? Are there any omissions?
4 Does the abstract give the reader a clear idea of what is in the report?
5 Does the title indicate the nature of study?
6 Are the objectives of the study stated clearly?
7 Are the objectives fulfilled?
8 If hypotheses were postulated, are they proved or not proved?
9 Has a sufficient amount of literature relating to the topic been studied?
10 Does the literature review, if any, provide an indication of the state of knowledge in the subject? Is your topic placed in the context of the area of study as a whole?
11 Are all terms clearly defined?
12 Are the selected methods of data collection accurately described? Are they suitable for the task? Why were they appropriate for the task?
13 Are any limitations of the study clearly presented?

Box 10.1 Checklist for structuring a traditional research report

---

1. *Title:* look for a general theme or a metaphor that will carry your main point without distorting it too much.
2. *Abstract:* briefly outline the whole project. Locate the research and indicate the timescale and context within which it was conducted; provide an overview of the methods used for both collecting and analysing data; and convey to the reader the results of the research.
3. *Introduction:* set out the reason you decided to undertake the particular research project. What was significant about it?
4. *Literature review:* provide an account of the literature written on the subject and highlight what are the learnings from it. (Many researchers compile the introduction and the literature review in one section. This is a question of opinion and audience.)
5. *Methodology:* indicate the data collection and analysis methods you have adopted and explain why these seem to be the most appropriate. Also, include in this section how reliable were the data in both the data collection and data analysis phases.
6. *Results/Findings:* describe your results and use table and figures where appropriate.
7. *Discussion:* answer the research questions posed; discuss everything about your results that is important and surprising; make recommendations and identify the next questions that arise.
8. *Conclusion:* provide an overview of the project and review it.
9. *References:* include all the references used and preferably use the Harvard referencing system as it is the most accepted.
10. *Appendices:* add all the material that would have taken too much space if you were to include them in the research and that are not directly relevant to the project, but help illustrate something refereed in the main report. Taber (2007: 185) provides us with some examples of appendices:

    - sample questionnaires
    - sample interviews transcripts
    - transcripts of classroom dialogues
    - photocopies of students' work
    - photographs or stills from digital video-recordings of students at work (subject to permission being available)
    - photographs of displays or models put together by the students

---

14 Have any statistical techniques been used? If so, are they appropriate for the task?
15 Are the data analysed and interpreted or merely described?
16 Are the results clearly presented? Are tables, diagrams, and figures well drawn?
17 Are conclusions based on evidence? Have any claims been made that cannot be substantiated?
18 Is there any evidence of bias? Any emotive terms or intemperate language?
19 Are the data likely to be reliable? Could another researcher repeat the methods used and have a reasonable chance of getting the same or similar results?

20 Are recommendations (if any) feasible?

21 Are there any unnecessary items in the appendix?

22 Would you give the report a passing grade if you were the examiner? If not, perhaps an overhaul is necessary.

Colin Hook (1995: 291–2), in his book *Studying Classrooms*, provides a helpful checklist of questions that can be used to review one's research in any format you decide to present it:

- Did I collect the information as planned? Did it provide the information I needed?
- What problems did I have? What could I have done better? Should I employ other data-gathering methods?
- Did I gather all relevant available information? Should I have gathered pupils' opinions, parental views, and other teachers' feelings?
- In what ways can I use the information to make more effective teacher decisions? Is further information required?
- Can the information obtained be interpreted in other ways? Are my interpretations and conclusions valid?
- Have I presented the information in a clear way? Does the information indicate future teaching actions?
- Can I discuss the information with pupils, colleagues or parents?
- Who else could have been involved, how and when?
- What did I, the pupils, parents, colleagues, etc., get out of the investigation?
- What changes should I make in future investigations? Do my pupils, colleagues, etc., have suggestions?
- Can I interest colleagues in co-ordinating action research approaches, to collaborate in future studies?
- Do other teachers share my concerns? Do other teachers have skills which may help me in self-monitoring?

Making your classroom research report formative

Up to this point we have been concerned with the technical aspects of report writing. Now we need to turn to the heart of the matter – how to make our research inform action; how to make one's research report formative.

Fiddy and Stronach (1987) were one of the first to argue that we need to move from theories of transmission to theories of utilization of research data. Why is it, they ask, that we, as evaluators and researchers into educational practice, are so uninterested in the pedagogical relations between ourselves and our clients, especially since the evidence seems to be that our clients learn little for us, and value us still less? Their response is illuminating: they argue for the abandonment of external critique, the rejection of models for formative evaluation research, the end to writing reports, the development of pedagogy (rather than methodology), of new kinds of educational research, and for the reintegration of research and development.

Cousins and Leithwood (1993) also point out that researchers should take a knowledge utilization perspective. In their study, which linked information use and school improvement, they concluded that participants' perceptions of the sophistication, relevance and timeliness of information sources had direct impact on information utilization for school improvement. In previous work on the utilization of evaluation results they identified a number of 'guidelines' on how to ensure that an evaluation leads to action (Cousins and Leithwood 1986). As this work is eminent and prolific and could be applied to all kinds of research, including action research, I have taken the liberty of adapting their conclusions by replacing the word 'evaluation' (used by the authors) with the word 'research'. So, they claim that research results are utilized most effectively when:

- research is appropriate in approach, methodological sophistication and intensity;
- the decisions to be made were significant to users and considered appropriate for the application of formally collected data;
- research findings were consistent with the beliefs and expectations of the users;
- users were involved in the research process and had a prior commitment to the benefits of the research;
- users considered the data reported in the research to be relevant to their problems;
- a minimum amount of information from other sources conflicted with the results of the research.

(Cousins and Leithwood 1986: 360)

So, let's take this train of thought a little further. Let us assume that a classroom researcher has generated some valid 'knowledge'. What key conditions must be present if someone is to take action congruent with the knowledge? Here, Louis and Miles (1992: 289) take a cut at what might be required:

- *Clarity*: The knowledge must be understood clearly – not be fuzzy, vague or confusing.
- *Relevance*: The knowledge is seen as meaningful, as connected to one's normal life and concerns – not irrelevant, inapplicable, impractical.
- *Action images*: The knowledge is or can become exemplified in specific actions, clearly visualized. Without such images, knowledge-based action is unlikely.
- *Will*: There must be motivation, interest, action orientation, and a will to do something with the knowledge.
- *Skill*: There must be actual behavioural ability to do the action envisioned.
- Without skill, the action will either be aborted or done incongruently with the knowledge undergirding it.

One can conclude from the foregoing discussions that a formative classroom research report:

- pays explicit attention to the change process;
- focuses on users' issues;
- involves uses in the process;
- develops a pedagogy for learning from the research;
- utilizes a methodology consistent with its purpose;
- integrates research and development.

Action upon one's results should be the ultimate goal for all classroom researchers. Research, and in particular qualitative research, is less of a methodology and more a way of life! It is an approach that is applicable across a range of settings, describes and analyses phenomena on their own terms, and helps us to think constructively and to generate meaning out of complex and problematic situations. Consequently, it is also an approach that empowers individuals and increases feelings of efficacy. This sense of efficacy can only develop if we report our methodological procedures and establish a genuinely collaborative and critical research community that is committed to informed action.

Other formats for reporting research

Classroom researchers should not feel constrained by the traditional research report format when sharing the product of their research, as there are any number of approaches that can be used for reporting research. As Giroux (1992: 21) suggests, we need a 'politics and pedagogy developed around new languages capable of acknowledging the multiple, contradictory and complex subject positionings people occupy within different social, cultural and economic locations'. The important thing is for the information to be valid and to have been carefully analysed and the fundamental point is that action should result from the research. Researchers in education have become increasingly interested in different forms of interpreting and representing data (Percelli 2004a, 2004b; Schratz 2001). Here are a few examples:

- *Cartoons or photography*: often classroom researchers use the cartoon format or photographs to get a key finding from their research across in a powerful and accessible way (for example see Figure 10.1).
- *Video or film*: a visual representation using video or digital camera provides concrete images that an audience can relate to their own situation.
- *Dance or theatre*: once again a visual representation, a performance using students or professional dancers or actors has the potential to have a profound impact on the audience.
- *Fiction*: using data or constructs from the research to tell a story often encourages reflection and discussion more effectively than the traditional report. As long as the quotations or events are 'real', then a fictional setting may enhance the message.
- *Diaries*: using extracts from one's diary to present insights from the research is valuable data.

- *Poetry*: this is another form of highlighting the learnings of one's research.
- *Data reduction and display*: displaying reduced data is often a powerful way of stimulating discussion. This approach allows large amounts of data to be displayed economically and it could be accompanied by another page of questions, commentary or explanation that highlighted the main issues.
- A '*patchwork*' *approach*: Winter (see for example Winter *et al.* 1999) has pioneered what is known as the patchwork approach. Here researchers are encouraged to use a combination of approaches to present the different stages of the research process. So, researchers could use film, poetry, reports and any other way they choose to communicate their findings.

Finishing a research report could feel like sitting an exam without being quite sure what the question is, but in the knowledge that the world will read and mark your paper according to an unpredictable whim. The mental blocks, the mad desire to postpone writing for more research or for another coffee is normal. But, one thing is certain. It is worth it.

Dissemination of results

At the beginning of this chapter I briefly discussed how powerful a classroom research report can be. I even claimed that reporting classroom research results has the potential to transform classroom practices around the world. This implies that the research will be disseminated. Classroom researchers should be aware that research is incomplete until it is in the public domain. Thus, decisions about who is going to disseminate the results, and coming back to our discussion earlier about the report's audience, to whom it will be disseminated and for what use, have to be made.

There are a variety of ways in which you can disseminate the results of your research. The most immediate way of course is sharing the research within your own school. Teachers have the opportunity through staff meetings, presentations in the school's professional development days and informal discussions with colleagues not only to change practices across the school, but also to engage in professional dialogue about classroom research and promote a culture of inquiry within the school. Currently, many schools encourage their teachers to undertake small research projects and some of them require newly qualified teachers to conduct a classroom research project in their first term.

Another way of communicating research is through school networks. In England there is an increasing number of informal and formal school networks which allow the quick exchange of information between schools, which of course is a smart school improvement strategy. Formal networks such as those of the Specialist Schools and Academies Trust (SSAT) and the erstwhile National College of School Leaders (NCSL) networked learning communities project bring together practitioners at a local level and then connect local networks to the regional and national. Hence, the dissemination of such results is one on a bigger scale.

Figure 10.1 Reporting research on a cartoon format.

Publications can also make your work accessible to wider audiences and could include:

- chapters in books: there is an increasing number of books published by universities and organizations such as the GTCE, the SSAT and the NCSL (see Chapter 2 for an example of two case studies published by the NCSL), presenting classroom research examples. There is also an increasing number of schools that publish research conducted by their own staff within the school but also externally;
- papers in academic journals;
- articles in teacher magazines.

However, the quickest, most powerful and nowadays possibly the most accessible approach to dissemination is the Internet – this is certainly true for developed countries and is becoming true for many developing ones. As mentioned earlier, technology has opened up opportunities for people to connect with others across the world and share information instantly. Classroom researchers are now publishing their results in their schools', network's and their own personal websites. Imagine a colleague in China reading your research, identifying similarities between your school and theirs and deciding to adopt the practice suggested by your research in order to improve teaching and learning in their school!

Before concluding this section, it is worth reflecting more imaginatively on how classroom researchers can support their dissemination efforts. One particular example involves a re-think of the audience for classroom research 'and its intended purpose. Miles and Huberman's (1994: 305) 'Matrix for Objectives of Dissemination Strategy Planning' could effectively support classroom researchers' dissemination efforts. This is because it requires researchers to consider their audiences and sub-audiences and the effects it provides, which range from the simple awareness that the message exists to implementation and routinization. This matrix is seen in Figure 10.2.

	Size of audiences			
Level of Diffusion and Use	Innovators: those few with special interest, skill, motivation	Key persons: gatekeepers, leaders of opinion	Majority of potential audience	Everyone who might be affected
Awareness				
Reception of basic message				
Understanding				
Acceptance				
Adoption decision				
Utilization/ Implementation				
Integration				
Routinization				

Figure 10.2   Matrix for Objectives of Dissemination Strategy Planning (Miles and Huberman 1994: 305).

Further reading

Sadly, teachers' research is still not acknowledged as being a vibrant vehicle for the production of theory for educational sustainability and is often viewed as more of a professional development activity (see, for example, Furlong 2004). Classroom researchers have the responsibility of changing such perceptions and cultures by presenting their findings in the most appropriate manner and getting the dissemination process right.

The discussion of reporting research and dissemination in this chapter has been quite extensive and the main sources were cited. In addition, the various collections of case studies referred to elsewhere in the book provide examples of different ways and styles of reporting. The texts by Rob Walker (*Doing Research*, 1989), Denscombe (*The Good Research Guide*, third edition, 2007), Judith Bell (*Doing Your Research Project*, fourth edition, 2005), Colin Hook (*Studying Classrooms*, 1995), Jean McNiff and Whitehead (*Action Research for Teachers*, 2005) and *All You Need to Know about Action Research*, 2006) and Fox et al. (*Doing Practitioner Research*, 2007), Taber (*Classroom-based Research and Evidence based Practice*, 2007) provide further advice.

11 Teaching and learning as the heartland of classroom research

One of the themes of this latest edition is the emphasis on moral purpose as the motivation for continuing professional development. This is no 'wishy-washy' idealism but a practical and strategic effort at designing learning experiences that enable every student to reach their potential irrespective of their background. It is this core idea that is at the basis of the current commitment to 'personalized learning'.

Personalized learning is an idea that is capturing the imagination of teachers, parents and young people around the world. It is an idea that has its roots in the best practices of the teaching profession and it has the potential to make every young person's learning experience stretching, creative, fun and successful. This emphasis provides a bridge from prescribed forms of teaching, learning skills, curriculum and assessment to an approach that is predicated on tailoring schooling to individual need, interest and aptitude.

In his pamphlet *'Learning about personalisation: how can we put the learner at the heart of the education system?'* Charlie Leadbeater (2004: 16) clearly and sensitively identifies personalized learning as the key driver for the transformation of schooling.

> The foundation of a personalised education system would be to encourage children from an early age and across all backgrounds, to become more involved in making decisions about what they would like to learn and how. The more aware people are of what makes them learn, the more effective their learning is likely to be.

He continues:

> Personalised learning does not apply market thinking to education. It is not designed to turn children and parents into consumers of education. The aim is to promote personal development through self realisation, self enhancement and self development. The child/learner should be seen as active, responsible and self motivated: a co-author of the script which determines how education is delivered.

And:

> The script of a system characterised by personalised learning . . . would start from the premise that the learner should be actively engaged in setting their own targets, devising their own learning plans and goals, choosing from a range of different ways to learn. . . . By making learning the guiding principle of the system, personalisation challenges some of the current divide and boundaries that exist – for example between formal and informal learning; between academic and vocational learning and between different ages and types of learners.

In one sense, personalized learning represents a logical progression from the standards and accountability reform strategies of the 1990s. These strategies marked an important first phase in a long-term large-scale reform effort. But in order to sustain system-wide improvement, societies are increasingly demanding strategies characterized by diversity, flexibility and choice.

In line with this, my view is that the genesis of personalization lies somewhere slightly different from the political emphasis with which it is currently associated. The foundations of personalization may be partly political, but mainly they reflect an ethical root. As I have already claimed, it is moral purpose that drives personalization. We see it most vividly in the concern of the committed, conscientious teacher to match what is taught, and how it is taught, to the individual learner as a person. That is not just a question of 'sufficient challenge' or aligning pedagogy to the point of progression that each learner has reached, even though that is vitally important. It is also part of the teacher's concern to touch hearts as well as minds, to nourish a hunger for learning and help equip the learner with a proficiency and confidence to pursue understanding for themselves.

The concrete expression of the phrase 'every child is special' – and the creation of an education system which treats them so – is what personalized learning is all about. That means overcoming the false dichotomies and the 'either/ors' which have bedevilled schooling for so long, so that for all pupils learning means 'both/and' – both excellence and enjoyment, skills and enrichment, support and challenge, high standards and high equity, present success and long-term participation, deep engagement and broad horizons – and in so doing, breaking the link between socio-economic disadvantage and attainment. That is the goal for personalized learning and understanding how to reconcile these apparent dichotomies provides fertile ground for the contemporary teacher-researcher.

At the heart of personalized learning is its impact, not just on test scores and examination results, but on the student's learning capability. If the teacher can teach the student how to learn at the same time as assisting them to acquire curriculum content, then the twin goals of learning and achievement can be met at the same time. We made this point in *Models of Learning – Tools for Teaching* (Joyce *et al.* 2002: 7) when we argued that it is the teacher's task not simply to 'teach', but to create powerful contexts for learning. We expressed that idea and the essence of personalized learning in this way:

> Learning experiences are composed of content, process and social climate. As teachers we create for and with our children opportunities to explore and build

important areas of knowledge, develop powerful tools for learning, and live in
humanising social conditions.

It is the integration of curriculum content, teaching and learning strategies and the
school cultures that enhance self-confidence that in my opinion provide the parameters for the work of teacher-researchers. But there is a significant barrier to progress in
this area: despite the contemporary emphasis on the importance of classroom practice,
the language or discourse about teaching remains in general at a restricted level. There
is a need for a far more elaborate language with which to talk about teaching and more
sophisticated frameworks against which to reflect on practice. Even in those instances
where more precision of language is achieved, say in the debate on whole-class teaching, there are few operational definitions against which teachers can assess their own
practice and thereby develop and expand their range of classroom practices. Quality
teaching and learning needs to be underpinned by more elaborate and explicit frameworks for learning and teaching.

In this chapter I discuss some of the evidence on effective teaching and learning.
This is for three reasons. The first is in order to provide a sharper focus for classroom
research activities that relate to teaching and learning. The second is to offer specifications that can contribute to broader and richer discourse about the nature of teaching
and learning. Third, it is principally through pedagogy that the teacher is best able to
create increasingly personalized learning experiences for their students.

Although the evidence on effective teaching can help teachers become more
creative in creating powerful learning environments for students, such research and
strategies, however, should not be regarded as panaceas to be followed slavishly.
Research knowledge and the various specifications of teaching can have many limitations, especially if they are adopted uncritically. Such knowledge only becomes useful
when it is subjected to the discipline of practice through the exercise of the teacher's
professional judgement. For, as Lawrence Stenhouse (1975: 142) said, such proposals
are not to be regarded 'as an unqualified recommendation, but rather as a provisional
specification claiming no more than to be worth putting to the test of practice. Such
proposals claim to be intelligent rather than correct.'

As has been seen throughout this book, outstanding teachers take individual and
collective responsibility to base their teaching on the best knowledge and practice
available. But they then take those ideas and strategies and critically reflect on them
through practice in their own and each other's classrooms. It is through reflection that
the teacher harmonizes, integrates and transcends the necessary classroom management skills, the acquisition of a repertoire of models of teaching, and the personal
aspects of their teaching into a strategy that has meaning for the students. This is the
heartland of the synergy between teaching and learning and classroom research.

In developing the theme of this chapter I will discuss the nature of powerful learning; describe a framework for thinking about teaching; outline the concept of a model
of teaching; give examples of three common teaching models; and reflect on the nature
of teaching style and the integration of content and process in classroom practice.

Powerful learning

There is now an increasingly sophisticated literature on how learning occurs and on the ways in which the learning experience can be organized to make a positive difference to students. The impact is not just on test scores and examination results, but also on the student's learning capability. This is the heart of the matter: teachers teaching the students how to learn at the same time as assisting them to acquire curriculum content.

The purpose of teaching therefore is not only to help students to acquire curriculum knowledge but also to assist them in becoming powerful learners. The most effective curricular and teaching patterns induce students to construct knowledge – to inquire into subject areas intensively. The result is to increase student capacity to learn and work smarter. The trick of course is to find ways of raising levels of attainment while at the same time helping students become more powerful learners by expanding and making articulate their repertoire of learning strategies.

Powerful learning refers to the ability of learners to respond successfully to the tasks that they are set, as well as the tasks they set themselves – in particular to:

- integrate prior and new knowledge;
- acquire and use a range of learning skills;
- solve problems individually and in groups;
- think carefully about their successes and failures;
- evaluate conflicting evidence and to think critically;
- accept that learning involves uncertainty and difficulty.

The deployment of such a range of learning strategies is commonly termed metacognition, which can be regarded as the learner's ability to take control over their own learning processes. The key point is that within whatever context learning takes place, it involves an 'active construction of meaning'. This carries implications for the management of learning opportunities. As learning is interactional, it occurs only when the learner makes sense of particular experiences in particular contexts. This 'making sense' involves connecting with an individual's prior knowledge and experience. Thus, new learning has to relate to, and ultimately 'fit with', what individuals already understand. Learning should therefore be seen as a process as much as producing end results.

This interactive view of learning is mirrored later in the chapter by a discussion of how a teaching strategy can also be a model of learning. But here I am getting ahead of myself. Having briefly discussed the process of learning we now need to give some attention to the skills of learning that need to be taught and acquired.

If we are serious about personalized learning then we need to be clear as to the typology of the skills students should gain in order to develop their personal effectiveness and employability. These skills fall into three categories:

- functional skills;
- thinking and learning skills;
- personal skills.

The argument so far has led us to a position where it is clear that skills are a vital part of what it means to be educated. There is currently:

- insufficient clarity on the skills students should gain; and
- no clear or coherent development of skills across most national curriculum.

The goal must therefore be to:

- define a single framework of skills in which students should gain mastery across the curriculum; and
- set out the ways in which these skills can best be delivered.

Having defined the three skills sets in which students should gain mastery it is worth looking in a little more detail at what such a framework entails.

Functional skills are literacy, numeracy and ICT. In most countries these are regarded as key priorities and therefore tend to be taught and assessed in the core subjects of Mother tongue, Maths and ICT.

Thinking and learning skills are those young people need to acquire in order to become effective learners. Gaining mastery of these skills equips students to raise their achievement by developing their ability to:

- improve their achievement by applying a wide range of learning approaches in different subjects;
- learn how to learn, with the capability to monitor, evaluate, and change the ways in which they think and learn;
- become independent learners, knowing how to generate their own ideas, acquire knowledge and transfer their learning to different contexts.

The specific thinking and learning skills[1] that I would suggest seem appropriate here are as follows.

Enquiry
- ask relevant questions;
- pose and define problems;
- plan what to do and how to research;
- monitoring progress in tackling a problem;
- predict outcomes and anticipate consequences;
- test conclusions, review solutions and improve ideas.

Creative thinking
- apply imagination to question and challenge ideas;
- generate and extend ideas;

---

[1] These skills are based on the 'Thinking Skills' as set out in the National Curriculum Handbooks for Primary and Secondary teachers in England (DfEE/QCA 1999a,b). They also constitute part of the 'aspects of learning' as set out in the 'Excellence and Enjoyment: Learning and Teaching in the Primary Years' materials, developed by the Primary National Strategy (DfES 2004b).

- suggest hypotheses;
- look for alternative innovative approaches and outcomes.

Information processing
- locate and collect relevant information;
- sort, classify, sequence, compare and contrast;
- analyse relationships.

Reasoning
- give reasons for opinions and actions;
- draw inferences and make deductions;
- use precise language to explain what they think;
- make decisions informed by reasons or evidence.

Evaluation
- assess evidence;
- understand criteria for judging the value of own and others' work or ideas;
- judge the value of what they read, hear and do;
- have confidence in their judgments.

Personal skills are those young people need to acquire in order to develop their personal effectiveness. Gaining mastery of these skills equips students to manage themselves and to develop effective social and working relations. The specific skills that I suggest should comprise Personal Skills are as follows.[2]

Communication (and personal presentation)
- speak effectively for different audiences;
- listen, understand and respond appropriately to others;
- participate effectively in group discussions;
- read fluently a range of literary and non-fiction texts and reflect critically;
- write fluently for a range of purposes and audiences, including critical analysis of own and others' writing.

Diligence, reliability, and capability to improve
- plan, organize and timetable effectively;
- initiative and self-motivation;
- willingness to learn and progress;
- reflect on own work and identifying ways to improve;
- understand how decisions taken now can affect the future.

Working with others (social skills and team work)
- contribute to small-group and whole-class discussion and tasks;
- work with others to meet a challenge: negotiate, resolve differences and support others;
- social skills and awareness and understanding of others' needs;
- leadership skills.

---

[2] The majority of these skills are currently set out as part of the 'Key skills' and 'other aspects of learning' in the National Curriculum Handbooks for Primary and Secondary teachers in England (DfEE/QCA 1999a,b).

Moral and ethical awareness

- Spiritual: understand sense of self, strengths and weaknesses, unique potential, and will to achieve;
- Moral: understand difference between right and wrong, concern for others, consequences of actions and forgiveness;
- Social: understand responsibilities and rights of being a family and community members (local, national and global), how to relate to others and work for common good;
- Cultural: understand and respect own and other cultural traditions, appreciate and respond to a variety of experiences.

This framework provides clarity on the skills students should gain. But to ensure students gain mastery of these skills there needs to be agreement on how the skills should be:

- embedded in teaching and learning, especially since in most systems these skills are not well taught in all schools and consequently students' skill development is patchy;
- developed coherently across the curriculum especially as again in most systems these skills are not specified or developed in a systematic way and progression is assumed rather explicit.

In terms of Functional Skills it would seem sensible that in most systems, as in England, literacy, numeracy and ICT should be (a) taught and assessed in the core subjects of English, Maths and ICT; and (b) have clear levels of progression written into National Curriculum attainment targets and tests.

This leaves Thinking and Learning Skills and Personal Skills to accommodate. As Thinking and Learning Skills and Personal Skills are cross curricular (i.e. they transcend subject boundaries) they are therefore best acquired and developed through teaching and learning across the curriculum. In line with the argument at the end of this chapter, the most appropriate way of embedding these skills is through improved guidance and training in teaching and learning across the curriculum.

This skills framework is consistent with trends in other countries. For example, the OECD's (2005) Definition and Selection of Competencies (DeSeCo) Project classified individuals' key competencies for a successful life into three broad categories:

1 **Use tools interactively** (both physical and socio-cultural ones)
    a. Use language, symbols and texts interactively
    b. Use knowledge and information interactively
    c. Use technology interactively.
2 **Interacting in heterogeneous groups and specifically to:**
    a. Relate well to others
    b. Co-operate, work in teams
    c. Manage and resolve conflicts.
3 **Acting autonomously**
    a. Act within the big picture

    b.   Form and conduct life plans and personal projects
    c.   Defend and assert rights, interests, limits and needs.

So in summary, the clarity provided by a single skills framework allied with better guidance and training on pedagogy will itself create greater coherence across any national curriculum. This is the necessary foundation for ensuring that the essence of personalization is available for every student. As has been argued at length, the central characteristic of effective teachers is their ability to create powerful learners as well as knowledgeable students. The purpose of the framework for teaching proposed below, is to suggest a way in which all teachers can do just that.

A framework for thinking about teaching

In *School Improvement for Real* (Hopkins 2001) I introduced a framework for thinking about teaching and learning. I briefly refer to it again here as it still seems to me to provide a useful starting point in the quest to develop a language and practice for teaching. Figure 11.1 illustrates the four elements of the framework that interestingly are often regarded as being contradictory rather than complementary. Let us look at each of them in turn.

    I start with 'teaching skills' because these are the basic building blocks of teacher competence. These are the everyday classroom management skills that most teachers became familiar with during their initial training and that they continue to refine as part of their reflection on professional practice. These are behaviours such as: content coverage, engaged time (i.e. students learn more when they are on task for a high proportion of class time), active teaching, structuring information, wait time and effective questioning.

Figure 11.1   Four ways of thinking about teaching.

There is an extensive research literature on teaching effects that are replete with cues and tactics necessary for effective teaching. Consistently high correlations are achieved between student achievement scores and classroom processes (Brophy 1983; Brophy and Good 1986). The research evidence on those teaching behaviours most closely associated with student achievement gains is now very sophisticated. An excellent summary is provided by Bert Creemers (1994: 88) in his book *The Effective Classroom*. They are taken from his 'basic model of educational effectiveness' that sees the quality of instruction as having three main components, that is curriculum, grouping procedures and teacher behaviour. These are all of course essential aspects of the skill sets teachers need to personalize learning. The characteristics of teacher behaviour seen in Box 11.1 all have strong empirical support in the research literature.

The second component is what I have called 'teaching relationships'. These are less technical and are more related to the teacher's commitment to their students and belief in the power of high expectations. A supportive, rigorous and optimistic learning environment is fundamental for high levels of student achievement. For me, a key

---

Box 11.1 Characteristics of teacher behaviour associated with student achievement gains

Teacher behaviour
- **Management of the classroom** to create a situation where learning can take place. This implies an orderly and quiet atmosphere in the classroom, although learning itself requires more than a well-organized class. Moreover, effective teaching itself contributes to the management of the class.
- **Provision of homework.** If properly organized, homework contributes to effectiveness. This implies a clear structure of assignments, and provision and evaluation of homework.
- **Expectations** teachers (and schools) have can influence their students' outcomes. We can expect those expectations to become apparent in the actual teacher behaviours.
- **Clear goal setting.** This includes a restricted set of goals, and an emphasis on basic skills and on cognitive learning and transfer. The content should be chosen in line with these goals.
- **Structuring the content.** This includes the ordering of the content according to the hierarchy ordered goals. The use of advanced organizers can also structure the content for students. The use of prior knowledge can increase students' own contributions and responsiveness for learning.
- **Clarity of presentation**, which implies the elements mentioned above but also refers to the transfer process itself (avoiding vagueness and incomplete sentences).
- **Questioning** (by means of low- and higher-order questions) keeps students at work and can be used to check their understanding.
- **Immediate exercise after presentation.** Like questioning, exercises provide a check for understanding and can be used to clarify problems.
- **Evaluating** whether the goals are obtained, by means of testing, providing feedback and corrective instruction.

aspect of teaching is the teacher's ability to generate and sustain an authentic relationship with their students. For example, the teacher 'who made a difference' is a common topic of conversation following an admission that 'I am a teacher'. To many educators a prime indicator of the 'effective' school is one in which high proportion of pupils 'have a good or "vital" relationship with one or more teachers'.

The influence of expectations is often a subtle one, and is felt within a myriad of classroom interactions. The ways in which the teacher sets tasks, arranges groups, locates the responsibility for learning and provides feedback, are all illustrations of how teachers can give messages of high expectations and support that condition and enhance student behaviour. It implies establishing the classroom as a safe and secure learning environment in which pupils can expect acceptance, respect and even warmth from their teachers, without having to earn these – they are intrinsic rights that are extended to all pupils, without prejudice, simply because they are there.

I had a somewhat paradoxical example of this recently when I was in a school in Antofagasta, a mining town in the north of Chile. The school was new, built by the local mining company and situated right next to a *favela*. It was one of the most deprived shanty towns I have ever seen. During the visit the headteacher took me aside and said animatedly: 'Do you know David that best tool we have for helping these children is not our brain but our heart?' He was a kind man and I knew what he meant. But I only half agreed with him. Of course those children needed love and support and acceptance, but they also needed the knowledge and skills to enable them to escape from the *favela*, to transcend their context and not to be imprisoned within it. A teaching relationship in the way I am describing here embodies both and is at the heart of personalized learning.

These two perspectives on high quality teaching are not discrete. It is the practice of fine teachers to combine these elements through a *'process of reflection'* to create an individual style. This is the third element of the framework. The concept of 'teaching style' has been well documented in the literature (see for example the series of studies by Bennett 1976, 1988, and Galton and his colleagues 1980, 1999). Instead of focusing on discrete teacher behaviour, as does the 'process–product' research associated with specific teacher effects, this research explores the relative effectiveness of different teaching styles or collections of teacher behaviours. Consequently, it may be that critical systematic reflection is a necessary condition for quality teaching. This is not reflection for reflection's sake, but in order to continue to develop a mastery of one's chosen craft. It is through reflection that the teacher harmonizes, integrates and transcends the necessary classroom management skills and the personal aspects of their teaching into a strategy that has meaning for their students.

In my experience it is these three elements well integrated into a distinctive individual approach that most people would regard as being the definition of a good, indeed very good, teacher. In England for example, such a teacher would be highly regarded both by external inspectors and by their peers. But for me this is a necessary but not a sufficient condition for the quality of teaching required to personalize learning. As we saw earlier in the chapter, personalized learning is about developing learning capability and involving students in creating their own meaning and learning pathways. In some ways, and perhaps this is a little unfair, the approach to teaching I have just described could be regarded as just a refinement, albeit a sophisticated one, of the traditional 'transmission' or 'recitation' approach to teaching. This method is in stark contrast to the approach to teaching envisioned by advocates of personalized learning, where the teacher is cast in an entirely different role – that of a creator of increasingly powerful learning experiences. It is this approach to teaching that provides the fourth element in the framework – 'teaching models'.

Earlier in the chapter I made the point, as I have just done above, that it is the teacher's task not simply to 'teach', but to create powerful contexts for learning. I then quoted from our book *Models of Learning – Tools for Teaching* (Joyce et al. 2002). Let me now complete the quotation (Joyce et al. 2002: 7) in support of the argument that a good teaching strategy can also be a powerful learning strategy:

> Our toolbox is the models of teaching, actually models for learning that simultaneously define the nature of the content, the learning strategies, and the arrangements for social interaction that create the learning environments of our students.
>
> Through the selection of appropriate models, content can become conceptual rather than particular, the process can become constructive inquiry instead of passive reception, and the social climate can become expansive not restrictive. Our choices depend on the range of our active teaching repertoire and our efforts to expand it by developing new models and studying those developed by others.

It is the integration of 'content, process and social climate' that explains how the learning experience can be organized and personalized to make a positive difference to students. The impact is not just on test scores and examination results, but also on the students' capacity to learn. As I have already said, if the teacher can teach the student how to learn at the same time as assisting them to acquire curriculum content, then the twin goals of learning and achievement can be met at the same time.

Thus, imagine a classroom where the learning environment contains a variety of models of teaching that are not only intended to accomplish a range of curriculum goals, but are also designed to help students increase their competence as learners. At the risk of gilding the lily, allow me a final quote from *Models of Learning – Tools for Teaching*:

> In such classrooms the students learn models for memorising information, how to attain concepts and how to invent them. They practise building hypotheses and theories and use the tools of science to test them. They learn how to extract information and ideas from lectures and presentations, how to study social issues and how to analyse their own social values. These students also know how to profit from training and how to train themselves in athletics, performing arts, mathematics and social skills. They know how to make their writing and problem solving more lucid and creative. Perhaps most importantly, they know how to take initiative in planning personal study, and they know how to work with others to initiate and carry out co-operative

tasks. As students' master information and skills, the result of each learning experience is not only the content they learn but also the greater ability they acquire to approach future learning tasks with confidence and to create increasingly effective learning environments for themselves.

(Joyce *et al.* 2002)

Bruce Joyce (2002) developed this approach in his pioneering work *Models of Teaching* (Joyce and Weil 1996) that was first published in 1972 and is now in its seventh edition. Joyce describes and analyses over thirty different models of teaching – each with their own 'syntax', phases and guidelines – that are designed to bring about particular kinds of learning and to help students become more effective learners. It is in this way that the use of 'teaching models' form part of an overall strategy for enhancing teacher professionalism and the key tool for personalizing learning.

Models of learning – tools for teaching

Models of teaching simultaneously define the nature of the content, the learning strategies, and the arrangements for social interaction that create the learning environments of students. Models of teaching are also models of learning. How teaching is conducted has a large impact on students' abilities to educate themselves. Each model has its own core purpose that relates not only to how to organize teaching, but also to ways of learning. So, for example, if in whole-class teaching the teacher uses the advance organizer model to structure a presentation, the student can use the same method as a means of extracting information and ideas from lectures and presentations. Some examples of the relationship between teaching and learning strategy are given in Box 11.2.

It is important to be clear about what is meant by a 'model of teaching'. As the

Box 11.2 Examples of the relationship between model of teaching and learning skills	
Model of teaching	*Learning skill*
Advanced organizer (or whole class teaching model)	Extracting information and ideas from lectures and presentations
Group work	Working effectively with others to initiate and carry out cooperative tasks
Inductive teaching	Building hypotheses and theories through classification
Mnemonics	Memorizing information
Concept attainment	Attaining concepts and how to invent them
Synectics	Using metaphors to think creatively

idea is exotic to the repertoires of many teachers, one needs to be quite concrete in explaining the concept. This is what I will attempt to do in the following section. An initial distinction would be to regard the evidence on teaching skills as providing the teacher with tactical knowledge, whereas the research on 'models of teaching' gives teachers strategic knowledge about how to create whole classroom settings to facilitate learning.

In *Models of Learning – Tools for Teaching* (Joyce *et al.* 2002) and the *Creating Conditions for Teaching and Learning* (Hopkins *et al.* 2000) handbook based on experiences in IQEA schools, a range of contrasting and complementary teaching strategies are described. These are drawn from Joyce's original four families of teaching models, namely the information processing, the social, the personal, and the behavioural families. Here are brief descriptions of three of the models of teaching and learning, followed by a more curriculum-focused example.

The whole-class teaching model

In active whole-class teaching the teacher controls pupils' learning and seeks to improve performance through direct instruction, whole-class questioning, discussion and learning activities (adapted from Hopkins and Harris 2000).

CASE STUDY

A class of Year 7 pupils is being introduced to rhythm in poetry as part of a unit on sound effects in language. The objectives of the lesson are to refine pupils' listening powers in particular their sense of volume, beat and pace; to appreciate the force of repetition and variation of tempo; to understand the relationship between meaning and beat; to appreciate how writers use these elements to create dramatic effects in their writing. The teacher has chosen Vachel Lindsay's ballad, The Daniel Jazz, as an example.

The lesson begins with the title of the poem. The class is asked to work out what it means. Who was Daniel? What has jazz got to do with him? There is a whole class discussion to ascertain prior knowledge of the class using a range of questioning techniques. Taking the medley of ideas, the teacher builds up a complete version of the story for the class.

The teacher then develops the jazz/story connection and challenges the class to say what they understand by 'jazz writing'. Students are asked to write down at least two ideas on the relationship between music and words. Students share their ideas with the person next to them and together they produce two or three more ideas.

After a few minutes the teacher asks for responses to the questions and elicits terms which might include: DRUM BEAT, RHYTHM, NOISE, LOUD, FAST, SLOW, BASS, TIMING, REPETITION and so on. Some of these concepts are written on the board and stay as reference points for the rest of the lesson.

The teacher then displays the first ten lines of The Daniel Jazz. Teacher reads the first four lines and asks if any of the words on the board apply to this section of the poem. Class recites the lines together emphasizing the beat. A Sun newspaper report of the Daniel incident at a local zoo is introduced to the class. The class tries to recite it but fail. The difference between the two pieces of writing is posed as a question to the class.

In pairs, the class is asked to identify any differences in pace and rhythm in the first 20 lines of the poem. After a few minutes pairs report back with examples. At this point the teacher can assess the degree to which the concepts are being understood and adjust teaching accordingly. More demonstration may be needed to reinforce the concepts of rhythm and pace.

A provided worksheet asks pupils to identify the slow and fast lines in the 20 lines they are now getting familiar with and explain in the writing space provided what makes them slow and why the writer has varied the pace. Partners discuss their results and then the teacher asks for some examples praising and refining pupil contributions as is appropriate.

The conclusion to the lesson is an accretive recital. Two pupils say the first line, then two more join in for the second and so on until the whole class are jazzing their way through the lines, feeling the beat.

This model of teaching enables pupils to order, absorb, understand and relate different areas of knowledge efficiently. It is not a matter of instruction alone. As well as enabling students to process information, the model also allows for pupil interaction so that they learn from each other as well as the teacher and extend their repertoire of social skills. Whole-class teaching is about talking with pupils, listening to them and guiding their learning activities.

Whole-class active teaching is essentially composed of three components or phases:

1   Pupils are formally presented with a problem, issue, area of knowledge or set of skills through lecture or demonstration.
2   Pupils develop understanding through systematic questioning and disciplined enquiry.
3   Pupils apply understanding through a series of set tasks.

The model pre-supposes a coherent instructional programme based on a clear set of overarching goals. The model though is not inclusive to these goals. The instructional model works as part of an integrative teaching and learning plan that may include cooperative group work and independent study. Employing a range of teaching activities influences pupil motivation and is likely to engage them in learning. Non-stop teacher presentation or instruction involving taking notes, answering questions from textbooks and recycling information in homework is tedious and repetitive. Mixing the palette of teaching approaches is more likely to engage pupils in learning, as will mixing modes of delivery and format.

It is important to emphasize that whole-class teaching is a strategic approach to teaching that not only focuses on basic skills and cognitive processes, but also on promoting learning strategies, problem solving and social support. Teachers using the whole-class model address these more complex instructional goals by using a range of techniques to structure strategic learning. Some of these key strategies are:

Understanding: This is a prerequisite to clarity and involves matching the new information to the learners' present knowledge. Does the teacher:

- determine students' existing familiarity with the information presented?
- use terms that are unambiguous and within the students' experience?

Structuring: This involves organizing the material to promote a clear presentation; stating the purpose, reviewing main ideas, and providing transitions between sections. Does the teacher:

- establish the purpose of the lesson?
- preview the organization of the lesson?
- include internal summaries of the lesson?

Sequencing: This involves arranging the information in an order conducive to learning, typically by gradually increasing its difficulty or complexity. Does the teacher:

- order the lesson in a logical way, appropriate to the content and the learners?

Explaining: When explaining principles and relating them to facts through examples, illustrations or analogies, does the teacher:

- define major concepts?
- give examples to illustrate these concepts?
- use examples that are accurate and concrete as well as abstract?

Presenting: This refers to volume, pacing, articulation and other speech mechanics. Does the teacher:

- articulate words clearly and project speech loudly enough?
- pace the sections of the presentation at rates conducive to understanding?
- support the verbal content with appropriate non-verbal communication and visual aids?

(adapted from Good and Brophy 2003)

In summary, the whole-class model of teaching includes the following five phases:

1 *Review*

- Review the concepts and skills from the previous lesson (and if appropriate the homework).

2 *Presenting information*

- Lecture or talk:

  - Preview the outline and scope of the lecture.
  - Introduce key terms or concepts.
  - Lecture proceeds in small steps, starting with what is familiar and using lively explanations and illustrations.

- Demonstration:
  - Preliminaries – a guide as to what to observe and expect.
  - Preview – purpose is outlined.
  - Rehearsal – teachers go through each step.
  - Reprise – procedures are repeated.

3 *Involving pupils in discussion*

- Focus on meaning and promoting student understanding through fast-paced discussion.
- Assess student comprehension through high-quality questioning.

4 *Engaging pupils in learning activities*

- Design activities to focus on content.
- Implementation of learning activities.

5 *Summary and review*

- Pupils ask follow-up questions, share findings and conclusions.
- Teacher reinforces key points, emphasizes central ideas and sums up achievements.

The cooperative group work teaching model

As a model of teaching, cooperative group work has a powerful effect in raising pupil achievement because it harnesses the synergy of collective action. It combines the dynamics of democratic processes with the processes of academic enquiry. It encourages active participation in learning and collaborative behaviour by developing social as well as 'academic' skills. Thus the model requires pupils to practise and refine their negotiating, organizing and communication skills, define issues and problems, develop ways of solving them including collecting and interpreting evidence, hypothesizing, testing and re-evaluating.

The model is highly flexible and draws on a wide range of methods – individual research, collaborative enquiry and plenary activities – and allows the integration of them all into a powerful teaching tool. The teacher is able to conduct a more subtle and complex learning strategy that achieves a number of learning goals simultaneously. Thus, styles can vary from didactic to 'light touch' teaching where the teacher is more an adviser and guide than a director. Two popular approaches to cooperative group learning are 'numbered heads' and the 'jigsaw'. Here are two examples of these approaches:

CASE STUDY

Numbered heads

In an English lesson the teacher is focusing on the punctuation of direct and indirect speech. First, the class is divided into named groups of four and each pupil is allocated a number. From a displayed passage of unpunctuated dialogue and description each group is asked to identify the direct speech. Everyone knows that after two minutes of discussion there will be silence signalled by a bell ringing and that one of them will have their number called and will have to respond. This motivates groups to share information and make sure everyone knows the answer. It gives every pupil a chance to shine and, because they have the group behind them, no one is made anxious about answering. Successful responses bolster both individual and collective confidence, which can be boosted further by some form of team award system.

Jigsaw

In food technology a teacher sets up a question or problem for enquiry and divides pupils into equal-sized groups called Home Groups. Typical topics might include food hygiene in the home, safe practice in the kitchen, processed versus organic foodstuffs, dangerous additives and so on. Each group is given an identical task and suggested list of roles/jobs. For five minutes groups discuss the 'problem' and allocate roles/jobs. The Home groups then divide and those with identical jobs form new Expert groups whose function is to collect relevant information. After a period of research the original Home groups are reformed and expert knowledge pooled to solve the problem or map the issue.

There are many other examples of cooperative learning strategies (Hopkins and Harris 2000):

Twos to fours or snowballing Children work together in pairs, perhaps upon a mathematical problem or science experiment. They then join with another pair to explain what they have achieved, and to compare this with the work of the other pair. This provides a valuable opportunity to express understanding, and to respond to the views of others in a supportive context.

Rainbow groups A way of ensuring that children experience working alongside a range of others is to give each child in a group a number, or a colour. When the group has worked together, all the children of the same number or colour form new groups to compare what they have done.

Envoys Often, in group work, the teacher is concerned that they will be under pressure from many different directions. Envoying helps children to find help and support without necessarily having recourse to the teacher. If a group needs to check something, or to obtain information, one of the group can be sent as an 'envoy' to the library, or book corner, or another group, and then will report back. Another use is to ask groups to send an envoy to a different group to explain what they have done, obtain responses and suggestions, and bring them back to the group.

Listening triads This strategy encourages children, in groups of three, to take on the roles of talker, questioner or recorder. The talker explains or comments on an issue or activity. The questioner prompts and seeks clarification. The recorder makes notes, and at the end of the (brief) time, gives a report of the conversation. Next time the roles are changed.

Critical friends A group member is responsible for observing the ways in which the group works together. Using a simple guide list (which children can devise), the observer watches and listens as the children work. The group then discusses this information. This helps children to develop their own evaluative strategies.

Effective group work involves an agreed set of ground rules that are based on self-respect for individuals and directed at creating efficient working patterns. These ground rules are negotiated as part of an introductory all-class session and refined by each group afterwards to suit their particular concerted needs. Framed as negatives or positives these 'commandments' should establish norms of civilized and democratic behaviour and if developed collaboratively will be accepted and followed more readily. The rules should be simple, reasonable and just. They include, for example:

- No one should interrupt another.
- No one should abuse another.
- No one should ignore another.
- Criticism must be justified and evidenced.
- Different opinions should be respected.
- Praise should be given.
- All members should offer help and share knowledge.

For cooperative methods of learning to be effective, they have to be planned, implemented and monitored very carefully. An ideological commitment to the idea is not enough and, indeed, can result in poorly conceived group activities that may quickly become a shambles. While cooperative methods have an enormous potential for encouraging success in the classroom, this is unlikely to be the outcome unless they are introduced in a systematic and coordinated way. Facilitating effective small group learning means helping group members perceive the importance of working together and interacting in helpful ways.

In summary, there are a wide range of strategies that comprise the cooperative group work teaching model. They are all, however, underpinned by the following principles (Johnson and Johnson 1993).

- *Positive interdependence*, when all members of a group feel connected to each other in the accomplishment of a common goal. All individuals must succeed for the group to succeed.
- *Individual accountability*, holding every member of the group responsible to demonstrate the accomplishment of the learning.
- *Face-to-face interaction*, when group members are close in proximity to each other and enter into a dialogue with each other in ways that promote continued progress.
- *Social skills*, human interaction skills that enable groups to function effectively (e.g. taking turns, encouraging, listening, giving help, clarifying, checking, understanding, probing). Such skills enhance communication, trust, leadership, decision making, and conflict management.
- *Processing*, when group members assess their collaborative efforts and target improvements.

The inductive teaching model

Inductive teaching is a model from the information-processing family. Its main purpose is to encourage pupils to build, test and to use categories to organize their thinking about a particular topic or subject area.

CASE STUDY

A Year 10 class is being introduced to different styles of portrait painting as part of their GCSE course. Initially the teacher gives each individual an A4 handout containing numbered photographs of different kinds of portraits. The portraits represent a range of styles and are from different centuries. For five minutes, the teacher gets the class to look at the photographs individually. The class is then divided into pairs and the teacher instructs each pair to categorize the portraits by grouping certain photographs together using the numbers to group the categories. The pairs set about this task placing the portraits into groups and giving each category a name. The teacher makes it clear that some portraits could be placed in several categories. She also reassures the pupils by telling them that any categories that can be named and justified are acceptable.

After 15 minutes or so, the teacher pauses this activity and asks several of the pairs to share their classification with the whole class and their reasons for classifying the portraits in this way. The pairs offer a series of numbers that are written up by the teacher for the whole class to view. While this is happening, other pupils look at their own classifications to ascertain whether they have reached similar conclusions or not. Having provided a set of numbers the other pupils are then asked by the teacher to guess the rationale behind the classification. One pair offers 'seventeenth century' as one category while another offers 'cubism' as a category. Eventually the initiators of the classification are asked to tell the class why they grouped the data together and the teacher helps the whole class look for links between the data chosen.

After several pairs have provided their categories and the class has worked out their reasons for grouping the data together, the teacher then hands each pair some additional photographs of portraits. The pairs are then asked to reconsider their categories with respect to the new data. The pupils are given time to allocate the new data within existing categories, or to re-categorize the whole data set. Once they have done this task the teacher once again asks selected pairs to share their classification and the labels they have given each category.

The teacher lists the different categories and asks the pupils to add any categories not represented by the list. The teacher then asks the pupils to choose one category and to paint a portrait in this style.

The inductive teaching model is a powerful way of helping pupils to learn how to construct knowledge. The model focuses directly on intellectual capability and is intended to assist pupils in the process of mastering large amounts of information. Within teaching there are numerous occasions when pupils are required to sort and classify data. However, in many cases the sorting process is viewed as an end in itself. Pupils are usually required to understand the 'one correct way of classifying'. Teachers know that there are usually many ways of classifying but they choose one for simplicity.

The inductive method allows pupils to understand a variety of classifications in a structured way that includes a variety of teaching techniques within one method. Without opportunity for re-classification or hypothesizing, learning potential is limited and the development of high-order thinking is restricted. The inductive model of teaching consists of a number of discrete phases that cannot be rushed or omitted. Inductive inquiries are rarely brief because the very nature of the inquiry requires pupils to think deeply. The key activity in the inductive model is the collecting and sifting of information in order to construct categories or labels. This process requires pupils to engage with the data and seek to produce categories in which to allocate the data. It requires them to generate hypotheses based upon this allocation and to test out these hypotheses by using them to guide subsequent work.

The flow of the inductive model involves:

- identifying the information relevant to a topic or a problem;
- grouping individual items into categories that have common attributes;
- classifying the information and developing labels for the categories (this also involves identifying and exploring critical relationships and making inferences);
- creating hypotheses and predicting consequences.

The inductive teaching model follows a sequence of different phases. In the first phase pupils are presented with information or data sets and are required to sort the data into categories. The data sets are derived from a subject area and are intended to facilitate learning about a particular topic or theme. The data sets can be assembled by the teacher in advance of the lesson or collected by the pupils with guidance from the teacher. If assembled by the teacher, the data sets will be prepared with certain concepts in mind. To engage pupils in this model, teachers need to begin by presenting data sets to them and in subsequent lessons to encourage pupils to create and generate their own data sets. It is important that pupils have experience of the inductive model in all its phases and have success in learning with this model before embarking upon more sophisticated and complicated data sets.

To be really effective, data classification needs to occur several times. The initial phase of the classification is particularly important because this is where concepts are generated and applied. Following this initial phase, additional data or new information that requires some re-classification or refinement of the categories may be added. Adding new data means that concepts are challenged, requiring pupils to think again about their initial classification. Through this iterative process pupils obtain control over the data and can understand related concepts more readily.

Inductive teaching increases pupils' ability to form concepts and to create linkages between different concepts. It also enables pupils to have a wider perspective on the topic in question and to think more broadly about the subject matter. Another, important aspect of the inductive model is the collective nature of the enquiry and the group responsibility to contribute to the compilation of categories. By allowing individuals to share their ideas with the whole class, different perspectives on the same data and challenges to thinking are inevitable.

There are many other advantages to the use of the model:

- It engages pupils in higher-order thinking.
- It involves variety in that the stages are taught in different ways so it supports a variety of learning styles.
- Once the data has been prepared, it can be easily kept from one year to another and its tangibility means that it is likely to get incorporated into schemes of work.
- Once the data has been prepared, it is easy to share among members of staff and across different schools.
- Providing teachers keep to the stages of the model, it provides a varied and stimulating way to learn.

In summary, the inductive model of teaching involves the following six phases (Joyce and Calhoun 1998):

Phase One: Identify the domain

- Establish the focus and boundaries of the initial inquiry.
- Clarify the long-term objectives.

Phase Two: Collect, present, and enumerate data

- Assemble and present the initial data set.
- Enumerate and label the items of data.

Phase Three: Examine data

- Thoroughly study the items in the data set and identify their attributes.

Phase Four: Form concepts by classifying

- Classify the items in the data set and share the results
- Add data to the set.
- Reclassification occurs, possibly many times.

Phase Five: Generate and test hypotheses

- Examine the implications of differences between categories.
- Classify categories, as appropriate.
- Reclassify in two-way matrices, as well as by correlations, as appropriate.

Phase Six: Consolidate and transfer

- Search for additional items of data in resource material.
- Synthesize by writing about the domain, using the categories.
- Convert categories into skills.
- Test and consolidate skills through practice and application.

A brief note on the nature of teaching style and the integration of content and process

In this chapter I have tried to argue that teaching and learning should provide the central focus for the work of the teacher-researcher – it should be their heartland. The position I have taken is that the teacher-researcher needs to become increasingly specific about those teaching strategies that promote more effective learning. This is for two reasons. First, this is the best way to communicate professional knowledge to other teachers. Second, in the belief that a good teaching strategy is also a good learning strategy it is by the same token the best way to communicate them to our students. The danger however is that the discourse in this chapter appears overly technical and instrumental. That is an illusion – we need clarity on the concepts and precision on principles if we are to put professional knowledge, as Lawrence Stenhouse once said, to the test of practice. 'Putting to the test of practice' however requires a capacity to integrate, unite and transcend functionalist approaches. I hope that is clear by now. If not let me in concluding this chapter cite two further examples of the ways in which the teacher-researcher stands at the fulcrum of establishing a professional practice for education.

First, it is ultimately my belief that effective teaching and learning has to be seen within a holistic framework. The comparative study of policies aimed at improving teacher quality we conducted for the OECD identified six characteristics of high-quality teachers (Hopkins and Stern 1996: 10):

- commitment;
- love of children;
- mastery of subject didactics;
- a repertoire of multiple models of teaching;
- the ability to collaborate with other teachers;
- a capacity for reflection.

Although it is convenient to group teachers' desired capacities and behaviours into categories, these attributes all interact in practice. For example, one French teacher elegantly defined teacher quality as 'savoirs, savoir-faire, et savoir-être', this is translatable perhaps as 'knowledge, knowing how to do, and knowing how to be' (Hopkins and Stern 1996: 503).

Second, and in the same way it is at the school level that there needs to be a powerful integrative force. As Lawrence Downey (1967) once evocatively put it, 'A school teaches in three ways, by what it teaches, by how it teaches and by the kind of place it is.' It is a consideration of the context and conditions that support effective teaching and learning that provides a focus for the following chapter and I hope for much of the book.

Let me illustrate this thought through extending the earlier discussion of the importance of 'learning to learn' and ways of achieving this within a whole school context. The recent emphasis in schools on 'learning to learn' has the great advantage that successful teachers become better skilled themselves in integrating the teaching and learning of skills into subject content. There are a variety of strategies that are being employed and these include:

- subject specific programmes that contribute to pupils' understanding, thinking and learning of key skills in a subject context;
- discrete skills programmes (learning to learn lessons) that enable an explicit focus on skills with reference to a broad range of subject content and contexts;
- cross-curricular programmes that ally clarity on learning skills with a focus on subject content to help students transfer their learning between lessons.

It is difficult to say which approach is better than the other. In our experience, however, it depends a) on what fits best into the schools context, and b) how well the programme is being implemented. Above all however it is how well these programmes link together curriculum, teaching strategies and the school's whole approach to learning. Our view is that any of these programmes should be systematically imbedded in the curriculum and have strong links between teaching and learning. Figure 11.2 shows how the integration of such a programme into the curriculum could take place. There are three elements of the figure that when linked together serve to summarize the key issues in this chapter.

First the school as in A must have adopted a clear model of learning that is consistently applied. Many models are suitable as long as they are developmental, i.e. move from low to high learning skills. In the figure I have used Gagne's (1965) classification. Frameworks developed by Bloom (1956) or Claxton (1999) would also be suitable.

The second element at B is the judicious and strategic application of the models if learning – the tools for teaching approach described earlier. The key point of course is that any model of learning has the potential to develop specific learning skills. So, the curriculum planning task becomes ensuring i) that there is clarity on the specific

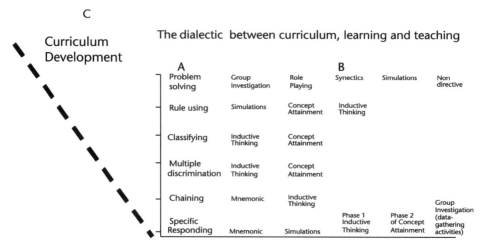

Figure 11.2 The dialectic between curriculum, learning and teaching.

learning skill that needs to be developed; and ii) that then is matched to an appropriate model of teaching.

When as in C, this approach is applied to the whole school and has a methodology for progressively developing learning skills across the curriculum. This occurs horizontally – that in any term or year a student is consistently being exposed to a range of learning strategies – and vertically – that these learning strategies are progressively developed at a more sophisticated level with more demanding curriculum content as the student progresses through school.

Finally, a comment on the debate around whether 'whole-class' or 'group activity' should dominate, or what should be the balance between whole-class, small group, and individual activities. Settling that question leads to the broader question of what will work best for children, because it is the models of learning and teaching that are chosen, rather than the grouping arrangements adopted, that will directly affect student achievement. In these classes, students are taught directly models for learning that they use when working as members of the class community, in small collaborative groups, and as individuals. The more efficient models of teaching assume that the whole class will be organized to pursue common learning objectives within which individual differences in achievement are comfortably accommodated. Thus, their creators have a vision of the whole class and a vision of small group work and individual work as part of the overall educational scheme (Joyce and Calhoun 1997: 16). Or as Bruce Joyce elegantly phrased it, the operational repertoire of the teacher is the critical element in the calculus of effects.

Further reading

Much of this chapter has been based on previous writing on teaching and learning. The key text here is *Models of Teaching* (Joyce and Weil 1996). In *Models of Learning – Tools for Teaching* (Joyce *et al.* 2002), we adapted the original manuscript for a trans-American audience, and *Creating the Conditions for Teaching and Learning* (Hopkins and Harris 2000) reports on the use of these materials in IQEA schools. In terms of the different models of teaching described in this chapter, further information on whole-class teaching can be found in Good and Brophy (2003) and Creemers (1994); on cooperative group work, Robert Slavin (1995), Sharan and Shachar (1988) and Johnson *et al.* (1993) are the most accessible sources; and on inductive teaching, Joyce and Calhoun's (1997) *Learning to Teach Inductively* is mandatory. The literature on how children learn (Wood 1998), the different types or 'multiple intelligences' (Gardner 1991, 1993) and the descriptions of a range of learning styles (Kolb 1984) are helpful in designing increasingly effective learning experiences within authentic school improvement contexts. James *et al.* (2006a) *Learning How to Learn: Classrooms, Schools and Networks* as well as James *et al.* (2006b) *Learning How to Learn: Tools for Schools* are an essential read on learning to learn. Useful sources for the research on teaching also include Kyriacou (1997, 1998), DeBono (1991), Claxton (1999) and Miujs and Reynolds (2001), together with the other studies reported earlier in this chapter.

12 Teacher research, the creation of professional learning communities and the transformation of schooling

In the first edition of this book I was clear that teacher research should embody a 'classroom exceeding' perspective and argued for enhanced collaborative action amongst teacher-researchers. Subsequent editions have expanded on that theme as I began to emphasize the importance of the role of the teacher-researcher in educational reform. Since the end of the 1980s, the amount of change expected of teachers and schools has increased enormously. As well as the curriculum and organizational changes with which most are all too familiar, there are a wide range of central policy initiatives in England and Wales that are potentially supportive of teacher and school development. Whether by accident or design, changes in the funding and delivery of staff development, schemes for school self-evaluation, teaching and learning reviews, assessment of learning performance management, and school development planning are all supportive of what David Hargreaves (1994) once called the 'new professionalism'. With a little imagination, all of these activities can combine or 'braid' together to form an 'infrastructure' at the school level to support the management of change and the professional development of teachers. Our school improvement experience convinces me of the crucial role classroom observation and research can play in supporting the professional growth of teachers and the process of school transformation.

In this chapter, I intend to extend this discussion beyond the school and make an argument for the role that the teacher-researcher can play in system-wide reform. In *Every School a Great School* (Hopkins 2007) I argued that to achieve this aspiration one needed to re-calibrate the balance between 'national prescription' and 'schools leading reform' in favour of the latter. It is only in this way that the conditions can be created at the school and classroom level where every student has the opportunity to reach their potential. I therefore begin this chapter with a brief description of the system reform argument; then outline the four drivers that will facilitate the rebalancing mentioned above and the role of the teacher-researcher in achieving this; having set the scene I will provide further illustrations of the ways in which teacher-researchers can support the work implied by the four drivers, that is, professional development, enhancing the professional judgement of teachers, networking, and how it all comes together in an approach to school improvement. I conclude the book with a reflection on the holistic nature of teacher research.

An argument for system reform

There is a general lesson to be drawn for large-scale/systemic reform from the global experience since the mid-1990s. It is in the logic of large-scale reform that an early narrow focus on key skills produces an initial rapid increase in standards. To move beyond this plateau of achievement requires a system-wide school improvement approach that can deliver continuous improvement beyond the early gains. In other words, large-scale reform has characteristically focused on short-term objectives, whereas systemic change envisages a multi phased process that ensures that early gains do not level off, but continue to improve as a consequence of employing strategies that at the same time raise achievement and build capacity.

It is implicit in this argument that there is a growing recognition that schools need to lead the next phase of reform. In *Every School a Great School* (Hopkins 2007) I used an analysis of the English experiment with large-scale reform to set out the following propositions:

- Most agreed that standards were too low and too varied in the 1970s and 1980s and that some form of direct state intervention was necessary.
- After early success progress plateaued and the question became whether pre-scription still offered the recipe for sustained large-scale reform in the medium term.
- There was a growing recognition that schools need to lead the next phase of reform. But this must categorically not be a naïve return to the not so halcyon days of the 1970s when a thousand flowers bloomed and the educational life chances of too many of our children wilted.
- The implication is that we need a transition from an era of prescription to an era of professionalism, in which the balance between national prescription and schools leading reform will change.

However, achieving this shift is not straightforward. As Michael Fullan (quoted in Hopkins 2007) has said, it takes capacity to build capacity, and if there is insuffi-cient capacity to begin with it is folly to announce that a move to 'professionalism' provides the basis of a new approach. The key question is 'how do we get there?', because we cannot simply move from one era to the other without self-consciously building professional capacity throughout the system. This progression is seen in Figure 12.1.

It is worth taking a little more time unpacking the thinking underlying Figure 12.1. Five points need making.

The first is to emphasize that this not an argument against 'top down' change. It is clear that neither 'top down' nor 'bottom up' change work just by themselves; they have to be in balance – in creative tension. The balance between the two at any one time will of course depend on context.

Second, it must be realized that in England in 1997 it was obvious that more central direction was needed. This reflects the balance towards national prescription as seen in the left-hand segment of Figure 12.1.

Figure 12.1 Towards system-wide sustainable reform.

Third, it should be no surprise to realize that the right-hand segment is relatively unknown territory. It implies horizontal and lateral ways of working with assumptions and governance arrangements very different from what we know now. The main difficulty in imagining this landscape is that the thinking of most people is constrained by their experiences within the power structure and norms of the left-hand segment of the figure.

The fourth point is both complex and critical. In terms of the figure, effective system-wide sustainable reform requires a movement from the left to the right segment, with all that implies. The left to right movement is necessarily incremental as it builds on, rather than contradicts, the success of previous phases. Yet, and this is the crucial point, the achievement of creating the educational landscape implied by the right-hand segment represents a step change from what has gone before. Yes, the difference between left- and right-hand segments represents a radical change or a transformation; but the process or journey from left to right will be incremental, building on past success and reshaping in the light of learning from experience. It is in this way that the language of school improvement (logical incremental steps building on past experience) and transformation (a qualitatively different state from what was known previously) is reconciled.

Finally, of course it is not being suggested that you always have to start from the left-hand side of the figure and move in some sort of uniform way to the right. That is just how it was in England in 1997. Other systems may well be in the middle and need to move left briefly to firm up certain conditions before rapidly proceeding into the right-hand segment. Some may believe that they are already in the right-hand segment.

If this diagram has any value it is as a heuristic – its purpose is to help people think rather than tell them what to do.

Four drivers for system reform

I need to reiterate that the transition from 'prescription' to 'professionalism' is not straightforward. In order to move from one to the other strategies are required that not only continue to raise standards but also build capacity within the system. This point is key; one cannot just drive to continue to raise standards in an instrumental way – one also needs to develop social, intellectual and organizational capital. Building capacity demands that we replace numerous central initiatives with a national consensus on a limited number of educational trends. There seems to me to be four key drivers that if pursued relentlessly and deeply will deliver both higher standards and enhanced professional capacity. These are personalized learning, professionalized teaching, networks and collaboration and intelligent accountability. All have significant implications for teacher-researchers.

As seen in the 'diamond of reform' below (Figure 12.2) the four trends coalesce and mould to context through the exercise of responsible system leadership. Before relating the concept of system leadership to teacher research, let me briefly describe each of the four drivers.

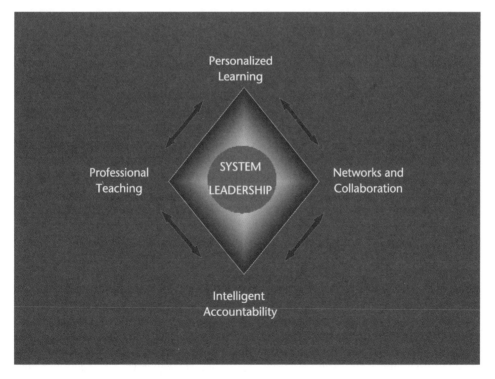

Figure 12.2   Four key drivers underpinning system reform.

Personalized learning

As we have seen, the current focus on personalization is about putting students at the heart of the education process so as to tailor teaching to individual need, interest and aptitude in order to fulfil every young person's potential. Many schools and teachers have tailored curriculum and teaching methods to meet the needs of children and young people with great success for many years. What is new is the drive to make the best practices universal. A successful system of personalized learning means clear learning pathways through the education system and the motivation to become independent, e-literate, fulfilled, lifelong learners. Obviously personalized learning demands both curriculum entitlement and choice that delivers a breadth of study and personal relevance, as well as emphasizing the development of the student's meta-cognitive capacity, in other words, 'learning how to learn'. The personalization, however, is in terms of flexible learning pathways through the education system rather than personalized goals or institutional tracking, which have often been shown to lower performance expectations for students and to provide easy ways out for teachers and schools allowing them to defer problems rather than solve them. The drive for high standards applies to all. In the previous chapter we explored the implications of personalized learning for the teacher-researcher.

Professionalized teaching

Significant empirical evidence suggests that teaching quality is the most significant factor influencing student learning that is under the control of the school. It is also clear that the forms of teaching that promote high levels of student learning vary in some instances quite dramatically from country to country. The phrase 'professionalized teaching' implies that teachers are on a par with other professions in terms of diagnosis, the application of evidence-based practices and professional pride. The image here is of teachers who use data to evaluate the learning needs of their students, and are consistently expanding their repertoire of pedagogic strategies to personalize learning for all students. It also implies schools that adopt innovative approaches to timetabling and the deployment of increasingly differentiated staffing models. More detail on how the teacher-researcher can help support the development of professional learning communities is given later.

Intelligent accountability

This refers to the balance between nationally determined approaches to external accountability on the one hand and the capacity for professional accountability within the school that emphasizes the importance of formative assessment and the pivotal role of self-evaluation, on the other. In any debate on accountability it is important to distinguish between means and ends, methods and purpose. There are two key purposes for accountability. The first is as a tool to support higher levels of student learning and achievement; the second is to maintain public confidence. The means of achieving this will inevitably vary from situation to situation. In general where there are high levels of student achievement and small variations of performance between schools then pressures from external accountability will be modest. In those situations where there is a need for more robust forms of external accountability it should always be designed to support teacher professionalism and the school's capacity to utilize data to enhance student performance. We look at the teacher-researcher role in enhancing the professional judgements of teachers a little later in the chapter.

Networking and collaboration

This relates to the various ways in which networks of schools can stimulate and spread innovation as well as collaborate to provide curriculum diversity, extended services and community support. The prevalence of networking practice supports the contention that there is no contradiction between strong, independent schools and strong networks, rather the reverse. Effective networks require strong leadership by participating heads and clear objectives that add significant value to individual schools' own efforts. Without this networks wither and die, since the transaction costs outweigh the benefits they deliver. Although evidence of effectiveness is still accumulating, it is becoming clear that networks support improvement and innovation by enabling schools to collaborate on building curriculum diversity, extended services and professional support to develop a vision of education that is shared and owned well beyond individual school gates. Again the teacher-researcher role in networking is discussed a little later.

In *Every School a Great School* (Hopkins 2007) I argued that although these key drivers provide a core strategy for systemic improvement, it is system leadership that adapts them to particular and individual school contexts. I then describe system leaders as those who reach beyond their own school to create networks and collaborative arrangements that not only add richness and excellence to the learning of students, but also act as agents of educational transformation. Although it is often the senior leadership in the school who adopt these roles and take on these functions, this is not necessarily the case. The implicit argument in this section has been that particularly in terms of the four key drivers these are functions that are directly in the domain of teacher-researchers and where they too can exercise professional leadership. We now look at four areas of professional practice where teacher-researchers play an active role.

Professionalized teaching – building a culture of professional development

We have already noted the happy phrase the 'new professionalism' coined by David Hargreaves (1994). His argument was that, paradoxically, much of the recent legislation is having the unintended consequence of eroding the traditional culture of individualism in teaching by forcing structural changes that are generating new forms of collaboration. The 'new professionalism' implies a change in the values and practices of teachers that embraces the ethos of teacher research as structural changes are encouraging a move from 'individualism to collaboration' and from 'hierarchies to teams'. It is also clear that under the right conditions, significant and rapid progress can be made in enhancing the learning of students (Hopkins 2001: Ch. 10). In these instances, it is a strong vision coupled with intensive staff development on instructional practices and 'capacity building' that has led to significant increases in levels of student achievement. The important point in this context is that once again the skills and aptitudes of the teacher-researcher are well suited to this new professional role.

In making his argument, Hargreaves sets out two propositions about the relationship between teacher and school development. The first is that there is little school development without teacher development. The second is that there is little teacher development without school development. The truth of the first proposition is axiomatic. This book and virtually every citation in it are based on that premise. The second proposition is more controversial; but it is at the heart of the difference between this and the original version of this book that was published in 1985. Put simply, I believed then that to improve schools we needed to improve teachers, and to build a community of teacher-researchers. Now I believe that to sustain the ethic of teacher development we need to anchor our work to a whole-school context and focus it unrelentingly on the teaching and learning process.

We have not as yet built an infrastructure for staff development within our schools. Such an infrastructure would involve portions of the school week being devoted to staff development activities, such as curriculum development and implementation, new models of teaching, regular observation sessions and on-site coaching. Integral to these activities is a commitment to reviewing one's performance as a prelude to development. It is within this context that classroom research is a fundamental staff development activity.

Bruce Joyce and Beverly Showers' (1995) work on staff development, in particular their peer coaching strategy, has in recent years transformed our thinking on staff development. It is here that there is the closest link with classroom research techniques, especially observation. Joyce and Showers identified a number of key training components which, when used in combination, have much greater power than when used alone. The major components of training are:

- presentation of theory or description of skill or strategy;
- modelling or demonstration of skills or models of teaching;
- practice in simulated and classroom settings;
- structured and open-ended feedback (provision of information about performance); and
- coaching for application (hands-on, in-classroom assistance with the transfer of skills and strategies to the classroom).

Based on this analysis, Joyce and Showers (1984: 85) summarized the 'best knowledge' we have on staff development like this:

- the use of the integrated theory-demonstration-practice feedback training programme to ensure skill development;
- the use of considerable amounts of practice in simulated conditions to ensure fluid control of the new skills;
- the employment of regular on-site coaching to facilitate vertical transfer; and

- the preparation of teachers who can provide one another with the needed coaching.

Joyce (1992) has also distinguished – helpfully in my opinion – between the two key elements of staff development: the workshop and the workplace. The workshop, which is equivalent to the best practice on the traditional INSET course, is where we gain understanding, see demonstrations of the teaching strategy we may wish to acquire, and have the opportunity to practise them in a non-threatening environment. If, however, we wish to transfer these new skills back into the workplace – the classroom and school – then merely attending the workshop is insufficient. The research evidence is very clear that skill acquisition and the ability to transfer vertically to a range of situations requires 'on-the-job support'. This implies changes to the workplace and the way in which we organize staff development in our schools. In particular, this means the opportunity for immediate and sustained practice, collaboration and peer coaching, and studying development and implementation. We cannot achieve these changes in the workplace without, in most cases, drastic alterations to the ways in which we organize our schools. Yet we will not be able to transfer teaching skills from INSET sessions to a range of classrooms without them. Fortunately, at least for teacher-researchers, as seen in the examples scattered throughout this book, the workplace conditions they create for themselves mesh with and are similar to the core activities of classroom research.

What is being proposed here is a wide range of staff development activities that represents a fairly sophisticated infrastructure for sustained professional development. A key element in all of this is the provision of in-classroom support or in Joyce and Showers' term 'peer coaching' (Joyce and Showers 1995). It is the facilitation of peer coaching that enables teachers to extend their repertoire of teaching skills and to transfer them from different classroom settings to others.

During the implementation of this approach during our IQEA school improvement projects, as is seen later, we have emphasized the use of peer coaching to support student learning (see for example, Joyce *et al.* 1999, Chapter 7). When the refinements noted below are incorporated into a school improvement design, peer coaching can virtually assure 'transfer of training' for everyone:

- Peer coaching teams of two or three are much more effective than larger groups.
- These groups are more effective when the entire staff is engaged in school improvement.
- Peer coaching works better when heads and deputies participate in training and practice.
- The effects are greater when formative study of student learning is embedded in the process.

The constellation of staff development activities just described makes the structural link between the collaborative and reflective work of teachers and enhanced levels of student achievement clear and achievable. The staff development focus has the potential to unite both the focus on teaching and learning and capacity building. In highly effective schools it is this that provides the essential infrastructure for school improvement.

Intelligent accountability – enhancing the professional judgement of teachers

Underpinning any approach to 'intelligent accountability' is the teacher's skill in using data to make judgements on and select strategies for enhancing student learning. We have previously (Ainscow *et al.* 2000: 11) set out the case for enquiry-driven improvement efforts as follows:

> We have observed that those schools which recognise that enquiry and reflection are important processes in school improvement find it easier to sustain improvement effort around established priorities, and are better placed to monitor the extent to which policies actually deliver the intended outcomes for pupils. Central to the conditions, which promote the effective use of enquiry and reflection as developmental tools, are:
>
> - Systematic collection, interpretation and use of school-generated data in decision-making.
> - Effective strategies for reviewing the progress and impact of school policies and initiatives.
> - Widespread involvement of staff in the processes of data collection and analysis.
> - Clear ground rules for the collection, control and use of school-based data.

Unfortunately, in a large number of schools the range of data available is being underused. Of course, some schools are much better organized in this area, and have clear systems and procedures for collecting, analysing and interpreting information which is seen as relevant to particular aspects of the school or particular decisions. Even in these cases, however, a more general commitment to enquire into and reflect on the school's progress is rare – more often it is the issue that is identified then the information collected, rather than data being collected to help identify what the issue should be.

I would not want to suggest here that everything that takes place in a school can be noted, nor that all information has equal significance. But our work with schools that have adopted a sustained commitment to improvement initiatives has led us to identify the habits of enquiry and reflection as important forces for improvement and the role of the teacher-researcher as being critical in ensuring this.

The best of practice in outstanding schools suggests that student progress is regularly monitored. This is a key principle of effective assessment for learning practice. Many schools are checking student progress at least once each half term. Two points seem clear from this experience: first, the process needs to be carried out systematically; second, the skills of teacher-researchers are those necessary to carry out this process successfully. We addressed both of these issues in some detail in *The Empowered School* (Hargreaves and Hopkins 1991). Although principally concerned with development planning and located in a different era, some of the advice we offered there still has resonance for the work of the teacher-researcher in planning a systematic process of progress checking and enhancing the professional judgement of teachers.

We defined a 'progress check' in *The Empowered School* (Hargreaves and Hopkins 1991: 67) as an act of evaluation *in the course of* implementation. It is a response to the question: how are we doing so far? Many progress checks are intuitive, a 'feel' for whether things are going well or badly. This is a natural part of monitoring one's activities: it becomes more systematic if these intuitive reactions are shared within the team, and evidence on student learning is produced to support them. Regular *progress checks* involve:

- giving somebody in the team responsibility for ensuring that the progress checks take place;
- deciding what will count as evidence of progress in relation to student learning;
- finding quick methods of collecting evidence from different sources;
- reviewing student progress at team meetings;
- deciding on what changes need to be made to teaching practice in general and work programmes for individual students in particular.

Success checks typically take place at the end of the academic year. The team now decides how successful the teaching and curriculum programme as a whole has been and what changes need to be made for the following year. Checking success need not be complex or time-consuming. It will consist largely in collating, and then drawing a conclusion about, the earlier progress checks.

In *The Empowered School* David Hargreaves and I argued that the process of checking on progress and success in development planning requires teachers to use their professional judgement in a systematic way (Hargreaves and Hopkins 1991; Chapter 9). It is not the mechanistic completion of progress and success checks that is important, but rather it is the enhancing of the teachers' professional judgement that is the crucial aspect of embedding an ethos of enquiry and reflection within a school. This process provides the interface between development planning, classroom research and school improvement.

Teachers already, as part of their everyday activities, monitor and evaluate their own actions as well as the behaviour and work of pupils. If teachers did not rely on their *intuitive professional judgement*, they would not be able to cope with the complexities of their work. There are occasions, however, when it cannot be wholly relied on as a basis for making a decision. Such occasions are when teachers are not entirely confident about their intuitive judgement, or the issue is of considerable importance or significance. In these circumstances, teachers make a *considered professional judgement*, which requires some action to check the intuitive judgement. A considered professional judgement is reached through reflection and further investigation. Using intuitive and considered professional judgements is a routine part of being a teacher. Both are a natural and inherent part not only of assessing progress for evaluation but more generally of the school improvement process.

Innovations often create new working circumstances with which the teacher is less familiar. Since teachers usually want the innovation to succeed, there may be a bias towards noticing the most favourable evidence. Professional judgement may therefore be less trustworthy than usual. In these cases a *refined professional judgement* is required. This is an opportunity for enhancing professional judgement, and is achieved:

- through discussion with colleagues about the extent of progress or success in school improvement work;
- by establishing agreement on standards used to make judgements;
- through mutual observation in the classroom;
- through the use of informed opinion.

When it is well structured, development work provides ample opportunities for teachers to talk with others, to seek agreement on standards, to observe one another and to read relevant documentation: all are means of refining the professional judgements which are so essential for evaluation and school improvement. It is here where the potential of evaluation as school improvement is realized. Extending teachers' professional judgements therefore links the professional development of the individual teacher to the development of the school as a whole as well as improving the quality of teaching and learning.

There are circumstances when teachers need to *complement* even a refined professional judgement with additional evidence. Such occasions are when others need to be persuaded of the validity of teachers' judgements, or when there are benefits to all if teachers' judgements are backed by independent evidence. Collecting complementary evidence is usually more time-consuming than making professional judgements, so careful thought needs to be given to questions such as: what kind of complementary evidence is appropriate to documenting success? How can it be collected as quickly and easily as possible without adding substantially to existing workloads? There are different types and sources of complementary evidence, and it is these that reflect what is often regarded as more formal approaches to evaluation:

- observations (e.g. mutual observation during teacher appraisal);
- views and opinions (e.g. short questionnaire to colleagues, students or parents);
- written materials (e.g. a 'book look' of students' work);
- statistical information (e.g. trends in student attendance rates);
- more formal research (e.g. by a colleague on a 'Masters' course).

To summarize, the foundation of intelligent accountability is the use of regular progress and success checks. Although these frameworks are important in underpinning a process of assessment, it is the enhancing of the professional judgements of teachers that sustains and adds value to the process.

Networking and collaboration – creating effective conditions

There has been much international interest in the role of networks in supporting school improvement (e.g. OECD 1999). There are, however, various interpretations of the network concept. Although networks bring together those with like-minded interests, they are more than just opportunities to share 'good practice'. The following definition of networks emerged from an analysis of effective networks identified by the OECD (quotation and discussion in this section based on Hopkins 2000, Chapter 10):

> Networks are purposeful social entities characterised by a commitment to quality, rigour, and a focus on outcomes. They are also an effective means of supporting innovation in times of change. In education, networks promote the dissemination of good practice, enhance the professional development of teachers, support capacity building in schools, mediate between centralised and decentralised structures, and assist in the process of re-structuring and re-culturing educational organisations and systems.

The qualities exhibited by such networks are, however, not easily acquired. A number of key conditions need to be in place if networks are to realize their potential as agents of educational innovation. Once again the skills of teacher-researchers can facilitate successful networking and teacher-researchers themselves have proven to be outstanding network leaders. In terms of school improvement, a number of conditions for effective networks can be identified:

- *Consistency of values and focus* – it is important that networks have a common aim and purpose, and that the values underpinning the network are well articulated and 'owned' by those involved. This consistency of values and purpose also relates to the need for the focus of the network to be consistent with the overarching policy framework.
- *Clarity of structure* – effective networks are well organized with clear operating procedures and mechanisms for ensuring that maximum participation is achieved within and between schools. These structures promote involvement that is broad-based, preferably with a whole organization or systemic focus, rather than being narrow, limiting or particular.
- *Knowledge creation, utilization and transfer* – the key purpose of networks is to create and disseminate knowledge to support educational improvement and innovation. Such knowledge and practice needs to be based on evidence, focus on the core features of schooling, and are subject to robust quality assurance procedures.
- *Rewards related to learning* – those who belong to networks need to feel that their involvement is worthwhile. Rewards for networking are best related to supporting professional development and the encouraging of learning. Effective networks invest in people.
- *Dispersed leadership and empowerment* – highly effective networks contain skilful people who collaborate and work well together. The skills required by

network members are similar to the skill sets associated with effective teams and include a focus on dispersed leadership and empowerment.

- *Adequate resources* – networks need to be adequately resourced particularly in terms of time, finance and human capital. It is not necessarily the quantum of resource that is important; more crucially there needs to be flexibility in the way in which it is deployed.

In line with the argument of this chapter, networks in education have a key role to play in supporting school improvement and system reform. Accordingly, networks need to be regarded as support structures for innovative schools, not only in disseminating 'good practice', but also in overcoming the traditional isolation of schools, and to a certain extent even challenging traditional hierarchical system structures. In the past, most school systems have operated almost exclusively through individual units, be they teachers, departments, schools or local agencies. Such isolation may have been appropriate during times of stability, but during times of change there is a need to 'tighten the loose coupling', to increase collaboration and to establish more fluid and responsive structures. Networks provide an important way of doing this and have powerful potential for extending the teacher as researcher role.

To summarize, networks have the potential to support educational innovation and change by:

- providing a focal point for the dissemination of good practice, the generalizability of innovation and the creation of 'action oriented' knowledge about effective educational practices;
- keeping the focus on the core purposes of schooling, in particular in creating and sustaining a discourse on teaching and learning;
- enhancing the skill of teachers, leaders and other educators in change agent skills and managing the change process;
- building capacity for continuous improvement at the local level, and in particular in creating professional learning communities, within and between schools;
- ensuring that systems of pressure and support are *integrated* not segmented (for example, professional learning communities incorporate pressure and support in a seamless way);
- acting as a link between the centralized and decentralized schism resulting from many contemporary policy initiatives.

As has been argued at length in this chapter, the main reason why reforms have not had the desired impact is because Government policy on education has not been adequately informed by what is known about teacher and school development. If one issue is certain it is that the future of schooling requires a systemic perspective, which implies a high degree of commitment to school improvement, teacher development and an unrelenting focus on student achievement and learning. Networks, within and outside schools, provide a means for doing just that.

Pulling it all together – locating classroom research within a model of school improvement

In pulling the argument of this chapter together it may be helpful to give an extended example of how the conventional teacher as researcher role can be extended to encompass school improvement and system-wide reform. The example given here is of one school, but the implications are for schools working in local areas to form networks and thus achieve local transformation. This takes us beyond the parameters of this particular book but examples can be found in a number of our publications (Higham, Hopkins and Matthews, forthcoming; Hopkins 2007; Hopkins and Higham 2007; Hopkins and Pont 2007). The example is taken from our 'Improving the Quality of Education For All' (IQEA) school improvement project. In common with a number of school improvement projects throughout the world, IQEA has sought to develop the capacity of schools to accommodate and use external change in order to maximize student outcomes. IQEA focuses on the teaching/learning process and the conditions that support it in the knowledge that, without an equal focus on the development capacity or internal conditions of the school, innovative classroom work will soon become marginalized. The IQEA project works from an assumption that schools are most likely to strengthen their ability to provide enhanced outcomes for all pupils when they adopt ways of working that are consistent with both their own and the current reform agenda. Indeed, the schools we are currently working with are using the external drive to improve teaching and learning as a basis for conducting their developmental work at the classroom level.

At the outset of IQEA we attempted to outline our own vision of school improvement by articulating a set of principles that provided us with a philosophical and practical starting point (Ainscow *et al.* 2000; Hopkins 2001, 2002). These principles represent the expectations we have of the way project schools pursue school improvement. They serve as an *aide-mémoire* to the schools and to ourselves. We feel that the operation of these principles creates synergism – together they are greater than the sum of their parts.

- School improvement is a process that focuses on enhancing the *quality of students' learning*.
- The vision of the school should be one which embraces *all* members of the school community as both learners and contributors.
- The school will secure its *internal priorities* through adopting external pressures for change and in so doing enhance its capacity for managing change.
- The school will seek to use data, action research and *enquiry* to drive forward and inform with school improvement efforts.
- The school will seek to develop structures and create conditions that encourage collaboration and lead to the *empowerment* of students and teachers.

More recently, schools within the project have sought to integrate work at both levels by focusing on different models of teaching in order to expand teacher's instructional repertoires. There is mounting evidence that the content of a lesson notwithstanding, the use of appropriate teaching strategies can significantly increase student achievement. A major goal for school improvement, therefore, is to help teachers become professionally flexible so that they can select, from a repertoire of possibilities, the teaching approach most suited to their particular content area, and the age, interests and aptitudes of their students. One of the characteristics of successful schools is that teachers talk about teaching. In IQEA schools this involves:

- teachers discussing with each other the nature of teaching strategies;
- establishing specifications or guidelines for the chosen teaching strategies;
- agreeing on standards used to assess student progress as a result;
- mutual observation and partnership teaching in the classroom.

This focus has provided a basis for staff development and planning at the school level, as well as peer observation and innovation in the classroom. Having selected a particular model of teaching, each school places priority on embedding the model into the teachers' classroom practice. When this has been achieved, other models are subsequently added to further enhance the quality of teaching and learning within the school. This experience suggests that focusing on models of teaching has enabled IQEA schools to build the capacity for change at both the school and classroom levels. It has also created a coherent programme of staff development within IQEA schools that impacts directly and positively on student achievement and learning. It is the recent focus on models of teaching in IQEA schools that provides the focus of the following example and the implicit message that the IQEA group were in fact whole school teacher-researchers.

CASE STUDY

Swanwick Hall School is an 11–18 comprehensive school in eastern Derbyshire with a fully comprehensive intake but a skew to the less able. The school joined the East Midlands IQEA partnership in 1997 because many of the 'school improvement measures' used in school prior to that time were not classroom based. Ruth Watts, the deputy head, describes what this emphasis on teaching and learning has meant:

- There exists a better deal for pupils in terms of interest and variety, which caters for a greater range of learning styles.
- Most staff development time has been concentrated on teaching and learning which pleased virtually all staff.
- The impetus for change belongs to a volunteer group of staff ranging across departments and experience (it includes the headteacher and several NQTs) working collaboratively with the heads of faculty group. This means that the staff does not feel driven by senior management or external pressures as much as they did previously.

After extensive discussion, the IQEA group decided that all staff should concentrate on the model of inductive teaching for the first year of development. The main reasons for this decision were:

- The model is applicable to all departments.
- No one understood it previously so all staff were learning together and sharing ideas across departments.
- The different phases cater for different styles of teaching, including individual and group work, so there is variety in the lessons.
- The six phases make it quite a complex model, which requires understanding, so the staff had something to talk about. Comments were heard like 'Phases 1–4 are fine but then I struggle with phases 5 and 6. Any ideas?'
- The latter phases involve higher order thinking skills, which were underdeveloped in school at the time.
- Though the data for inductive teaching often requires considerable time in planning, it can be used from year to year, once it exists. This has meant that building the teaching model into schemes of work has not been too difficult.

Once the volunteer group had practised the model and videoed themselves, they were ready to organize a whole-school inservice day with time to learn about the model and then prepare work for inductive teaching in departments. Volunteer staff, who had never done any Inset work before, talked to the rest of the staff at the following training day. This produced a much more powerful message than an expert from outside school.

Over the next 12 months a variety of ways were found to share ideas on inductive teaching:

- There were more half inset days to report back on progress and develop more data sets for new lessons.
- There was co-planning and co-teaching while the volunteer IQEA group covered colleagues' lessons.
- Ideas and strategies were shared via videos.
- After every staff development session, each department completed a questionnaire for the IQEA group who published a 'State of Inductive teaching' report for staff.
- Lists were produced of topics taught inductively, with lists of the year groups involved. These ranged from Year 7 to Year 13 with no obvious bias to any particular key stage.
- Heads of faculty meetings were used as ways of sharing ideas and problems, e.g. how to include reluctant staff, building the model into schemes of work, etc.
- Students were questioned about their perceptions of teaching and learning and the results were published.
- A year later the inservice day was started with a 'curriculum tour', that is all departments put on a 20-minute workshop on topics they had taught inductively. This again proved to be a highly successful staff development session.

The pattern for the second year of IQEA was very similar to the first. The focus for Year 2 was cooperative group work and mnemonics, while remembering that it was still important to check that inductive teaching was well embedded into schemes of work. Virtually all departments engaged in cooperative group work, especially pairs/fours, jigsaw techniques and numbered heads (see Chapter 11). The third year of IQEA was more open-ended. Monitoring progress and sharing ideas became a little harder but only because the impetus for development comes from departments and individual teachers rather than being centrally controlled.

Subsequent activity at Swanwick included:

- developing the use of some of the newer models across more staff;
- linking work on behaviour for learning more specifically to the IQEA initiative;
- using the 'cooperative learning standards' more widely together with some of the ideas from accelerated learning;
- collecting more data from staff and pupils about progress and perceptions;
- increasing the number of staff able to give workshops on teaching and learning to other schools in the networks. (During the academic year 2000–01 for example, over 20 staff have been involved in delivering school improvement workshops around England and Wales, and even as far away as Hong Kong!)

It is in these ways that successful schools such as Swanwick Hall are pursuing their improvement efforts to improve pupil achievement and progress in a much more explicit way. There are three key messages from this example and the evidence of research and practice that provide insights into how to do this and the role of the teacher-researcher in achieving this is again critical.

1 *Keep the focus on student learning.* The increasing national emphasis on student academic outcomes is very welcome. There is a danger however that the focus on SAT scores, and GCSE and A level results will concentrate attention on attainment at the expense of the quality of pupils' learning. Achievement at whatever level is based on pupils' ability to respond effectively to the tasks they are set, and this depends on how well they can take control over their own learning (Mortimore 1993). It is these skills and strategies as well as the focus on academic outcomes that need to become integrated into the targets a school sets itself for pupil progress and achievement.

2 *Maintain consistency across the school.* Schools that add value to the learning, progress and attainment of their pupils are consistent in their teaching practices, the educational values that they hold, the high levels of expectation that they have and their low tolerance of failure. Pupils in highly effective schools are clear about what is required from them, feel secure in their learning and school environment, and respond positively to the academic and social demands placed upon them.

3 *Clarify the link between effective teaching and student learning outcomes.* Effective teachers and effective schools take seriously the link between classroom practice and student learning outcomes; particularly in terms of what the students

learn, how the students learn, the pace of learning and the high expectations existing in the classroom. Teaching strategies reflect not just the teacher's classroom management skills, but also, as we saw in Chapter 11, the ability of the teacher to help students to acquire new knowledge through, for example, learning how to extract information from presentations, to memorize information, to build hypotheses and concepts, to use metaphors to think creatively, and to work effectively with others to initiate and carry out cooperative tasks (Joyce and Calhoun 1997).

Coda

In his evocative essay, *The Tree*, John Fowles (1979) talks of the importance of 'seeing nature whole'. He argues against the contemporary reductionist and utilitarian view of the environment that alienates us from the source of nature itself. By fragmenting nature, by categorizing it, by breaking it up into little pieces so that we can 'understand it', we lose its essence. The more we try to control nature in this way, the more we move away from and fail to grasp its vital spirit. So it is with teacher development. The more we regard teachers as functionaries, the more we move towards reductionist notions of 'competency' and dull the spark of creative artistry, the more we impoverish the teaching and learning in our schools.

Much has changed in education since the first edition of this book was published. Although many of the changes are to be welcomed, not all of them have in my opinion been for the best. I am particularly concerned that some of the changes have come at the expense of teacher development. One of the ways of restoring the balance, I believe, is to re-emphasize the role of the teacher-researcher, emphasize the focus of teacher research on pedagogy and firmly locate this within a whole school context. In these final paragraphs I expand a little on this theme and argue, in the spirit of John Fowles, for seeing teacher and school development 'whole'.

I have tried in this and the previous chapter to demonstrate that classroom research is at the root of key school improvement activities such as acquiring a repertoire of teaching strategies, staff development and networking. I have also argued that because of the recent changes, teachers now, more than ever, need to apply the ethic of teacher research to these areas of professional development. But it increasingly seems to me that teacher research alone is not enough. Reflective classroom practice needs to be linked to whole school development and a focus on teaching and learning.

Schools involved in the Improving the Quality of Education for All project (see Hopkins 2002), for example, use their development plan as an overarching strategy to focus innovative efforts on a limited number of priorities, in a way that generates ownership and galvanizes support. The priorities tend to relate to teaching and classroom organization in a broad sense, and these schools use some form of classroom observation or 'peer coaching' to help staff work together and to learn from each other. The effectiveness of this approach is considerably enhanced when the observation is underpinned by an agreed specification of the teaching strategy to be employed. This provides a 'standard' for the mutual observation, as well as a language for talking about teaching. Indeed, peer coaching is proving to be a powerful means for establishing ownership, of acquiring new teaching strategies and eventually transforming the culture of the school.

Even more power is achieved when schools work together on their school improvement activities. There are now a number of cohorts of schools in this country and elsewhere that are basing their development work on IQEA principles. They are finding that establishing networks, which build in systems for coordination, dissemination and evaluation, provide teachers with greatly increased energy, support, and confidence. We are also finding that a school's improvement work becomes more rapidly institutionalized when it is initiated as part of a network. The variety of networks supported by the Specialist Schools and Academies Trust provide an outstanding example of how principled networking can support teacher and school development on the one hand, and enhanced learning and achievement of students on the other.

This and the other examples scattered throughout the book suggest that what are needed are powerful and integrative implementation strategies that directly address the nature of teaching and the culture of the school. Our current work with these schools suggests that it is through linking more precise specifications of teaching to classroom research strategies within the context of the development plan that progress is made. Strategies for school improvement that do not link teaching to whole-school activities are 'doomed to tinkering'. In short, we need to see teacher and school development whole. When we do this we not only begin to meet the real challenge of systemic educational reform, but we also create classrooms and schools where both our children and their teachers learn.

Further reading

This chapter has touched on a broad range of issues that has a vast supporting literature. As regards school self-evaluation, the GRIDS handbooks (Abbott *et al.* 1988; McMahon *et al.* 1984), Macbeath (1999) and MacBeath *et al.* (2003) and Blanchard (2002) are essential reading. Of interest also are Phil Clift and colleagues' (1987) *Studies in School Self Evaluation*, as well as our own work on school-based review (Bollen and Hopkins 1987; Hopkins 1987, 1988). The link between school self-evaluation and inspection is described in OFSTED booklets and in MacBeath (2006) *School Inspection and Self-evaluation*. Our research on development planning resulted in the DES booklet *Planning for School Development* (Hargreaves *et al.* 1989), *The Empowered School* (Hargreaves and Hopkins 1991) and the more recent reconceptualization of development planning around a central focus on teaching and learning and student achievement (Hargreaves and Hopkins 1994; Hopkins and MacGilchrist 1998). The work of Barbara MacGilchrist and her colleagues at the institute of Education, London has been both helpful and insightful, in particular *Planning Matters* (1995) and *The Intelligent School* (1997). Our own work on school improvement, on which much of this chapter has been based, provides research accounts and tools, handbooks and training materials, as well as more academic reviews (Ainscow *et al.* 2000; Beresford 1998; Hopkins 2001, 2002; Hopkins *et al.* 1994, 1996, 1997, 1998). Finally, the literature on school improvement in general is also growing. Comprehensive treatments are found in *The New Structure of School Improvement* (Joyce *et al.* 1999), *Innovation and Change* (Rudduck 1991), the *What's Worth*

Fighting For? series (Fullan and Hargreaves 1992; Hargreaves and Fullan 1998), *Changing our Schools* (Stoll and Fink 1996) and *Change Forces* (Fullan 1993). Durrant and Holden (2006) *Teachers Leading Change: Doing Research for School* of the *Improvement of the Leading Teachers, Leading Schools Series*, and Jackson and Street (2005) 'Collaborative enquiry: why bother?' in Street and Temperley's *Improving Schools through Collaborative Enquiry* of the *Improving Schools Series* are particularly useful here as they bring research and school improvement together. Last but by no means least, the standard texts on educational change are Michael Fullan's (2007) *The New Meaning of Educational Change* (fourth edition), and *The International Encyclopaedia of Educational Change* in four volumes (Hargreaves *et al.* 1998).

Appendix
Ethics for classroom research

It is paramount that classroom research teachers, as part of the wider research community, are fastidious in taking into consideration and meeting ethical standards posed by such communities. First, in this section, we will briefly refer to a framework established for social researchers before examining the ethical principles and considerations that apply specifically to classroom research.

There are a number of approaches to research ethics. According to the Economic and Social Research Council (ESRC 2005: 7):

> research ethics refers to the moral principles guiding research from its inception through to its completion and publication of results and beyond – for example the curation of data and physical samples after the research has been published.

The six key principles underpinning ethical research, wherever applicable, should include (ibid: 5):

- Research should be designed, reviewed and undertaken to ensure integrity and quality.
- Research staff and subjects must be informed fully about the purpose, methods and intended possible uses of the research, what their participation in the research entails and what risks, if any, are involved. Some variation is allowed in very specific and exceptional research contexts for which detailed guidance is provided in the policy Guidelines.
- The confidentiality of information supplied by research subjects and the anonymity of respondents must be respected.
- Research participants must participate in a voluntary way, free from any coercion.
- Harm to research participants must be avoided.
- The independence of research must be clear, and any conflicts of interest or partiality must be explicit.

These guidelines, as one can easily recognize, are intentionally vague so that researchers are able to interpret them in ways that fit the needs of the specific research they are undertaking (Smyth and Williamson 2004: 10), also allowing researchers to make ethical decisions based on their own morality and the issues raised by their research project. And classroom researchers should do exactly that.

Action researchers must trust the ethical decision they take, when these do not come in contrast with the above key principles, but also with the ones of their particular organization. As Kemmis and McTaggart (1988: 43–4) remind us, classroom researchers' 'actions are deeply embedded in an existing social organization and the failure to work within the general procedures of that organization may not only jeopardize the process of improvement but existing valuable work. Principles of procedure for action research accordingly go beyond the usual concerns for confidentiality and respect for the persons who are the subjects of enquiry and define in addition, appropriate ways of working with other participants in the social organization. The principles outlined below reflect the commitment implicit in the methods of action research to participation and collaborative work, and negotiation within, and ultimately beyond, existing social and political circumstances.

> **Observe protocol:** Take care to ensure that the relevant persons, committees and authorities have been consulted, informed and that the necessary permission and approval has been obtained.
>
> **Involve participants:** Encourage others who have a stake in the improvement you envisage to shape the form of the work.
>
> **Negotiate with those affected:** Not everyone will want to be directly involved; your work should take account of the responsibilities and wishes of others.
>
> **Report progress:** Keep the work visible and remain open to suggestions so that unforeseen and unseen ramifications can be taken account of; colleagues must have the opportunity to lodge a protest to you.
>
> **Obtain explicit authorization before you observe:** For the purposes of recording the activities of professional colleagues or others (the observation of your own students falls outside this imperative provided that your aim is the improvement of teaching and learning).
>
> **Obtain explicit authorization before you examine files, correspondence or other documentation:** Take copies only if specific authority to do this is obtained.
>
> **Negotiate descriptions of people's work:** Always allow those described to challenge your accounts on the grounds of fairness, relevance and accuracy.
>
> **Negotiate accounts of others' points of view (e.g. in accounts of communication):** Always allow those involved in interviews, meetings and written exchanges to require amendments which enhance fairness, relevance and accuracy.
>
> **Obtain explicit authorization before using quotations:** Verbatim transcripts, attributed observations, excerpts of audio and video recordings, judgements, conclusions or recommendations in reports (written or to meetings).
>
> **Negotiate reports for various levels of release:** Remember that different audiences demand different kinds of reports; what is appropriate for an informal verbal report to a faculty meeting may not be appropriate for a staff meeting, a report to council, a journal article, a newspaper, a newsletter to parents; be conservative if you cannot control distribution.
>
> **Accept responsibility for maintaining confidentiality.**
>
> **Retain the right to report your work:** Provided that those involved are satisfied with the fairness, accuracy and relevance of accounts which pertain to them; and that the accounts do not unnecessarily expose or embarrass those involved;

then accounts should not be subject to veto or be sheltered by prohibitions of
confidentiality.

Make your principles of procedure binding and known: All of the people
involved in your action research project must agree to the principles before the
work begins; others must be aware of their rights in the process.[1]

Classroom researchers have also to acknowledge their ethical responsibility towards
their own personal biases. Our own background, values and beliefs and cultural understandings inevitably have an impact on our decisions about the research. We construct
reality through our own ideas and 'truths' which many, and justifiably, would argue
that is 'our truth'. However, research needs to be as objective as possible, and as any
claim to objectivity or to a 'value free' position is an illusion, personal biases have to be
identified throughout the research process and strategies to minimize them have to be
employed.

If we were to match the classroom researchers' ethical considerations with each of
the research stages, as at any stage during research ethical issues could materialize
(Manion 1994), then we should be able to confidently answer the following questions:

Preparation stage

1   Should you do the research at all?
2   What ethical issues may arise from your research?
3   If your research includes children, what ethical issues could arise from the ages
    of the children involved?
4   Whose interests is the research serving?

Before the data collection

1   Whose consent do you need?
2   Have you fully explained to the participants the reasons for the research, its
    methods and possible implications?
3   Have you made clear to participants that they have the right to withdraw at
    any stage of the research?
4   Are participants assured confidentiality?
5   How have you made sure that the participants have understood the above?
    Have you used language that they comprehend?

During the data collection

1   Are you true to your promises to participants?
2   Is the research causing participants the minimum disruption?
3   Are you storing confidential data safely so that they are not accessible by
    others?
4   Are the data reliable and valid?

[1] Reprinted, with permission, from Deakin University (Kemmis and McTaggart 1982: 43–4).

During the data analysis

1   Are findings reliable and valid?
2   Have you been reporting parts of your findings periodically to stakeholders?

During the report writing and dissemination

1   Are you writing the truth?
2   Have you ensured that none of the participants can be identified?
3   Have you considered the different audiences and dissemination approaches for your research?

Bibliography

Abbott, R., Birchenough, M. and Steadman, S. (1988) *GRIDS School Handbooks*, 2nd edn (Primary and Secondary versions). York: Longman for the SCDC.

Acheson, K. and Gall, M. (1997) *Techniques in the Clinical Supervision of Teachers*, 4th edn. New York: Longman.

Adelman, C. (1981) *Uttering, Muttering*. London: Grant McIntyre.

Ainscow, M., Beresford, J., Harris, A. *et al.* (2000) *Creating the Conditions for School Improvement*, 2nd edn. London: David Fulton.

Ainscow, M., Hargreaves, D.H. and Hopkins, D. (1995) Mapping the process of change in schools, *Evaluation and Research in Education*, 9(2): 75–90.

Armstrong, M. (1980) *Closely Observed Children*. London: Writers and Readers.

Armstrong, M. (1982) The story of five stories: an enquiry into children's narrative thought. Unpublished mimeo.

Atweh, B., Kemmis, S. and Weeks, P. (eds) (1998) *Action Research in Practice: Partnership for Social Justice in Education*. London: Routledge.

Barber, M. and Sebba, J. (1999) Reflections on progress towards a world class education system, *Cambridge Journal of Education*, 29(2): 183–93.

Barrow, R. (1986) Research into teaching, the conceptual factors, *Educational Research*, 28(3): 220–30.

Becker, H. (1958) Problems of inference and proof in participant observation, *American Sociological Review*, 28: 652–60 (reprinted in McCormick, R. (ed.) (1982) *Calling Education to Account*. London: Heinemann).

Bell, J. (2005) *Doing Your Research Project*, 4th edn. Buckingham: Open University Press.

Bennett, N. (1976) *Teaching Styles and Pupil Progress*. London: Pergamon Press.

Bennett, N. (1988) The effective primary school teacher; the search for a theory of pedagogy, *Teaching and Teacher Education*, 4(1): 19–30.

BERA (2000) *Good Practice in Educational Report Writing*. http://www.bera.ac.uk/ publications/ pdfs/GOODPR1.PDF (accessed 13 September 2007).

Beresford, J. (1998) *Collecting Information for School Improvement*. London: David Fulton.

Beresford, J. (2003) *Creating the Conditions to Involve Pupils in their Learning*. London: David Fulton.

Beresford, J. (1999) Matching teaching to learning, *Curriculum Journal*, 10(3): 321–44.

Blanchard, J. (2002) *Teaching and Targets. Self Evaluation and School Improvement*. London: RoutledgeFalmer.

Bloom, B.S. (1956) *Taxonomy of Educational Objectives. Handbook I: The Cognitive Domain*. New York: David McKay Co Inc.

Bollen, R. and Hopkins, D. (1987) *School Based Review: Towards a Praxis*. Leuven: ACCO.

Bollington, R. and Bradley, H. (1990) *Training for Appraisal: A Set of Distance Learning Materials*. Cambridge: University of Cambridge Institute of Education.

Bolster, A. (1983) Towards a more effective model of research on teaching, *Harvard Educational Review*, 53(3): 294–308.

Bowen, B., Forsyth, K., Green, J. *et al.* (undated) *Ways of Doing Research in One's Own Classroom*. Cambridge: Cambridge Institute of Education, Ford Teaching Project.

Bradbury, H. and Reason, P. (2001) 'Conclusion: broadening the bandwidth of validity: issues and choice-points for improving the quality of action research', in P. Reason and H. Bradbury (eds) *Handbook of Action Research: Participative Inquiry and Practice*. London: Sage.

Briggs, A.R.J. and Coleman, M. (eds) (2007) *Research Methods in Educational Leadership and Management*, 2nd edn. London: Paul Chapman.

Brooker, R. and MacPherson, I. (1999) Communicating the processes and outcomes of practitioner research: an opportunity for self indulgence or a serious professional responsibility?, *Educational Action Research*, 7(2): 207–21.

Brophy, J. (1983) Classroom organisation and management, *The Elementary School Journal*, 82(4): 266–85.

Brophy, J. (1981) Teacher praise: a functional analysis, *Review of Educational Research*, 51: 5–52.

Brophy, J. and Good, T. (1986) Teacher behaviour and student achievement, in M. Wittrock (ed.) *Handbook of Research on Teaching*, 3rd edn. New York: Macmillan.

Bryman, A. (2004) *Social Research Methods*, 2nd edn. Oxford: Oxford University Press.

Cambridge University (1994) *Mapping Change in Schools: The Cambridge Manual of Research Techniques*. Cambridge: UCIE.

Campbell, D. and Russo, J. (1999) *Social Experimentation*. Thousand Oaks, CA: Sage.

Campbell, D. and Stanley, J. (1963) Experimental and quasi-experimental designs for research on teaching, in N. Gage (ed.) *Handbook of Research on Teaching*. Chicago, IL: Rand McNally.

Carr, W. (1995) *For Education*. Buckingham: Open University Press.

Carr, W. (ed.) (1989) *Quality in Teaching*. Lewes: Falmer Press.

Carr, W. and Kemmis, S. (1986) *Becoming Critical*. Lewes: Falmer Press.

Carr, W. and Kemmis, S. (2005) Staying critical, *Educational Action Research*, 13(3): 347–58.

Claxton, G. (1999) *Wise Up: The Challenge of Lifelong Learning*. London: Bloomsbury.

Clift, P., Nuttall, D. and McCormick, R. (1987) *Studies in School Self Evaluation*. Lewes: Falmer Press.

Cogan, M. (1973) *Clinical Supervision*. Boston, MA: Houghton Mifflin.

Cohen, L., Manion, L. and Morrison, K. (2007) *Research Methods in Education*, 6th edn. London: Routledge/Falmer.

Congdon, P. (1978) Basic principles of sociometry, *Association of Education Psychologists Journal*, 4(8): 5–9.

Cook, T.D. and Campbell, D.T. (1979) *Quasi-Experimentation: Design and Analysis for Field Settings*. Chicago, Ill: Rand McNally.

Corey, S. (1953) *Action Research to Improve School Practice*. New York: Teacher's College Press.

Cousins, J.B. and Leithwood, K.A. (1986) Current empirical research on evaluation utilization, *Review of Educational Research*, 56(3): 331–64.

Cousins, J.B. and Leithwood, K.A. (1993) Enhancing knowledge utilization as a strategy for school improvement, *Knowledge: Creation, Diffusion, Utilizatio*, 14: 305–33.

Creemers, B. (1994) *The Effective Classroom*. London: Cassell.

Croll, P. (2000) *Systematic Classroom Observation*, 2nd edn. Lewes: Falmer Press.

Cronbach, L.J. (1975) Beyond the two disciplines of scientific psychology, *American Psychologist*, 30: 116–27.

Daniels, D.H., Beaumont, L.J. and Doolin, C.A. (2001) *Understanding Children: Interview and Observation Guide for Educators*. Maidenhead: McGraw Hill/Open University Press.

Deakin University (1998) *The Action Research Reader*. Victoria: Deakin University Press.

DeBono, E. (1991) *Teaching Thinking*. London: Penquin Books.

Delamont, S. (1992) *Fieldwork in Educational Settings*. Lewes: Falmer Press.

Delamont, S. (1983) *Interaction in the Classroom*. London: Methuen.

Delamont, S. (1984) *Readings on Interaction in the Classroom*. London: Methuen.

Denscombe, M. (2007) *The Good Research Guide*. Buckingham: Open University Press.

Denzin, K.N. and Lincoln, Y.S. (eds) (2003) *Collecting and Interpreting Qualitative Methods Volume 3*. London: Sage.

DES (Department of Education and Science) (1989) *Planning for School Development*. London: HMSO.

DfEE/QCA (Department for Education and Enjoyment/Qualifications and Curriculum Authority) (1999a) *Flexibility in the Secondary Curriculum*. London: DfEE/QCA.

DfEE/QCA (Department for Education and Enjoyment/Qualifications and Curriculum Authority) (1999b) *The National Curriculum: Handbook for Primary Teachers in England*. London: HMSO.

DfES (Department for Education and Skills) (2004b) *Excellence and Enjoyment: Learning and Teaching in the Primary Years*. London: DfES.

Dillon, J. (1983) Problem solving and findings, *Journal of Creative Behaviour*, 16(2): 97–111.

Downey, L. (1967) *The Secondary Phase of Education*. Boston, MA: Ginn.

Doyle, W. (1987) Research on teaching effects as a resource for improving instruction, in M. Wideen and I. Andrews (eds) *Staff Development for School Improvement*. Lewes: Falmer Press.

Dunn, W. and Swierczek, F. (1977) Planned organizational change: toward grounded theory, *Journal of Applied Behavioural Science*, 13(2): 135–57.

Durrant, J. and Holden, G. (2006) *Teachers Leading Change: Doing Research for School Improvement* (Leading Teachers, Leading Schools Series). London: Sage.

Ebbutt, D. (1985) Educational action research: some general concerns and specific quibbles, in R. Burgess (ed.) *Issues in Educational Research*. Lewes: Falmer Press.

Ebbutt, D. and Elliott, J. (eds) (1985) *Issues in Teaching for Understanding*. York: Longman.

Economic and Social Research Council (2005) *Research Ethics Framework (REF)*, http://www.esrcsocietytoday.ac.uk/ESRCInfoCentre/Images/ESRC_Re_Ethics_Frame_tcm6-11291.pdf (accessed 20 July 2007).

Elbaz, F. (1983) *Teacher Thinking – A Study of Practical Knowledge*. London: Croom Helm.

Elliott, J. (1976) *Developing Hypotheses about Classrooms from Teachers' Practical Constructs*. Cambridge: Cambridge Institute of Education, Ford Teaching Project.

Elliott, J. (1991) *Action Research for Educational Change*. Buckingham: Open University Press.

Elliott, J. (2005) Becoming critical: the failure to connect, *Educational Action Research*, 13(3): 359–74.

Elliott, J. and Adelman, C. (1976) *Innovation at the Classroom Level: A Case Study of the Ford Teaching Project*, Unit 28, Open University Course E 203: Curriculum Design and Development. Milton Keynes: Open University Educational Enterprises.

Elliott, J. and Ebbutt, D. (1985a) *Facilitating Educational Action Research in Schools*. York: Longman.

Elliott, J. and Ebbutt, D. (eds) (1985b) *Case Studies in Teaching for Understanding*. Cambridge: Cambridge Institute of Education.

Evertson, C. and Harris, A. (1992) What we know about managing classrooms, *Educational Leadership*, April: 74–8.

Fiddy, R. and Stronach, I. (1987) How can evaluation become formative? Norwich: CARE, University of East Anglia (mimeo).

Fielding, M. (2001) Students as Radical Agents of Change, *Journal of Educational Change*, 2: 123–41.

Fielding, M. (2004) Transformative approaches to student voice: theoretical underpinnings, recalcitrant realities, *British Educational Research Journal*, 30(2): 295–311.

Fielding, M. (1994) Valuing difference in teachers and learners: building on Kolb's learning styles to develop a language of teaching and learning, *Curriculum Journal*, 5(3): 393–417.

Fisher, R. (1966) *The Design of Experiments*, 8th edn. Edinburgh: Oliver and Boyd.

Flanders, N. (1970) *Analysing Teaching Behaviour*. Reading, MA: Addison-Wesley.

Fowles, J. (1979) *The Tree*. St Albans: Sumach Press.

Fox, M., Martin, P. and Green, G. (2007) *Doing Practitioner Research*. London: Sage.

Frost, D., Durrant, J., Head, M. and Holden, G. (2000) *Teacher-led School Improvement*. London: Falmer Press.

Fullan, M. (1993) *Change Forces: Probing the Depths of Educational Reform*. London: Falmer.

Fullan, M. (1997) *What's Worth Fighting For in the Principalship?*, 2nd edn. New York: Teachers College Press.

Fullan, M. (2000) The return of large-scale reform, *Journal of Educational Change*, 2(1): 5–28.

Fullan, M. (2007) *The New Meaning of Educational Change*, 4th edn. London: Cassell.

Fullan, M. and Hargreaves, A. (1992) *What's Worth Fighting For? Working Together For Your School*. New York: Teachers College Press.

Furlong, J. (2004) BERA at 30. Have we come of age?, *British Educational Research Journal*, 30(3): 343–58. www.bera.ac.uk/publications (accessed 13 August 2007).

Gage, N. (1978) *The Scientific Basis of the Art of Teaching*. New York: Teachers College Press.

Gagné, R.M. (1965) *The Conditions of Learning*. New York: Holt, Rinehart, and Winston.

Galton, M. (1978) *British Mirrors*. Leicester: University of Leicester School of Education.

Galton, M., Simon, B. and Croll, P. (1980) *Inside the Primary Classroom*. London: Routledge and Kegan Paul.

Galton, M. (1999) *Inside the Primary Classroom: Twenty Years On*. London: Routledge.

Gardner, H. (1991) *The Unschooled Mind: How Children Think and How Schools Should Teach*. New York: Basic Books.

Gardner, H. (1993) *Frames of Mind: The Theory of Multiple Intelligences*, 2nd edn. London: Fontana Press.

Gibson, R. (1986) *Critical Theory and Education*. London: Hodder and Stoughton.

Giroux, H. (1992) *Border Crossings: Cultural Workers and the Politics of Education*. New York: Peter Lang.

Glaser, B. and Strauss, A. (1967) *The Discovery of Grounded Theory*. New York: Aldine.

Goldhammer, R., Anderson, R. and Krajewski, R. (1993) *Clinical Supervision: Special Methods for the Supervision of Teachers*, 3rd edn. Stout: Rinehart and Winston Inc.

Good, T. (1989) Using classroom and school research to professionalize teaching. Keynote presentation at International Congress for School Effectiveness and Improvement, Rotterdam, 5th January.

Good, T. and Brophy, J. (2003) *Looking in Classrooms*, 9th edn. Boston: Allyn and Bacon.

Gray, J., Hopkins, D., Reynolds, D. *et al.* (1999) *Improving Schools. Performance and Potential.* Buckingham: Open University Press.

Halsall, R. (ed.) (1998) *Teacher Research and School Improvement: Opening Doors from the Inside.* Buckingham: Open University Press.

Hamilton, D., Macdonald, B., King, C. *et al.* (eds) (1977) *Beyond the Numbers Game.* Berkeley, CA: McCutchan.

Hammersley, M. (ed.) (1993) *Controversies in Classroom Research*, 2nd edn. Buckingham: Open University Press.

Hammersley, M. and Atkinson, P. (1995) *Ethnography: Principles in Practice*, 2nd edn. London: Routledge.

Hammersley, M. (1987) Some notes on the terms of 'validity' and 'reliability', *British Educational Research Journal*, 13 (1): 73–81.

Hargreaves, D. (2004) *Personalising Learning – 2: Student Voice and Assessment for Learning.* London: SSAT.

Hargreaves, A. and Fullan, M. (1998) *What's Worth Fighting For Out There?* Australia: Australian Council for Educational Administration Inc.

Hargreaves, A., Lieberman, A., Fullan, M. and Hopkins, D. (eds) (1998) *International Encyclopaedia of Educational Change.* Dordrecht: Kluwer.

Hargreaves, D.H. (1994) The new professionalism: a synthesis of professional and institutional development, *Teaching and Teacher Education*, 10(4).

Hargreaves, D.H. (1995) School culture, school effectiveness and school improvement, *School Effectiveness and School Improvement*, 6(1): 23–46.

Hargreaves, D.H. and Hopkins, D. (1991) *The Empowered School.* London: Cassell.

Hargreaves, D.H. and Hopkins, D. (eds) (1994) *Development Planning for School Improvement.* London: Cassell.

Hargreaves, D.H., Hopkins, D., Leask, M., Connolly, J. and Robinson, P. (1989) *Planning for School Development.* London: DES.

Higham, R., Hopkins, D. and Matthews, P. (forthcoming) *System Leadership.* London: Routledge.

Hitchcock, G. and Hughes, D. (1995) *Research and the Teacher*, 2nd edn. London: Routledge.

Hook, C. (1995) *Studying Classrooms*, 2nd edn. New York: Hyperior Books.

Hopkins, D. (1982) Doing research in your own classroom, *Phi Delta Kappan*, 64(4): 274–5.

Hopkins, D. (1984a) Teacher research: back to the basics, *Classroom Action Research Network Bulletin*, 6: 94–9.

Hopkins, D. (1984b) Towards a methodology for teacher based classroom research, *School Organization*, 4(3): 197–204.

Hopkins, D. (1987) *Improving the Quality of Schooling.* Lewes: Falmer Press.

Hopkins, D. (1988) *Doing School Based Review.* Leuven: ACCO.

Hopkins, D. (1989) *Evaluation for School Development.* Milton Keynes: Open University Press.

Hopkins, D. (2000) Powerful learning, powerful teaching and powerful schools, *The Journal of Educational Change*, 1(2): 135–54.

Hopkins, D. (2001) *School Improvement for Real.* London: Routledge/Falmer.

Hopkins, D. (2002) *Improving the Quality of Education for All*, 2nd edn. London: David Fulton.

Hopkins, D. (2007) *Every School a Great School*. Maidenhead: McGrawHill/Open University Press.

Hopkins, D. and Harris, A. (2000) *Creating the Conditions for Teaching and Learning*. London: David Fulton.

Hopkins, D., Harris, A., Singleton, C. and Watts, R. (2000) *Creating the Conditions for Teaching and Learning. A Handbook of Staff Development Activities*. London: David Fulton.

Hopkins, D. and Higham, R. (2007) System leadership: mapping the landscape, *School Leadership & Management*, 27(2): 147–66.

Hopkins, D. and Levin, B. (2000) Government policy and school development, *School Leadership and Management*, 20(1): 15–30.

Hopkins, D. and MacGilchrist, B. (1998) Development planning for pupil achievement, *School Leadership and Management*, 18(3): 409–24.

Hopkins, D. and Pont, B. (2007) *Innovative Approaches to Contemporary School Leadership*, Paris: OECD.

Hopkins, D. and Stern, D. (1996) Quality teachers, quality schools, *Teaching and Teacher Education*, 12(5): 501–17.

Hopkins, D., Ainscow, M. and West, M. (1994) *School Improvement in an Era of Change*. London: Cassell.

Hopkins, D., Bollington, R. and Hewett, D. (1989) Growing up with qualitative research and evaluation, *Evaluation and Research in Education*, 3(2): 61–80.

Hopkins, D., West, M. and Ainscow, M. (1996) *Improving the Quality of Education for All*. London: David Fulton.

Hopkins, D., West, M. and Beresford, J. (1998) Creating the conditions for classroom and teacher development, *Teachers and Teaching*, 4(1): 115–41.

Hopkins, D., West, M., Ainscow, M., Harris, A. and Beresford, J. (1997) *Creating the Conditions for Classroom Improvement*. London: David Fulton.

Hull, C., Rudduck, J. and Sigsworth, A. (1985) *A Room Full of Children Thinking*. York: Longman.

Hustler, D., Cassidy, T. and Cuff, T. (eds) (1986) *Action Research in Classrooms and Schools*. London: Allen & Unwin.

Jackson, D. and Street, H. (2005) Collaborative enquiry: why bother? in H. Street and J. Temperley (eds) *Improving Schools Through Collaborative Enquiry* (Improving Schools Series). London: Continuum.

James, M., Black, P., McCormick, R., Pedder, D. and Wiliam, D. (2006a) Learning how to learn, in classrooms, schools and networks: aims, design and analysis, *Research Papers in Education*, 21(2): 101–18.

James, M., Black, P., Carmichael, P., Conner, C., Dudley, P., Fox, A., Frost, D., Honour, L., MacBeath, J., McCormick, R., Marshall, B., Pedder, D., Procter, R., Swaffield, S., and Wiliam, D. (2006b) *Learning How to Learn: Tools for Schools*. London: Routledge.

Johnson, D.W. and Johnson, R.T. (1993) *Circles of Learning*. Aedina, MN: Interaction Book Company.

Johnson, D.W., Johnson, R.T. and Holubec, J. (1993) *Cooperative Learning in the Classroom*, 6th edn. Edina, MN: Interaction Book Company.

Joyce, B. (1992) Cooperative learning and staff development research: teaching the method with method, *Cooperative Learning*, 12(2): 10–13.

Joyce, B. and Showers, B. (1984) Transfer of training: The contribution of coaching, in

D. Hopkins and M. Wideen (eds) *Alternative Perspectives on School Improvement*. Lewes: Falmer Press.

Joyce, B. and Showers, B. (1995) *Student Achievement Through Staff Development*. White Plains, NY: Longman.

Joyce, B. and Weil, M. (1996) *Models of Teaching*, 5th edn. Englewood Cliffs, NJ: Prentice-Hall.

Joyce, B. and Calhoun, E. (1997) Learning to Teach Inductively. Mimeo, Pauma Valley, California.

Joyce, B. and Calhoun, E. (1998) *Learning to Teach Inductively*. Needham Heights, MA: Allyn and Bacon.

Joyce, B., Calhoun, E. and Hopkins, D. (1999) *The New Structure of School Improvement: Inquiring Schools and Achieving Students*. Buckingham: Open University Press.

Joyce, B., Calhoun, E. and Hopkins, D. (2002) *Models of Learning – Tools for Teaching*, 2nd edn. Buckingham: Open University Press.

Kemmis, S. (1983) Action research, in T. Husen and T. Postlethwaite (eds) *International Encyclopaedia of Education: Research and Studies*. Oxford: Pergamon.

Kemmis, S. (1988) Action research in retrospect and prospect, in Deakin University, *The Action Research Reader*. Victoria: Deakin University Press.

Kemmis, S. (2005) Knowing practice: searching for saliences, *Pedagogy, Culture and Society*, 13: 391–426.

Kemmis, S. (2006) Participatory action research and the public sphere, *Educational Action Research*, 14(4): 459–76.

Kemmis, S. and McTaggart, R. (1988) *The Action Research Planner*, 3rd edn. Victoria: Deakin University (1st edn, 1981).

Kolb, D.A. (1984) *Experiential Learning*. Englewood Cliffs, NJ: Prentice-Hall.

Kounin, J.S. (1970) *Discipline and Group Management in Classrooms*. New York: Holt, Rinehart and Winston.

Kyriacou, C. (1997) *Effective Teaching in Schools*, 2nd edn. Cheltenham: Stanley Thornes.

Kyriacou, C. (1998) *Essential Teaching Skills*, 2nd edn. Cheltenham: Stanley Thornes.

Lawton, D. (1989) *Education, Culture and the National Curriculum*. London: Hodder and Stoughton.

Leadbeater, C. (2004) *Learning about Personalisation: How can We put the Learner at the Heart of the Education System*? Nottingham: Department for Education and Skills.

Lewin, K. (1946) Action research and minority problems, *Journal of Social Issues*, 2: 34–46.

Lincoln, Y. and Guba, E. (1985) *Naturalistic Inquiry*. Beverly Hills, CA: Sage.

Lincoln, Y. and Guba, E.G. (2005) Paradigmatic controversies, contradictions and emerging confluences, in N.K. Denzin and Y.S. Lincoln (eds) *The Sage Handbook of Qualitative Studies* (3rd edn). Thousand Oaks: Sage.

Lortie, D. (1975) *School Teacher*, Chicago, IL: University of Chicago Press.

Louis, K.S. and Miles, M. (1992) *Improving the Urban High School*. London: Cassell.

Macbeath, J. (1999) *Schools Must Speak for Themselves*. London: Routledge.

Macbeath, J. (2006) *Inspection and Self-evaluation. Working with the New Relationship with Schools*. London: Routledge.

Macbeath, J. and Sugimine, H. with Sutherland, G., Nishimura, M. and the students of the Learning School (2003) *Self-evaluation in the Global Classroom*. London: RoutledgeFalmer.

MacDonald, B. and Walker, R. (eds) (1974) *Innovation, Evaluation Research and the Problem of Control*. Norwich: CARE, University of East Anglia Press.

MacGilchrist, B., Mortimore, P., Savage, J. and Beresford, C. (1995) *Planning Matters*. London: Paul Chapman.

MacGilchrist, B., Myers, K. and Reed, J. (1997) *The Intelligent School*. London: Paul Chapman.

Magee, B. (1973) *Popper*. London: Fontana/Collins.

May, N. and Rudduck, J. (1983) *Sex Stereotyping and the Early Years of Schooling*. Norwich: University of East Anglia Press.

McCormick, R. and James, M. (1989) *Curriculum Evaluation in Schools*, 2nd edn. London: Routledge.

McIntyre, D., Pedder, D. and Rudduck, J. (2005) Pupil voice: comfortable and uncomfortable learnings for teachers, *Research Papers in Education*, 20 (2):149–68.

McKernan, J. (1996) *Curriculum Action Research*, 2nd edn. London: Kogan Page.

McLaughlin, M.W. (1990) The Rand Change Agent study revisited: macro perspectives, micro realities, *Educational Researcher*, 19(9): 11–16.

McMahon, A., Bolam, R., Abbott, R. and Holly, P. (1984) *GRIDS School Handbooks* (Primary and Secondary versions). York: Longman for the Schools Council.

McNiff, J. (1992) *Action Research: Principles and Practice*. London: Routledge.

McNiff, J. and Whitehead, J. (2005) *Action Research for Teachers: A Practical Guide*. London: David Fulton Publishers.

McNiff, J. and Whitehead, J. (2006) *All You Need to Know about Action Research*. London: Sage.

Miles, M. and Huberman, M. (1984) Drawing valid meaning from qualitative data: toward a shared craft, *Educational Researcher*, 13(5): 20–30.

Miles, M. and Huberman, M. (1994) *Qualitative Data Analysis: A Sourcebook of New Methods*. Beverly Hills, CA: Sage.

Mills, G. E. (2003) *Action Research: A Guide for the Teacher Researcher*. Upper Saddle River, NJ: Merrill/Prentice Hall.

Miujs, D. and Reynolds, D. (2001) *Effective Teaching: Evidence and Practice*. London: Paul Chapman.

Miujs, D. and Reynolds, D. (2001) *Effective Teaching, Research and Practice*. London: Paul Chapman.

Mortimore, P. (1993) School effectiveness and the management of effective learning and teaching, *School Effectiveness and School Improvement*, 4(4): 290–310.

Newmann, F., King, B. and Young, S.P. (2000) Professional development that addresses school capacity: lessons from urban elementary schools. Paper presented to Annual Meeting of the American Educational Research Association, New Orleans, 3rd April.

Nixon, J. (ed.) (1981) *A Teacher's Guide to Action Research*. London: Grant and McIntyre.

OECD (2005) *The Definition and Selection of Key Competencies* www.oecd.org (accessed 1 June 2006).

OECD (1999) *Innovating Schools*. Paris: OECD/CERI.

Office For Standards in Education (1998) *School Evaluation Matters*. London: OFSTED.

Oja, S.N. and Smulyan, L. (1989) *Collaborative Action Research*. Lewes: Falmer Press.

Open University (1976) *Personality and Learning, Course E201*. Milton Keynes: Open University.

Patterson, J., Purkey, S.C. and Parker, J. (1986) *Productive School Systems for a Nonrational World*. Alexandria, VA: ASCD.

Patton, M.Q. (1990) *Qualitative Evaluation Methods*. Beverly Hills, CA: Sage.

Percelli, V. (2004) Heavy fuel, in O'Reilly S., K., S. Weber and C. Mitchell (eds) *Just Who do We Think We Are? Methodologies for Self Study in Teacher Education*. London: Falmer.

Percelli, V. (2005) Re-imagining research, re-presenting the self: putting arts media to work in the analysis and synthesis of data on 'difference' and 'disability', *International Journal of Qualitative Studies in Education*, 18(1): 63–83.

Polanyi, M. (1973) *Personal Knowledge*. London: Routledge and Kegan Paul.

Pring, R. (1978) Teacher as researcher, in D. Lawton, P. Gordon, M. Ing *et al.* (eds) *Theory and Practice of Curriculum Studies*. London: Routledge and Kegan Paul.

Rapoport, R. (1970) Three dilemmas in action research, *Human Relations*, 23: 1–11.

Reed, A. and Bergemann, V. (2004) *Guide to Observation, Participation and Reflection in the Classroom with Forms for Field Use CD-ROM*. Maidenhead: McGraw Hill/Open University Press.

Riley, K. and Rustique-Forrester, E. with Fuller, M. *et al.*, (2002) *Working with Disaffected Students: Why Students Lost interest in School and What We Can Do About it*. London: Paul Chapman.

Robson, C. (2002) *Real World Research*, 2nd edn. Oxford: Blackwells.

Rowland, S. (1984) *The Enquiring Classroom: An Introduction to Children's Learning*. Lewes: Falmer Press.

Rudduck, J. (1981) *Making the Most of the Short Inservice Course*. London: Methuen.

Rudduck, J. (ed.) (1982) *Teachers in Partnership: Four Studies of Inservice Collaboration*. York: Longman.

Rudduck, J. (1984) Introducing innovation to pupils, in D. Hopkins and M. Wideen (eds) *Alternative Perspectives on School Improvement*. Lewes: Falmer Press.

Rudduck, J. (1991) *Innovation and Change*. Buckingham: Open University Press.

Rudduck, J. and Hopkins, D. (eds) (1985) *Research as a Basis for Teaching*. London: Heinemann.

Rudduck, J. and Sigsworth, A. (1985) Partnership supervision, in D. Hopkins and K. Reid (eds) *Rethinking Teacher Education*. London: Croom Helm.

Rudduck, J., Berry, M., Brown, N. and Frost, D. (2000) Schools learning from schools, *Research Papers in Education*, 15(3): 259–74.

Sachs, J. (2003) *The Activist Teaching Profession (Professional Learning)*. Buckingham: Open University Press.

Sagor, R. (2000) *Guiding School Improvement with Action Research*. Alexandria, VA: ASCD.

Sagor, R. (2005) *The Action Research Guidebook*. Thousand Oaks, CA: Corwin Press.

Sandford, N. (1970) Whatever happened to action research? *Journal of Social Issues*, 26(4): 3–23.

Schratz, M. (2001) A visual approach to evaluation in schools. Paper presented at the Second Visual Conference of the Centre for Applied Research in Education, University of East Anglia.

Schön, D. A. (1996) *Educating the Reflective Practitioner: Toward a New Design for Teaching and Learning in the Professions*. San Francisco, CA: Jossey-Bass, Inc.

Schön, D. (1991) *The Reflective Practitioner*. New York: Basic Books.

Schwandt, T. and Halpern, E. (1988) *Linking Auditing and MetaEvaluation*. Beverly Hills, CA: Sage.

Sharan, S. and Shachar, H. (1988) *Language and Learning in the Co-operative Classroom*. New York: Springer-Verlag.

Simon, A. and Boyer, E. (1975) *Mirrors for Behaviour: An Anthology of Classroom Observation Instruments*. Philadelphia, PA: Research for Better Schools Inc.

Simons, H. (1982) Suggestions for a school self evaluation based on democratic principles, in R. McCormick (ed.) *Calling Education to Account*. London: Heinemann.

Simons, H. (1987) *Getting to Know Schools in a Democracy*. Lewes: Falmer Press.

Slavin, R.E. (1995) *Cooperative Learning: Theory, Research, and Practice*, 2nd edn. Boston: Allyn & Bacon.

Smith, L. and Geoffrey, W. (1968) *The Complexities of an Urban Classroom*. New York: Holt, Rinehart and Wilson.

Smyth, M. and Williamson, E. (eds) (2004) *Researchers and their 'Subjects': Ethics, Power, Knowledge and Consent*. Bristol: Policy Press.

Stake, R.E. (1995) *The Art of Case Study Research*. Thousand Oaks, CA: Sage.

Stenhouse, L. (1970) *The Humanities Project*. London: Heinemann. (Revised edition by Rudduck, J. (1983) Norwich: University of East Anglia Press.)

Stenhouse, L. (1975) *An Introduction to Curriculum Research and Development*. London: Heinemann.

Stenhouse, L. (1979) Using research means doing research, in H. Dahl, A. Lysne and P. Rand (eds) *Spotlight on Educational Research*. Oslo: University Press.

Stenhouse, L. (1980) Product or process: a response to Brian Crittenden, *New Education*, 2(1): 137–40.

Stenhouse, L. (1983) *Authority, Education and Emancipation*. London: Heinemann.

Stenhouse, L. (1984) Artistry and teaching: the teacher as focus of research and development, in D. Hopkins and M. Wideen (eds) *Alternative Perspectives on School Improvement*. Lewes: Falmer Press.

Stoll, L. and Fink, D. (1996) *Changing our Schools*. Buckingham: Open University Press.

Strauss, A. (1987) *Qualitative Analysis for Social Scientists*. Cambridge: Cambridge University Press.

Strauss, A. and Corbin, J. (1998) *Basics of Qualitative Research*, 2nd edn. London: Sage.

Street, H. and Temperley, J. (eds) (2005) *Improving Schools through Collaborative Enquiry*. London: Continuum Press.

Taber, K.S. (2007) *Classroom-based Research and Evidence-based Practice. A Guide for Teachers*. London: Sage.

Walker, R. (1989) *Doing Research*. London: Routlege.

Walker, R. and Adelman, C. (1990) *A Guide to Classroom Observation*. London: Routledge.

Webb, R. (ed.) (1990) *Practitioner Research in the Primary School*. Lewes: Falmer Press.

Weinberg, D. (2002) *Qualitative Research Methods*. Oxford: Blackwell Publishers.

Whitman, W. (1855/1959) *Leaves of Grass*. New York: Viking.

Winter, R. (1989) *Learning from Experience*. Lewes: Falmer Press.

Winter, R., Buck, A. and Sobiechowska, P. (1999) *Professional Experience and the Creative Imagination*. London: Routledge.

Wood, D. (1998) *How Children Think and Learn*. Oxford: Basil Blackwell.

Wragg, E.C. (1999) *An Introduction to Classroom Observation*. London: Routledge.

Yin, R. (2003) *Case Study Research: Design and Methods* 3rd edn. London: Sage.

Young, R. (1989) *A Critical Theory of Education: Habermas and our Children's Future*. New York: Harvester Wheatsheaf.

Zeichner, K.M. and Noffke, S.E. (2001) Practitioner research, in V. Richardson (ed.) *Handbook of Research on Teaching*, 4th edn. Washington, DC: American Educational Research Association.

Index